Lands and Peoples

THE WORLD IN COLOR

Volume 6

CANADA   THE UNITED STATES

Grolier
INCORPORATED
New York

DISTRIBUTED IN THE UNITED STATES BY
THE GROLIER SOCIETY INC.

DISTRIBUTED IN CANADA BY
THE GROLIER SOCIETY OF CANADA LIMITED

Volume 6

TABLE OF CONTENTS

PAGE

The Arctic—*islands and frozen sea*   4

American Indians—*tribes of Canada and the United States*
    8 Pictures in Full Color   17

Canada—*monarch of the north*   32

The Atlantic Provinces—*rich in traditions of the sea*
    22 Pictures in Full Color   42

Quebec—*Canada's largest province*
    23 Pictures in Full Color   64

Ontario—*central province*
    20 Pictures in Full Color   80

The Western Provinces—*prairies, mountains and forests*
    21 Pictures in Full Color   96

Canadian Cities—*variety and striking contrasts*   120

Yukon and Northwest Territories—*the roof of North America*   144

The United States—*present and past*
    12 Pictures in Full Color   152

The Northeastern States—*from Maine to Maryland*
    24 Pictures, Graphs (Communications), in Full Color   200

The Southern States—*from Virginia to Texas*
    23 Pictures, Graphs (Culture), in Full Color   224

North Central States—*the Middle West*
    25 Pictures, Graphs (Economy), in Full Color   248

Mountain and Pacific States—*the far West*
    28 Pictures in Full Color   272

Alaska and Hawaii—*the forty-ninth and fiftieth states*
    14 Pictures in Full Color   304

United States Cities—*centers of culture and industry*   317

United States Parks—*conservation of natural beauty*
    18 Pictures in Full Color   376

Canada's Parks—*scenic grandeur, wildlife and history*   401

The Arctic

... islands and frozen sea

AT the northern top of the globe lie not one pole but two, a thousand miles apart. One is the North Magnetic Pole, to which all compass needles point. This pole is not fixed but slowly wanders. Today it is on Prince of Wales Island, part of an area rich in minerals, forests and, above all, animal life. The other, the geographic North Pole, one end of the axis on which the earth spins, is in a wilderness of ice and snow, a dead region that can barely support life. For it is not land at all but a thin crust of ice over the Arctic Ocean. Its thickness varies with the seasons but it is generally not more than ten feet thick, even in winter. The whole icecap is in constant motion. Torn by wind and current or cleaved by land masses, it breaks up into floes that pile up on one another in great pressure ridges.

Yet within a century ships may be sailing over it freely. For scientists believe that the icecap is melting; and, oddly enough, this melting may be the forerunner of a new ice age. They estimate that the icecap has lost almost a third of its thickness and an eighth of its area in the last fifty years. In the distant future only the midnight sun will distinguish the Arctic from other northern seas. At present, however, the winter ice covers nearly all the Arctic Ocean, reaching out to the huge Greenland icecap and to northern Canada, Alaska and Siberia but leaving clear waters toward the Atlantic, Norway and the coast of European Russia. On a globe it looks like a white hat that has slipped off the top of the world toward Alaska. The center of the icecap is some 360 miles from the North Pole and is called the "Pole of Inaccessibility."

The very name is a challenge to man. For over two thousand years men have sought the polar regions, goaded by a spirit of adventure, desire for wealth and plain curiosity, scientific and unscientific. The first was a Greek, Pytheas, in the fourth century B.C. He was followed, about a thousand years later, by Irish voyagers and the Norsemen, the most active of the early explorers. Based on Greenland and Iceland, they went some five hundred miles north of the Arctic Circle. European desire for the riches of the East in the sixteenth century prompted a search for a short polar route to the Orient. For three hundred years navigators searched for the Northwest Passage. Often in wooden sailing ships, with inadequate provisions and crude instruments, they mapped thousands of miles of bleak coast line. These maps are an enduring memorial to their names: Sir Martin Frobisher, John Davys, Henry Hudson, William Baffin, Vitus Bering and a host of others. Yet the Northwest Passage remained undiscovered until 1906 when Captain Roald Amundsen, a Norwegian, took a tiny ship through Bering Strait after a three-year voyage from the Atlantic.

The knowledge gained from the centuries of search enables aircraft to take their own Northwest Passage between Occident and Orient, slashing flying time by as much as 40 per cent. About half a million passengers have been carried since service began in 1954, and six airlines use the polar route.

The quest for the passage diverted attention from the North Pole itself. Intensive scientific exploration in the far north did not begin till the end of the eighteenth century. The British Navy led the way, but the Russians, Danes and Americans soon joined in. In 1848 Sir John Franklin's expedition was lost when its members perished in trying to escape overland from their ships trapped in the ice. Many attempts were made to find the remains and some seven thousand miles of

Canadian coast line were discovered in the process. Knowledge of the north increased rapidly, with discoveries by explorers of all nations and especially by Dr. Fridtjof Nansen, a Norwegian. He stayed aboard his ship while it drifted, with the movement of the icecap, across the Arctic Ocean. Finally, in 1909, an American, Robert Peary, reached the Pole.

He had used dogs and sleds, but in the modern era of international co-operation (ushered in by the eleven-nation investigation of Arctic magnetism and weather in 1882), aircraft and drifting ice stations began to be used. In 1926 Richard E.

POLAR BEARS—the only large land animals near the North Pole—amble surefootedly across the floes on the icy sea.

Byrd crossed the Pole by plane and Amundsen crossed by airship. In 1957 fifty-five nations co-operated in the International Geophysical Year, the U.S.S.R. and the United States establishing scientific stations on ice floes as part of the program. On at least one occasion the men had to flee their drifting camp when, with a booming noise, the ice cracked and the floe began to break up.

This work is of strategic as well as scientific importance because the shortest route for missile bombardment by the United States and the Soviet Union lies over the Arctic. Across northern Canada the enormous Distant Early Warning (DEW)-line radar fence has been built. It and its associated bases, burrowed into the permanently frozen subsoil, are serv-

NATIONAL FILM BOARD OF CANADA

iced along the centuries-old routes of the explorers, as well as by air. So much for Arctic defense. Attack is to be entrusted to atomic submarines, laden with missiles, cruising under the icecap. The ocean floor, though up to two miles deep, is by no means uniform, so the crews of such submarines as the USS Nautilus and the USS Skate must scan their sonar equipment anxiously for hidden mountains and shallows as well as downward-probing ice. But, once charted, service in the Arctic will be routine. Technology has turned this remote area into a front line. It is a front line that is a no man's land indeed.

By a sort of impromptu legal mathematics, Canada has defined the sub-Arctic possessions. South of parallel 60 it speaks of provinces, but north of that degree of latitude it calls them territories. Like most rules, however, this one has an exception, for a small triangle of Quebec protrudes north of the boundary.

The lands north of 60° are nearly half of Canada. When we remember that Canada is larger than the forty-eight

THE ARCTIC AREA is largely sea (unlike Antarctica, a land mass) on which a vast cap of ice floats. At the same time, many islands, some imbedded in the pack ice, fringe the ocean.

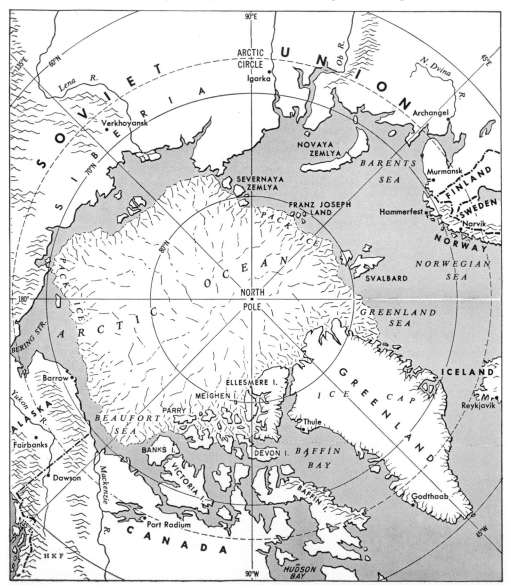

states of the United States south of the border we are prepared to find within these northern domains many conditions, several climates and at least three conspicuously distinct types of people. Vegetation and animals differ correspondingly.

Yukon Territory is mostly mountainous and forested. The high range along the southwest corner prevents the inland climate from being much affected by the Pacific, and there is only a little panhandle stretching north which is materially affected by the sea climate of the Arctic. Most of the Yukon has, therefore, a continental climate. The summers are hot, with temperatures ranging upward to 100° in the shade; the winters are cold, with the alcohol thermometers falling toward 80° below zero.

Boundary between Trees and Grass

The Northwest Territories comprise all the remaining land of Canada including the adjacent islands not included in any province. The forests and prairies of the Northwest Territories, east of the Yukon, are determined by the trend of midsummer sea winds. Therefore the boundary between tree land and grassland runs more or less northwestward from a point a little north of Churchill, on Hudson Bay, to the Arctic Ocean near the foot of the Cape Parry Peninsula, straight south from Banks Island. South or southwest of this line we have roughly the continental, or Yukon, climate, with intense summer heat and intense winter cold. Northeast of the line the winters are less cold and the summers less warm. The islands north of Canada are necessarily prairie, for the same reason, summer sea winds.

Greenland is about 83 per cent ice-covered. This is because the territory is mountainous and has a heavy precipitation from the surrounding waters. No Canadian island is so high and none of them is therefore ice-capped though there are considerable glaciers on three—Ellesmere, Axel Heiberg and Devon. There are some glaciers in Baffin Island but it is doubtful whether they are as large as those of British Columbia although probably larger than the ones so familiar to

tourists in Switzerland. There may be a glacier on Meighen Island. Apart from this there is far less permanent snow in the Canadian islands than there is in Switzerland and Austria. The Canadian mainland north of the Arctic Circle has no permanent snow. This is because mountains are absent and the winter snowfall is light. Portions of such states as New York and Michigan have an annual snowfall from two to five times as great as the average for the Canadian Arctic.

The old popular idea of Canada, Our Lady of the Snows, as part of the "frozen north," sometimes even exaggerated into "barren ground," has long been exploded. A northern editor once said that he well remembered the time when the millers of the Twin Cities of Minnesota had little confidence in the permanent wheat-producing power of northern North Dakota and believed that no serious competition would ever come from the British prairies to the north. But he added that Winnipeg alone then handled more wheat than the three largest wheat markets of the United States put together.

Summer Night Frosts Disappear

What surprises even Canadians is that summer frosts which injure wheat are actually more numerous south of the middle of Alberta than north of it. The point is that the maximum heat of the summer noonday, around 95° or 98° in the shade, remains about the same as you go north from the equator, while the sun shines more and more hours per day. The night is therefore shorter and the earth and air have less time to cool off between the last warming of the sunset and the first warming of the sunrise. When you get so far north that the midsummer nights are nearly gone the night frosts of midsummer are completely gone.

For this reason it is possible that farming will become a major occupation, though it probably will never surpass mining in importance. The development of mines has progressed rapidly and great quantities of gold and oil are now being produced. Furthermore, the area around Great Bear Lake is one of the world's chief

A TYPICAL MEMBER OF THE ROYAL CANADIAN MOUNTED POLICE

All members are trained as horsemen, though the force also uses autos and airplanes.

sources of radium and uranium ores.

But these new industries require people, and as more and more people move into the area, agriculture becomes increasingly important. The government agricultural station near Whitehorse produced fine crops of wheat and rye as early as 1948.

It is now believed that the land can produce more than enough to feed its growing population and it is possible that the wheat empire of Canada may stretch north into the subarctic Northwest Territories.

The books used to say that in the Northwest Territories of Canada the ground is always frozen and "the vegetation therefore poor or absent." But the ground frost really produces an effect just opposite to the one we had expected. A hundred miles south of the Arctic Circle one smart kick with a booted toe reveals in August ground underneath the warm sod perpetually frozen as hard as granite, but a hundred miles north of the Circle you still find growing upon this icy concrete trees of white spruce measured by the Forestry Commissioner of Canada at over seventy feet.

However, the most definite friendliness of the ground-ice for vegetation is seen on the prairies north of the forest. For the frost nullifies that yearly variation in rainfall which in most lands is considerable and in some extreme. Plants would die in Australia under rains as scant as those of the Arctic. But in northern Canada when a dry season produces increased heating of the soil, there follows a melting of a little of the ice below, so that all the plants have to do to quench their thirst abundantly is to reach with their roots an inch or two deeper than they usually do. There is accordingly neither in northern Canada nor in northern Siberia any appreciable variation in the productivity of the grasslands between the dry and wet years.

At Fort Yukon, Alaska, north of the Arctic Circle, a tested United States Weather Bureau thermometer has recorded 100° in the shade six feet above eternal frost. One of those six feet is soil which so completely imprisons the chill of the ground that the heat of the air just above it is that of the humid tropics, whether judged by an instrument or by the nerves of the people who swelter in it.

There is intense winter cold in the places of the greatest sub-Arctic summer heat. The spot that has 95° in the shade in July may have —75° in winter. However, the coldest places, both in Canada and Siberia, are found within the forest. Out on the prairie, which may be called "barren grounds" if you want to be terrifying or romantic, you seldom come within ten or fifteen degrees of weather as cold as that of the forest. This seems to be because the prairie condition is produced by the chill ocean winds of summer. These same ocean winds are correspondingly warmer in winter. Therefore you find that the minimum temperatures get less and less severe as you go north through Canada in January toward the Arctic Sea. Seventy-five below zero is recorded frequently in the Canadian forest, but fifty-five below has never yet been recorded on the north coast of Canada. Neither is there any weather bureau or other probably reliable record as low as —55° on any of the islands to the north of Canada.

These islands, however, are never extremely hot in summer. You must get far from the ocean to have great heat, and by the nature of things you cannot do this on an island. Similarly by the nature of things you will have the greater heat inland the larger the island. Tempera-

Siberia. But the important thing is that when you come to the end of the forest you only come to the beginning of the prairie. You may disguise that fact, if you like, by calling it "barren ground" in Canada or "tundra" in Siberia, but that is mostly quibbling. True enough, there is a difference between the Arctic and the Temperate Zone prairie, just as there is a difference between the prairies

WINTER TWILIGHT IN NORMAN WELLS, IN NORTHWESTERN CANADA

The town is on the Mackenzie River almost at the Arctic Circle. Originally it was a trading post but it has become important in recent years as the center of a rich oil field.

tures around 85° in the shade will be found in the centre of Victoria Island, 300 to 400 miles north of the Arctic Circle. None so high are probably found in Baffin or Ellesmere Islands. This is not because they are more northerly, but because they are both higher and swept by more persistent sea winds.

The forests of spruce extend more than a hundred miles north of the Arctic Circle in some of the river valleys of Canada and more than twice that far in

of Montana and Brazil. However, if you want to convey the idea that to the casual eye there is much similarity between treeless but well-watered grasslands in every zone, then the best common word is prairie.

There are some districts in the Arctic, no doubt, where mosses and lichens prevail above flowering plants both in number of species and in tonnage per acre. But in the Arctic as a whole there are 700 species of flowering plants against 500

IN THE SLANTING RAYS of the long summer twilight, an Eskimo family pauses to let its dogs rest. The group is on Bylot Island, north of its home area, Baffin Island.

of mosses and lichens combined; by tonnage there is at least ten times as much flowering vegetation in the Arctic as non-flowering. The whole state of Texas claims only five hundred species of native flowering plants.

Where there are flowers there are certain to be insects. Peary saw a bumble-bee out over the ocean half a mile north of the most northerly land on earth. De Long's men caught a live butterfly on the floating sea ice, and this was 700 miles north of the Arctic Circle and 10 or 20 miles from the nearest island.

A WASHING MACHINE, driven by gasoline engine, entrances a northern housewife.

Mosquitoes are the great plague and hardship in all inland parts of the sub-Arctic and on most Arctic islands. They get steadily more numerous as you go north through Canada from the United States boundary, until they are at their worst on or just south of the Arctic Circle. Then they get less as you continue north and are not serious any more 500 miles beyond the circle. There is a similar northward decrease of many other insects.

The varieties of Arctic and sub-Arctic climate and conditions strike you particularly in relation to the people. Some Eskimo live in a forest but others have never been within several hundred miles of a tree. Most Eskimo live on or near a seacoast but there are some who have never been to the ocean. Fully half of the 35,000 or so Eskimo of the world live on seals mainly, but there are a few who have never tasted seal meat. Most Eskimo have still their native speech, but a few speak no language but English. Many in Greenland are familiar with Danish, some in northeastern Siberia know Russian, and so the complexity grows.

The first Eskimo came in contact with Europeans on the coast of Labrador about 900 years ago, and others on the coast of Greenland soon thereafter; but my second expedition in 1910 visited several hundred Eskimo who had never seen a white man until they met our party. It is probable that the last Eskimo saw their first European when the Rasmussen Expedition

10

MUSIC FOR ESKIMO DANCING. As the musicians pound out a strong, rhythmic beat on their flat sealskin drums, they chant. The singing is based on a simple five-tone scale.

HOUSES OF ICE BLOCKS, or igloos, are used only in winter, on hunting or fishing expeditions. Some Eskimo never see an igloo but have stone or wood houses all year round.

CANADIAN ESKIMO enjoy a book produced by the Government. The book is mostly pictures, with a brief text in single syllables, a written language used in the eastern Arctic.

A HELICOPTER LANDS at Pond Inlet, on the northern shore of Baffin Island. The Eskimo happily scurry out of the way as they know the plane brings supplies, news or both. Transportation by air has wrought deep changes in the life of the north.

12

NATIONAL FILM BOARD OF CANADA

THE KAYAK, the covered canoe of the Eskimo, was always made of sealskin. Today, other materials, brought north by plane, are used, and the design has been streamlined.

came to them in 1923. Some Eskimo saw their first book or paper either in my own hands or Rasmussen's, but one of the oldest journals now published in the New World is as completely Eskimo as the *Spectator* is English or the *Atlantic Monthly* American, and has appeared every year since 1861.

Being the last people on the far edge of the earth, these northerners have been particular victims of our folklore and superstition. Apparently because it was a common European belief in ancient times that there were pigmies in the Far North, and also because cold is supposed to have a stunting effect, the Eskimo have been described until recently as a small or dwarfed people. They are more properly described as of medium size. Our idiom compels us to say "Eskimo and Indians" but the general scientific opinion is that they are merely one kind of Indian and should therefore be called Eskimo Indians, corresponding to Sioux Indians or Iroquois Indians.

There is a belief common even now that most Eskimo, or all of them, live in snow houses in winter, but the fact is that snow houses are about as local in the Arctic as adobe houses are in the United States. Europeans, wherever in the world you find their descendants, usually travel a great deal, see pictures and read books. Most Swedes, for instance, would know that there are adobe houses in New Mexico. But before the white man came

STATION ON THE DEW LINE. The "line" is a radar network that stretches across the whole continent of North America, north of the Arctic Circle, to give warning of attack.

WESTERN ELECTRIC

NEXT WINTER'S FOOD for the dogs in the land of the long night. On Baffin Island, Eskimo Idlouk and his son, Oodlootituk, pile rocks on a cache of killed seals.

the Eskimos had no books, they traveled comparatively little, and some of them dwelt as far from others, when measured by the routes they had to travel, as Canada is from Brazil. Snowhouses have been seen by less than a third of the living Eskimo population of today. Most of them, however, know snowhouses pretty well through hearsay. A good many have seen movies made where they are found.

Eskimos are, generally speaking, a people of restless intelligence. Make it really clear to one inhabitant of a village that it is possible to set down a black mark on a white surface that means one sound and another black mark that means another sound. Show him that by twenty-five or thirty such marks, each different from the others, he can represent most or all of the important sounds of his own language. That is all you need to do. Come back a year or two later and you will find half the village reading and writing, with the knowledge of these skills already spreading to neighboring communities.

This, of course, applies only to writing the native tongue. American teachers in Alaska find the same difficulty teaching English to Eskimos that they would find in teaching Latin in Utah or Texas. But in a mining town, Eskimo children learn English in school about as rapidly as the whites, if given the same opportunity. That is because they also hear it in the street.

Arctic travelers usually agree that the Eskimos are the happiest people on earth. This could not be even half true if their lot were as hard as we used to suppose. It is curious how our books formerly told us, first, that life in the Arctic is necessarily a continuous hand-to-hand struggle with frost and famine, and second that the Eskimos have elaborate carvings in ivory and that their garments are frequently made up of thousands of separate pieces artfully sewn together into complicated designs. The truth is in the carvings and in the clothing; the false inference relates to the supposed desperate struggle for life. A woman who could sew for herself a warm coat in two days, if she made it from two whole caribou skins, will instead spend more than half of each day for two or three months in cutting up a great many skins into almost an infinite number of small pieces and then matching the m together, eventually developing a coat that is neither so warm as the two-day garment would have been nor so durable. In like manner her husband spends whole extra days and half-days in carving the handle of a bag that would have served him as well if left plain.

The so-called civilized nations have in one city the contrast between stark poverty and surfeiting riches. Naturally there is within the vast Eskimo territories a similar contrast. There are indeed communities, and I have lived in some of them, where it is hard work to make both ends meet. I have seen this in Victoria Island, and in Iowa, with this difference, that the Iowa farmers never starve to death but the Eskimos sometimes do. That is primarily for transportation reasons.

We have, then, in the more or less far north, vast territories, thousands of miles of coastline, and great stretches of inland wood or prairie in which there live a varied but generally carefree and happy people known as Eskimos. The main thing that binds them together and makes them Eskimos is their common speech,

one of the most difficult languages in the world for an outsider to learn.

It is said that a business man in a great city can get along if he has a ready command of from three to five thousand words, but an Eskimo cannot deal with his neighbors in less than ten to twelve thousand words, each colloquially at the tip of his tongue. It is not merely the size of the vocabulary. An English noun, for instance, has four forms—*man, man's, men, men's;* a Greek noun has nine forms; but an Eskimo noun has or can have more than a thousand forms, each different

EWING GALLOWAY

A PROUD INDIAN mother in the Yukon River country cradles her baby on her lap.

from any other and each with a precise meaning of its own. Their verbs are even more complicated than the nouns. Besides all that, you have to acquire a new way of thinking before you can speak such a tongue easily—a polysynthetic language.

But when you have learned a good polysynthetic language, you will not by choice use, say, English or German, for it is so much more flexible, precise and concise. Record, for instance, some Eskimo folktale as it is dictated to you by a storyteller. Then translate it idiomatically and you will find one page of Eskimo giving about two and a half pages of English.

NAVAHO WOMEN are noted for their long, ebony-black hair, which they keep gleaming with "brushes" of stiff grass. The Navahos love color, especially tawny, desert hues.

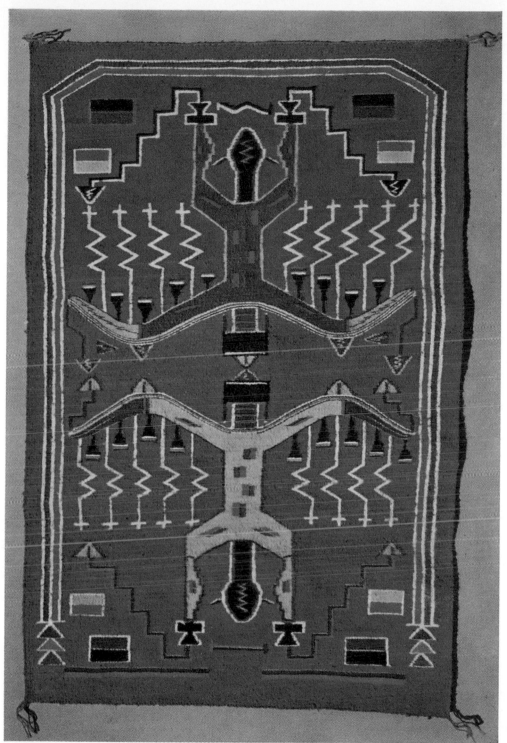

THUNDERBIRDS FLASH LIGHTNING from their wings in a modern Navaho blanket. Early patterns were mostly geometric, with few colors except the natural grays of the wool.

could out of forest products. Canoes were of birch bark in the north, elm bark in New York State, and dugouts were made of cypress in the south. Houses were of poles, covered with bark or matting. Buckets and dishes were of bark or basketry, with a little pottery. Clothing was of buckskin; bedding, of furs.

Here lived people of Algonkian speech. In the north, they were hunters only, like the Naskapi of Labrador. Farther south, they combined hunting and agriculture. It was Indians of the Narragansett tribe who taught the Pilgrim Fathers how to plant corn, four kernels to a hill, with beans between the rows and fish heads for fertilizer. To them or other Algonkians the white man owes the use of the clambake and the bean pot, which were Indian methods of fireless cooking. With their help the newcomers developed such foods

as johnnycake, buckwheat cakes, maple syrup and succotash.

"Succotash" is an Algonkian word. So are "woodchuck," "wigwam," "wampum," "squaw," "papoose," "tomahawk," not to mention scores of place names. How bare a map of eastern North America would be without such words as "Massachusetts," "Connecticut," "Adirondack," "Allegheny"!

Along Lake Superior and the upper Mississippi were other Algonkians, pushing their canoes through the wild-rice swamps or tending their cornfields in river valleys. School histories sometimes show pictures of their wigwams, which were frames of poles in domed or gabled shape, covered with bark or matting laid on like clapboards. More often they show pictures of the warriors, with heads shaved except for the scalp lock, and faces painted. Less often they tell about the Algonkian belief in the Great Spirit, the manito, whose power was in every plant, bird and animal. Boys approaching manhood used to go into the forest to fast and pray, hoping for a vision of one of the powerful beings that would give faith and strength for the life of hardship that lay ahead.

Indian Reservations as Homes

Algonkians of the east have now mixed with the general population or they are on small reservations, under the states, in the United States, not the national Government. Algonkians in what is now the Middle West sold their lands and moved still farther west of the Mississippi to reservations.

Another woodland group was the Iroquois, the famous Five Nations—Mohawk, Oneida, Onondaga, Cayuga and Seneca. Later they were joined by their kinsmen the Tuscarora from the south. In fact, the Iroquois seem to have moved up from the south, fighting their way through the Algonkians until they were established in the green valleys of central New York, while the Huron and others speaking the same language built their villages on the Canadian side of Lake Huron.

Even though women did the farm work, the Iroquois cornfields were always im-

SANTA FE RAILWAY

A MEDICINE MAN obeys the Navaho belief that sand painting must be erased by sundown.

mense. Among their cherished deities were the "three sisters"—the spirits of corn, beans and squash—as well as beings of the mountain and forest. The Iroquois did not go out alone to pray to their spirit helpers, as did the Algonkian hunter. The Iroquois held dignified ceremonies within the community long house, when dances were performed and tobacco incense was burned. Some of those dances are performed today, both in New York State and in Oklahoma. Sometimes masks were carved from living trees, to represent the wood spirits who could both cause and cure disease or injury.

The Fortress of the Iroquois

Iroquois villages were stockaded for defense and, inside, were the famous long houses. These were bark-covered dwellings almost as long as a Pullman car and divided into compartments in the same way. Each compartment was the home of a family, whose mother was its head; her husband left his own mother's home to come and live with her. Apparently that arrangement, used in many parts of the world, works just as well as the white man's way, with the father as head of the family. Families were gathered into clans, clans into tribes and the five (later six) tribes into a primitive United Nations. Their great assembly met once or twice a year to "take up the hatchet" or to "bury the hatchet"—that is, to make war or peace.

No wonder the Iroquois were able to conquer the neighboring Algonkians. They built up something like an empire which did not collapse until the American War of the Revolution. At that time their nations could not agree on which side to take and so their unity was broken. The Iroquois now live like whites, some on reservations in the United States and some in Canada. The Caughnawaga group of Canada have become famous as structural-steel workers.

The rich warm land that is now the Southern states was occupied by other Indians, farmers and hunters too, with a long history of settled living. These were the Muskhogeans: Creek, Choctaw,

THE TSIMSHIAN INDIANS in British Columbia have a family totem outside every home.

Chickasaw and Seminole. One Iroquoian tribe was among them, the Cherokee, who must have been dropped off as their kinsmen were moving northward at an earlier period.

These people are known in the United States Indian Office records as the Five Civilized Tribes, and they merit the name. It was probably the ancestors of some of them who built the famous mounds found in Ohio and for hundreds of miles north and south. Living closer to Mexico than

SAND PAINTING is an art of the Navaho medicine man. It is part of a religious rite performed to heal the sick. Though the artist drops sand freehand, he follows strict rules.

THE ZUNIS, of western New Mexico, are skilled at making silver jewelry, which is often set with turquoise. Though only simple tools are used, designs may be quite elaborate.

THE SONS AND DAUGHTERS of Cree Indian trappers attend the school at Lac La Ronge, Saskatchewan, in northern Canada. In this classroom, the children learn their three R's.

the northerners, the Muskhogeans may have learned to plant earlier. They built large villages, which the whites called towns, with houses of logs covered with earth for winter and spacious arbors for summer. Their women made fine pottery and baskets. Their men were fierce warriors whose clan signs on a blazed tree boldly told a victim just whom he must seek in vengeance.

The Civilized Tribes, like the Iroquois, had mother clans. These were gathered into towns with numbers of officials and a chief whom the whites called "king." On ceremonial occasions the king with his warriors and councillors sat on wooden benches around the town square. When new fire was made at the new year, in summer, they all took an emetic to purify themselves, made peace with each other, forgave debts and generally prepared for a co-operative year. The Five Civilized Tribes have made an admirable record as American citizens. Their land was bought in the 1830's and most of them moved to

Oklahoma. There they set up towns with the old names. They ran their own government and schools. Some of them already had constitutions; and Sequoya, the famous Cherokee leader, had provided his tribe with a written language. In 1907, when Oklahoma became a state, the tribal governments were dissolved. Many members by that time spoke English. Cherokee have become successful as lawyers, doctors, teachers, a vice-president of the United States (Charles Curtis) and, perhaps best known of all, the famous part-Cherokee Will Rogers.

Some tribal remnants have not moved. A few Cherokee cling to the Great Smoky Mountains where they have a reservation. Most of the Seminole, long before removal, had run away, as their name implies, to Florida. ("Seminole" comes from a Creek word that means "runaway.") There they fought the United States troops who tried to remove them. They were never really conquered, though they live peacefully today on their reserva-

24

tion in the swampy Everglades of Florida.

Crossing the Mississippi we come to the plains—the Great Plains where once thousands of buffalo roamed like a moving black carpet. We often think of the red men who hunted these buffalo as *the* Indians. Actually, they did not take up their roving life with horse and tepee until after the Spaniards had brought horses to the West, about 1600. Then Indians from many parts of the country pushed out to the rich plains to join the few already established along the rivers. The Cheyenne and Arapaho were Algonkians from the east. Apache came from the far north and Comanche from the west. The Sioux, or Dakota, best known of all, were relatives of the Muskhogeans, from the Mississippi Valley in the central United States.

Buffalo, the Mainstay of Life

Here, on the treeless plains, the main source of supply was the buffalo. Its skins, sewed together, formed the pointed tent which is called by the Siouan word *tepee*. The buffalo's sinews made sewing thread and bowstrings, its bones were tools, its stomach was a bag for meat. Practically all the rest of the animal was eaten, including a great many parts that whites would have refused. These parts were rich in vitamins, however, so that Indians got a fairly well-balanced diet without green vegetables. The meat was sun-dried for winter use into what the whites call "jerky." Pemmican, a Cree word, is dried meat pounded fine and packed in sacks. Add a few berries and greens in season and some buckskin for clothing and the Indian had all he needed. For decoration he wore the famous feather bonnet, though this was a privilege for the few. After the traders came, his clothes were richly embroidered with beads.

Since the plains Indians had no towns like the woodland people, they did not need much government. In the winter, when there were few buffalo, little groups camped by themselves. In summer, a whole tribe might get together for the great hunt and for the sun dance when they prayed for the welfare of the world. Individual warriors, also, went out to im-

plore the Great Mystery for success in war, which was the plainsman's whole career. It was not scalps they tried for but the honor accorded daring acts—to steal an enemy's horse from right outside his tepee, or to touch a dead enemy while his comrades fought around him. These Indians are now farming and running cattle on reservations in the west of the United States and in Canada.

In New Mexico and Arizona there are Indians still living in the style of centuries ago, wearing their old costumes, at least for ceremonies, speaking the old languages and observing the old religious rites. In the south of Arizona are the Pima, some of the first Indians in the United States to practice agriculture. Long before the whites came, they were building irrigation canals as much as sixteen miles long. In the western desert are the Papago who still pick the fruit of the giant cactus and drink its juice as a rite to make their crops grow.

Along the Rio Grande and west into the desert are the Pueblo peoples. *Pueblo* is Spanish for "village" and so the conquistadors named them, three hundred years ago. Their warm, sunny country provides neither forest nor buffalo plains, only sand and rocks with a few scrubby trees and desert bushes. What were the Indians to use for house and utensils? Their answer was the earth itself. Houses were made of stone or else adobe, which is the hard desert earth shaped into home-made bricks. There is summer rain in this country, so that it is possible to raise corn if it is the right variety. The Hopi have tough little plants that they place in the earth twelve inches deep and that give corn as in the other Pueblos, yellow-blue, black-red-white, and speckled.

Holiday Costumes of Pueblos

On feast days, you may see Pueblo Indians dressed in cotton that was grown and woven by themselves or in wool from the breed of sheep brought by the Spaniards. In some Pueblos the men wear their hair long, flowing beneath a bunch of parrot plumes. In others they wear strange masks, representing the rain spir-

A GROTESQUE MASK is carved by a twentieth-century Iroquois. His forefathers used such masks in healing ceremonies. They were cut from a living tree and usually painted.

A SEMINOLE ROBE is created on a sewing machine. Once the thousands of tiny pieces were seamed by hand. Some Seminoles still live in their old home, the Florida Everglades.

THE NAVAHO INDIANS make the walls of their houses from poles and the round roofs from earth. Near Lukachuka, Arizona, a family gathers outside a typical Navaho dwelling.

its on whom they call. As you walk among their neat little houses, you buy beautifully decorated pots made by the women or the charming water-color pictures that both boys and girls have begun to paint since they have gone to the government schools and found the new materials.

Out in the desert or the mountains are the Navaho and Apache, speaking Athapascan, a language from the north. Students think that they wandered down from the wild north centuries ago. The Navaho then mixed with Pueblo people, learned to grow corn and to weave; and when the Spaniards came, the Navaho learned about sheep and horses. Now, scattered over the desert, you may see their little domed huts, made of poles covered with earth, and white sheep and horses grazing near. Beside a hut, called a hogan, sits a woman at her loom, weaving one of the brilliant blankets in stripes and zigzags that are now sold all over the United States. The man, if he has not ridden off to the trading post or to a "sing," the Navaho name for a ceremony, may be making silver jewelry, an art learned from the Mexicans.

The Apache did not stop fighting until long after the Navaho, and many were the skirmishes they had with the United States cavalry. Now they have settled down and, as it turns out, their mountain homes furnish some of the best cattle and lumber country in the Southwest. On their five reservations, they run cattle, sheep and a lumber mill and they are talking about a tourist camp. Even so, some of them find time for the charming open-air ceremony in summer when they inaugurate their girls into womanhood.

North of this southwestern country are the arid lands of California and Nevada where the Indians lived on nuts, seeds, rabbits and any other food they could dig, pick or kill. Most of them have changed rather quickly to the white man's clothing and ways. In Idaho were hunters and fishers, also changing rapidly now that the land is farmed and the rivers dammed. On up into Alaska, we still find hunters, dressed in furs now and following the herds of caribou. Many of these speak Athapascan, like the Navaho and Apache.

The coast of Alaska, of western Canada, of Washington, Oregon and northern California is a different place. Here is a narrow strip where the Coast, or the Cascade, Range attracts plentiful rain. There are, or there were, huge forests of spruce and pine, alive with elk, deer, bear, fox and

28

mink. Cold rushing streams go down to the Pacific and in these, every summer, the salmon came to spawn.

Indians living here were as rich as those on the buffalo plains and they had more variety. The soft, straight wood of the evergreens allowed them to hew out planks, even with stone tools. They built houses that looked almost like an unpainted New England barn. They dug out huge canoes, some able to hold sixty men or to plow far into the Pacific after whales. Even their dishes were made of beautifully smoothed, inlaid wood.

Finally we come to the very rim of the continent. All around the northern seacoast, from southern Alaska to southern Greenland, lived the Eskimos. It must not be thought that they all lived in snow houses. What were once called the Water Eskimos lived on the more southerly coast, where they could be out in their skin canoes, or kayaks, for at least half the year. Some of these were in Alaska and some in Greenland. Their houses were of driftwood or of stone, covered with turf. In summer, they lived in skin tents, while they put out in canoes for hunting. One-man canoes, or kayaks, were used for seal, sea lion and birds. The big boat, or umiak, was for whales which they harpooned and towed in to shore. In autumn, they went inland hunting the caribou, which furnished their clothing. In winter, when the waters were frozen, they made trips by sled to hunt or trade.

All this is in the past. Long before World War II, white people had begun to live in Eskimo country as traders, teachers and government officials. Eskimos were moving from their old-style houses, changing to modern clothing and being employed in cannery and other work. The war speeded up the change, for men came in planes to the remotest parts of the Arctic for survey and study. In the United States, all Indians are now citizens, eligible to vote and to receive social-security payments.

In the 1950's the number of Indians living in the United States was about 500,000, many of whom lived on reserva-

tions. A reservation is a tract of land set apart by treaty for Indian use in return for other lands given up for settlement by whites. Indians need not occupy this land unless they wish, but the reserving of it by the Government is in payment of a debt. A recent law provides that they may trade or bequeath it to other Indians but not to whites. Thus each group is assured of some permanent place of its own in the country.

On each reservation in the United States the Government provides an administrative agent with a staff on which Indians are employed as fast as they can qualify. Where Indians live near public schools, the Government arranges with county or state for their attendance along with the whites.

In Canada, Indians often do not vote while they live on the reserves. These are the equivalent of reservations in the United States and are managed by the Department of Citizenship and Immigration, Indian Affairs Branch. If an Indian can prove that he is competent to handle his affairs in the modern manner, he may move off the reserve, be given the right to vote and live like any other citizen. The Canadian Government takes care of roads and general improvements. It builds and maintains the schools but these are staffed by the various churches. Some Indians go to the regular provincial schools. Medical services are given by the Department of National Health and Welfare. There are about 160,000 Indians living in Canada today.

Needy Indians are given allowances by the Indian Affairs Branch, but the Government makes every effort to help them become self-supporting. Many in the north are hunters and trappers, and projects have been instituted to increase the supply of beaver and muskrat. Farther south, they are farmers and day laborers. Assistance has been given them in agriculture, animal husbandry, fishing, logging and lumbering. As in the United States, an Indian band may elect a council and, through it, borrow money from the Government for group operations.

By Ruth M. Underhill

DON C. DIERS

A BEADED SIOUX COSTUME. When the white man appeared on the Plains, he brought fine beads with him. The Indians quickly substituted them for quills in dress decoration.

TOTEM POLES and totemic figures of the Northwest. The topmost carving, with down-turned nose, is a hawk symbol. At the left is a "welcome figure," with outstretched arms.

31

Canada

OCCUPYING about two fifths of North America, Canada is the world's second largest country in area (exceeded only by the Soviet Union). It has abundant natural resources, particularly minerals and water power, much of which still awaits development. At the same time, Canada has a relatively small population, approaching 18,000,000 in 1960. Beside this must be set the fact that the far north, bordering on the Arctic Ocean, has too severe a climate to invite much settlement under present conditions or to support agriculture. The population is concentrated in the south, although plenty of room is left for expansion in habitable areas.

Canada and the United States share the world's longest undefended border, a unique achievement in international relations. That either should ever attack the other is unthinkable. In fact, they act

together in maintaining the defense of North America, as in the DEW Line, the chain of radar stations stretching across the top of the continent.

Canada is, of course, just as American as the United States. Canada is equally a sovereign nation, with this difference: that it is a constitutional monarchy (Queen Elizabeth II of the United Kingdom is also the Queen of Canada) and a member of the Commonwealth of Nations. Canada won from Great Britain the last bit of control over its affairs in 1931. As in the United Kingdom the Queen is the ruler of Canada only in a symbolic sense, much as the symbol is revered. And the

... *monarch of the north*

Commonwealth is a loose association of free states.

In this century, particularly since the 1930's, the economic bonds between Canada and the United States have been growing apace. It is a natural result of being such close neighbors. Yet it puts a strain on their relations. The United States has about ten times the population of Canada as well as the world's mightiest industrial organization. As it has expanded it has sought investment as well as markets north of the border. The result is that about half of Canada's manufacturing industries are financed by United States capital. Nor is the border

any barrier to books, mass-circulation magazines, television and radio programs originating in the United States. The trend alarms many Canadians. Rightfully proud of their nationhood they fear the threat to their country's identity. The threat is, of course, innocent. People on both sides of the boundary realize that the United States has no designs on Canada. But the influence is hard to block or escape.

Canada is all the more determinedly going its own way in many fields. In international relations it has become the spokesman in the UN and various other organizations for many of the free world's "middle powers." The idea of the NATO was first proposed by former Prime Minister Louis St. Laurent. Canada insists that all NATO members, large and small, be treated and consulted as equals. In part because of the need for more man power, since World War II Canada has opened its doors much wider than the United States to European immigrants. In 1959 at the instigation of Canada a Commonwealth education program was introduced for the advancement of education in underdeveloped areas.

To encourage the careers of gifted Canadians at home, the Canada Council for the Encouragement of the Arts, Humanities and Social Sciences was created by act of Parliament in 1957. It was endowed with $100,000,000 out of public funds to provide grants to universities, symphony orchestras, theater and ballet companies, art galleries, scholars, artists, writers, composers. Today the Government-run Canadian Broadcasting Corporation provides educational radio and television programs reaching into all ten provinces.

Canada's national health program is equally widespread. The Hospital Insurance and Diagnostic Services Act came into force on May 1, 1957. In this sys-

OTTAWA, THE CAPITAL: Parliament Hill, upper center; Confederation Square and National War Memorial, lower center; Rideau Canal, which runs past the castle-like Chateau Laurier, lower right.

33

tem the costs are shared by the Federal (50 per cent) and provincial governments. Government grants are also forthcoming to help construct hospital facilities, purchase equipment, train professional personnel and make surveys of health services and resources. Federal Government social-welfare measures include aid for the needy and the aged or disabled, unemployment insurance and family allowances.

Transportation is growing rapidly. Besides the St. Lawrence Seaway, discussed elsewhere in this volume, 60,000 miles of railroads web the country and the 5,000-mile Trans-Canada Highway spans it. Between 1960 and 1970 Canada plans to spend $15,000,000,000 on roads, the costs to be shared by the Federal, provincial and municipal governments.

Canada is already one of the world's leading countries in hydroelectric development though only about a quarter of its water-power resources are yet in use. The possibilities in British Columbia and Labrador have hardly been touched. A transcontinental natural-gas line has been completed. Moreover, as the oil pipeline system grows, it will become more economical for Canada to draw on its rich western fields to supply eastern industries instead of importing oil.

The heart of this enormous half-continent was opened and exploited along two great waterways. The water routes of the St. Lawrence River and the Great Lakes were in the hands of the French until 1759; those of Hudson Bay and the rivers emptying into it were from the early seventeenth century more or less controlled by the British. The French-controlled waterway led to one of the most fertile and productive areas of the continent and gave access to the whole interior plain. The Hudson Bay waterway led to nothing but a vast and inhospitable country which had, however, almost unlimited supplies of furs.

When the British captured Quebec and put an end to the French empire in North America, the French colony had some 70,-000 inhabitants. To guarantee the loyalty of these people to its rule, the British Government permitted them to maintain the French language and the civil laws of France and to follow the Roman Catholic religion. The descendants of these 70,000 have grown today into a body of more than 4,000,000 French-speaking Canadians.

For some years after the taking of Quebec the English-speaking inhabitants of the new British colony of Canada consisted of a few traders and government officials and the occupying troops. But after the American War of Independence a large number of those who had supported the British in that conflict moved north and settled in the colonies of Nova Scotia, New Brunswick and Ontario. At length the colonies under Britain came to have more English-speaking people than French. By the time of the War of 1812 it was clear that the French population preferred to remain under the British flag rather than join the new republic of the United States.

Half a century later the development of railways had made communication easier, thereby cementing common interests of the colonies. Although still organized in several different units, the colonies began to consider forming a single British dominion which would extend from the Atlantic to the Pacific. In 1867 the British North America Act created a new political unit consisting of the province of Canada (combining Upper and Lower Canada, now Ontario and Quebec), Nova Scotia and New Brunswick, to "form and be one Dominion under the name of Canada." Provision was made for the subsequent inclusion of Prince Edward Island, British Columbia, the territory of the Hudson's Bay Company (out of which was created the three Prairie Provinces) and Newfoundland. All of these areas have since been incorporated.

The land area of this vast country covers 3,845,774 square miles, of which only 547,946 are considered suitable for agriculture and 1,345,840 square miles are under forest. The remaining 1,712,765 square miles are muskeg, rock and tundra. While unproductive on their surface, they contain immense mineral wealth.

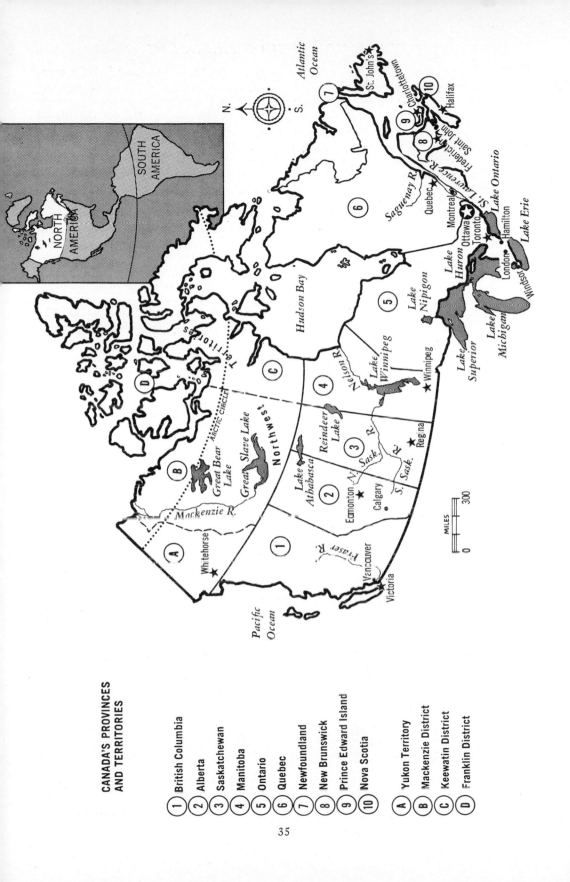

CANADA'S PROVINCES AND TERRITORIES

① British Columbia
② Alberta
③ Saskatchewan
④ Manitoba
⑤ Ontario
⑥ Quebec
⑦ Newfoundland
⑧ New Brunswick
⑨ Prince Edward Island
⑩ Nova Scotia

Ⓐ Yukon Territory
Ⓑ Mackenzie District
Ⓒ Keewatin District
Ⓓ Franklin District

Until recent years the exploration of this rock-and-muskeg area was delayed by the high cost of transportation, for the building of railways and the making of roads across its barren face was very difficult. The advent of the airplane and new methods of testing for ore bodies from the ground's surface has altered the picture, however. The mineral stores and possibilities of the shores of the Arctic will soon be as well known as those of long-settled and populous areas.

Most of the rock-and-muskeg land and a considerable part of the forest area lies in a geological formation known as the Canadian Shield or Laurentian Plateau. This is a shield-shaped region of denuded ancient rocks which embraces Hudson Bay, comes down to the shores of Lake Superior and Lake Huron, and occupies half of Canada's total land area. Scoured by glacial action, its rugged and irregular surface has not had time to develop a thick, fresh cover of soil, except in a few places such as the Clay Belt in northern Ontario and Quebec. Its trees are small and, until the rise of the newsprint industry based on pulpwood, its forest land was regarded

as a permanent wilderness; but the combination of suitable wood and streams for floating the logs, abundant water power and mineral wealth, has given the Shield great economic importance.

West of the Shield lie the prairies, the Canadian extension of the great, fertile central plain of North America, an expanse of rich soil where wheat growing extends far north into the Peace River country of Alberta. West of the prairies are the Rocky Mountains, the backbone of the continent, and beyond them are the Pacific coast and Vancouver Island, with great valleys of good land between forested mountains and a climate warmed by the Japan Current.

East and south of the Shield is the St. Lawrence Plain, gently sloping agricultural country containing half of Canada's population. Most of the nation's manufacturing has been drawn here by the transportation facilities of the St. Lawrence River and the Great Lakes and also by the cheap electric current produced by the waterfalls of the region. Because of the conformation of the Great Lakes, a part of this plain extends far down into

CANADIAN PACIFIC RAILWAY

THE CITADEL, A RELIC OF BOTH FRENCH AND BRITISH RULE

High above the St. Lawrence in the city of Quebec, zigzag the fortifications of the Citadel. Built in the 1820's, the present walls enclose earlier strongholds of the French.

THE QUEEN OF CANADA REVIEWS HER TORONTO GUARD OF HONOR

Elizabeth II is the sovereign of the Commonwealth dominions as well as of the United Kingdom.
Her Majesty and Prince Philip were in Toronto on their 1959 grand tour of Canada.

37

GREAT DIVIDE GATE ON MOUNT HECTOR IN YOHO NATIONAL PARK

The massive timber gate marks the border between Alberta and British Columbia and part of the Great Divide. On one side all streams flow to the Atlantic; on the other, to the Pacific.

CLATTERING CHUCK WAGONS RACE AT THE CALGARY STAMPEDE

Raising great clouds of dust in a fond salute to rough and ready frontier days, men of the Prairie Provinces join in a hard chuck-wagon race around the track at Calgary, Alberta.

the latitude of the United States and has a climate mild enough for the growing of tobacco and many delicate fruits.

The provinces by the sea lie still farther east of the Canadian Shield. They consist of two islands, Prince Edward Island and Newfoundland, the peninsula of Nova Scotia and the largely forested mainland area of New Brunswick. Geologically these form an extension of the Appalachian mountain chain of the United States, but their mountains have weathered to the point where they contain (except in Newfoundland) a good proportion of arable land and high-grade forest. The waters along their coasts are excellent fishing grounds. Industrially the Atlantic provinces are at some disadvantage because of their distance from the chief markets of the country.

The growth of Canada was slow until it was shown that wheat could be very suc-

cessfully grown in the prairies. Large-scale immigration began around 1900. In 1901 the country's population was a little over five million, of whom less than half a million were in the prairies; today the total is about fourteen million, of whom the prairies have over two and a half million.

Canada's annual production of wheat ranges from 300 to 560 million bushels, and the export of wheat and wheat flour is exceeded in money value only by that of newsprint paper. The other important exports are lumber and wood pulp, nickel, copper, asbestos, zinc, aluminum (made from foreign ores but with cheap Canadian water power), agricultural machinery, cattle and fish.

It can be seen that the economy of the country is highly specialized in the production of a few staple articles for which Canada has natural advantages. Since it needs great quantities of subtropical food-

N. Y. NEW HAVEN & HARTFORD RR. CO.

NIAGARA, AT THE BRINK OF THE GIGANTIC HORSESHOE FALLS

In a magnificent, irregular arc above a magic spray of mist, Horseshoe Falls sweeps toward wooded Goat Island. Beyond are Rainbow Bridge and the turgid spillings of American Falls.

GEORGE HUNTER

NORTHERN SASKATCHEWAN—A URANIUM MINE UNDER CONSTRUCTION

Above Lake Athabaska in the booming town of Beaver Lodge, building supervisors check blue-prints. The laced pile of steel rigging is the skeleton of a shaft for a uranium mine.

stuffs—raw cotton, machinery, coal, sugar and rubber—the volume of Canada's foreign trade is exceptionally heavy in relation to the country's population. As we have indicated the United States is Canada's chief trading partner, for the most part exchanging raw and semifinished materials in return for manufactured articles.

Yet it is no longer true that Canada is mainly an agricultural country. Farming yields only 13 per cent of the national income and engages only 15 per cent of the labor force. Nevertheless, though acreage increased only slightly, new methods and new kinds of machinery permitted farm production to double between 1940 and 1960. Actually, Canada is the world's sixth largest manufacturing country but almost all of the articles are bought at home.

Meanwhile, the Canadian population has become ever more urban. More than two thirds of the people live in cities or suburbs today. At the same time, Canada's birth rate has been rising rapidly. There was a 53 per cent increase in school attendance between 1950 and 1959. The result is overcrowded city schools and not enough qualified teachers. As in the United States, a solution to this problem has yet to be found.

In some respects Canada's political structure resembles that of Great Britain. In others it is like that of the United States. With the appointment of Vincent Massey in 1952, for the first time a Canadian citizen became governor general. A French Canadian, Major General George P. Vanier, was appointed governor general in 1959.

Except for the fact that membership in the Senate is not hereditary as it is in the English House of Lords, these political arrangements closely parallel those of Great Britain. In their internal structure, however, Canada's political parties resemble those of the United States. They hold conventions to select the party leader and to adopt a platform; when a party has a majority in the House of Commons, its leader becomes prime minister.

By B. K. SANDWELL

CANADA: FACTS AND FIGURES

THE COUNTRY

Occupies the upper half of the North American continent and adjacent islands, excepting the state of Alaska. The country has ten provinces and two territories, a total area of 3,845,774 sq. mi. and a population of nearly 18,000,000.

GOVERNMENT

Canada is an independent state within the British Commonwealth. The sovereign is represented by a governor general. Executive power is vested in a prime minister and a cabinet. Legislative power is entrusted to a parliament which consists of a 102-member Senate and a 265-member House of Commons. All British subjects of either sex, who are over 21 years of age and have resided in Canada for a year, are eligible to vote.

COMMERCE AND INDUSTRIES

While the country still depends in part on agriculture, it is rapidly being dominated by industry. The principal crops are wheat, oats, barley, rye, potatoes and a wide variety of fruit. Other prolific sources of income are furs, fish, wool, lumber, dairy products, hydroelectric power and minerals, particularly nickel, coal, asbestos, petroleum, gold, silver, copper and uranium. Much of Canada's revenue comes from such products as newsprint, food, beverages, textiles, chemicals, machinery, transportation equipment and electrical apparatus. Nearly every country in the world trades with Canada, but the United States is its outstanding customer. Monetary unit, the Canadian dollar.

COMMUNICATIONS

There are 60,000 mi. of railway; 235,000 mi. of surfaced roads; about 2,000 mi. of canals; over 50,000 mi. of scheduled airlines. The nation also has about 4,810,000 telephones. About 75% of Canadian homes have TV sets. There are 111 daily newspapers (91 in English and 13 in French).

RELIGION AND EDUCATION

Canada has no state church as 49 per cent of its population is Protestant and 46 per cent is Catholic. There are some 28,884 provincially controlled elementary and secondary schools; 1,212 academic private schools; 468 schools for Indians conducted by a Federal agency; 133 teacher-training schools; 283 colleges and universities.

CHIEF CITIES (Metropolitan)

Ottawa, capital, 345,000; Montreal, 1,625,000; Toronto, 1,360,000; Vancouver, 665,000; Winnipeg, 409,000; Hamilton, 328,000; Quebec, 310,000; Edmonton, 251,000; Calgary, 200,000.

The Atlantic Provinces

FACING the North Atlantic Ocean are Canada's four smallest provinces: Nova Scotia, New Brunswick, Prince Edward Island and Newfoundland. The first three have long been known as the Maritime Provinces. They jut out into the North Atlantic, and many of their communities are entirely dependent on the sea for a living.

These provinces boast some of the loveliest scenery in Canada. Tracts of inviting woodlands, sparkling beaches, clear lakes and rolling countryside grace the land. Most of it is rather thinly inhabited and is free of the blight that all too often comes with big cities. The whole region is a paradise for hunters, fishermen and nature lovers.

Much like some parts of the New England states, though, the Atlantic Provinces have retained their rural character at a cost. Lack of variety in resources, distance from the large markets of central Canada and other factors have prevented the development of big manufacturing industries. Though the Atlantic Provinces were settled very early, have a normal birth rate and have a steady if small flow of immigrants, they lose many of their young people every year. Despite the beauty of the area its sons and daughters seek the greater opportunities offered by the big cities to the west and south. Population growth, as a result, has been slow.

In Newfoundland, the largest food market east of Montreal, less than 25 per cent of the produce sold there comes from the four provinces. If all the tillable land in the Atlantic Provinces were worked efficiently, the farm output in the area could increase tenfold by 1970.

Leaders of the four provinces are not standing idly by, of course. Remedies have been and are being applied. The world-famous Antigonish Movement developed as a response to the problem of emigration from Nova Scotia at the dawn of the twentieth century. The Catholic clergymen who initiated the idea believed that emigration was responsible for the

AT PEGGY'S COVE, fishing hamlet on Nova Scotia's Atlantic shore, wind and wave scour the rocks beneath a veil of sea mist.

sumer co-operatives, even housing co-operatives. The success of the Antigonish Movement, furthermore, has inspired imitation all over the world, from Puerto Rico to Ceylon.

Since World War II the governments of the various provinces have joined in a number of enterprises to stimulate the economy further. Among the most important is the Atlantic Provinces Economic Council, a voluntary research and promotion organization founded in 1955. The council's purpose is to spur economic rehabilitation in the Maritimes. The four provincial prime ministers meet usually twice a year to co-ordinate economic planning. In 1958 they established the Atlantic Provinces Research Council. They act together to request federal government assistance. Ottawa has responded with financial support for a number of projects, including modernization of the Cape Breton coal mines and building of the Canso Causeway between the mainland and Cape Breton.

Not everyone is happy about the various campaigns being waged to encourage economic growth in the Atlantic Provinces. Some feel that the area's greatest asset is the relief it affords Canadians and Americans weary of big-city competition and crowding. This asset will become more and more important in the years to come if the big cities continue to expand as predicted. No one certainly wants to see industrialization mar the unique maritime countryside.

What might be called the outward coasts of Newfoundland and Nova Scotia are washed by the Atlantic, while the inward coasts of the four provinces (excluding Labrador) help form the boundaries of the Gulf of St. Lawrence. The tiniest of the provinces, Prince Edward Island—often called simply "the Island" —is set entirely within the gulf.

Since the Atlantic Provinces are nearer to Europe than any other part of North

... rich in traditions of the sea

region's economic ills. Present day leaders still hold this view. "Every ten years," a spokesman pointed out recently, "Nova Scotia has been losing what is about equal to the population of Prince Edward Island." The original leaders of the Antigonish Movement wanted to make remaining at home more rewarding. They encouraged the formation of co-operatives by farmers and fishermen to make the marketing of their products more profitable and the purchase of supplies cheaper. Credit unions were also set up. These serve as savings banks and the people can also borrow from them from time to time on no other security than their reputation for honesty.

The founding priests were also determined to stamp out illiteracy. The movement thus provides for elementary schools through its credit unions. The Antigonish Movement has long since spread throughout the four provinces. Its co-operatives now cover the whole region. There are marketing co-operatives, con-

America (except Greenland), it is not surprising that they were among the first regions to be reached and settled by Europeans. Newfoundland was visited by fishermen from western Europe early in the sixteenth century and perhaps before. Sir Humphrey Gilbert eventually took possession of the island in 1583 in the name of the English Crown. It thus became the first British colony in the New World. Permanent settlement, however, was slow in developing on Newfoundland. The fishermen who landed there to cure their catch did not remain in winter.

In 1604 French colonists under Pierre du Guast, Sieur de Monts, made the first settlement on Nova Scotia, which they called Acadie. At first they settled on an island in Passamaquoddy Bay, but they soon moved to the opposite side of the Bay of Fundy where they founded Port Royal, later called Annapolis Royal by the English. Soon afterward the British also claimed this region, and in 1621 it was granted by the British to a Scot, Sir William Alexander. He promptly named it Nova Scotia, the Latin for "New Scotland." The area covered the present Nova Scotia and also New Brunswick. This was the beginning of a long struggle between Britain and France for control of the two-pronged peninsula, a struggle that France finally lost. In 1713 the mainland was ceded to Britain but Cape Breton (Ile Royale) remained French until 1763.

When war with France flared up in 1755 the British expelled the French Acadians from the colony, who were forced to seek homes to the south. Settlers from New England replaced them, giving Nova Scotia its first large English-speaking population. In those years immigrants from Germany also arrived, and their descendants are still to be found in the county of Lunenburg. After 1800 a large number of Highland Scots came to Cape Breton Island and to the region around Pictou, where many of their descendants speak Gaelic to this day. But the greatest increase in population at any one time in Maritime history came with the American Revolution, when some thirty thousand loyalists left the rebellious colonies to find new homes in the colonies remaining within the British Empire. So large was the influx that Nova Scotia was divided in 1784 and the mainland north of the Bay of Fundy was formed into a new province called New Brunswick.

During the first half of the nineteenth century the Atlantic Provinces grew and prospered. Those were the days of wooden sailing ships, and Maritimers became famous for the crafts they built and sailed to all parts of the world. Products of the provinces, especially timber, enjoyed a favored position in the British market, and at the same time trade ties with nearby New England remained close. But after 1850, with the decline of the sailing ship and the coming of free trade in Britain (which meant a loss of preference in that market), the Atlantic Provinces entered upon less happy days. Some of their people favored joining the province of Canada to form a new nation, the Dominion of Canada. Such a union would give the seacoast provinces railway connections with the interior. With some misgivings Nova Scotia and New Brunswick entered Confederation in 1867, but Prince Edward Island stayed out until 1873 and Newfoundland did not enter until 1949. Citizens of the Atlantic Provinces have sometimes felt that they did not benefit from Confederation as much as did the inland provinces.

Certainly the interior of the continent grew much more rapidly. When navigation was open on the St. Lawrence, ships from Europe went directly to the great port of Montreal instead of stopping at Halifax or Saint John. The depression of the 1930's hit the Atlantic Provinces a heavy blow. The prices of their exports fell tragically. After 1940, however, better times returned as the provinces acquired a more diversified economic life.

Now let us look more closely at each of the provinces in turn, starting with Canada's newest province, Newfoundland, which includes Labrador. In shape Newfoundland resembles an equilateral triangle whose sides are cut with a great many jagged bays and inlets; thus there is a plentiful supply of good small harbors. The western shore of the island is marked by a range of high hills from which the land gradually slopes down to sea level on the eastern and southern coasts. The Labrador Current, which flows down the east coast, makes the climate cool, and the growing season is short. The days tend to be gray, with too little sunshine for good farming. A large part of the island is made up of unproductive barren lands and bogs, where neither trees nor crops will grow. Only a fraction of the soil is fertile enough to support agriculture.

The Seafaring Newfoundlanders

The inhabitants are mainly of English and Irish origin. Nearly all of them live on the coasts. Only minor settlements are to be found inland. Travel between one part of the island and another is generally done by sea, although there is a narrow-gauge railway running from Port aux Basques on the southwest coast to the capital city of St. John's on the southeast coast.

Labrador is a wild and rocky land lying east of Quebec and north of Newfoundland. It is uninhabited except along its coasts, where a few thousand Indians and Eskimos live by fishing and sealing.

Fishing dominates the economic life of Newfoundland today, as it has always done. For many hundreds of years men have gone out to the Grand Banks southeast of the island and to other fishing banks in search of cod, herring and other creatures of the deep. Less romantic but more efficient motor-driven trawlers have now largely replaced the sailing ships of former days. Salt cod has long been the leading product of the island's fisheries, but in recent years quick-freezing plants and refrigerator ships have been used to supply the growing market in fresh frozen fish. In one form or another half the population depends upon the fishing industry.

The next most important source of livelihood of the people of Newfoundland comes from the forests of small coniferous trees which cover nearly half the island. Several large pulp and paper companies carry on operations which employ thousands of men. Many hundreds of small sawmills are spread around the island. The lumber they cut is mostly for local use. The value of forest products is higher than that of the fisheries, but the forest industries employ fewer people.

Mining is the third most important industry of Newfoundland. Iron ore is taken from the Wabana mine on Bell Island, just northwest of St. John's, and is shipped to steel mills at Sydney, Nova Scotia. In the center of the island there is also a mine producing copper, lead and zinc. Work is now going on to exploit the extensive iron-ore deposits of northeastern Quebec, which reach into western Labrador.

The eastern location of Newfoundland and Labrador has made them vital links in communications and defense. During World War II, an important airfield was developed at Gander Bay, Newfoundland, and from it thousands of airplanes were ferried to Europe. Since Gander is one-third of the distance between New York and Ireland, it has become a major stopping-off point on transatlantic flights. Another great airport, built at Goose Bay in central Labrador, is a vital link in the air defenses of Canada and the United States.

The Tenth Province Is Born

From 1855 to 1934 Newfoundland was a self-governing dominion. During the depression of the 1930's, however, its economic position became so poor that representative government was suspended in favor of government by a British royal commission. During World War II, the island's position improved greatly and it became possible to restore representative government. This involved a choice of returning to the status of a separate dominion or entering into Canadian Confederation as the tenth province. By a narrow margin, Newfoundland made the second choice.

Since joining Confederation, the provincial government has encouraged European industrialists to establish plants on the island, and the large amount of new capital invested there should bring increased employment and prosperity to the inhabitants. Moreover, Confederation has brought such social benefits as family allowances, which mean a great deal to those with low incomes.

South and west of Newfoundland, across the Gulf of St. Lawrence, are the three traditional Maritime Provinces— Nova Scotia, New Brunswick and Prince Edward Island. They are joined, rather than separated, by the sea. They have excellent harbors from which ships and ferry boats regularly carry passengers from one province to another.

New Brunswick, east of the state of Maine, is less clearly a maritime region than are the other Atlantic provinces; nevertheless it has extensive coasts on the Bay of Fundy and the Gulf of St. Lawrence. Its north coast is formed by the deep indentation of Chaleur Bay, which separates the province from the Gaspé Peninsula of Quebec. New Brunswick is a rugged, hilly land, rectangular in shape. It is largely covered with forest, especially in the northern parts. Through its hills cut the largest rivers to be found in these provinces; one of them, the St. John, which rises in the state of Maine, is the mightiest on the Atlantic seaboard south of the St. Lawrence. This river flows into the Bay of Fundy where it forms an excellent harbor at the site of Saint John, New Brunswick's largest city. Other important rivers are the Restigouche, famous for its salmon, and the Miramichi, both of which flow eastward.

The population of New Brunswick is found mainly along the coasts and in the river valleys. The rugged north-central portion is almost uninhabited. The northern half of the province is predominantly French-speaking and many pioneer settlements have recently been established here. The population of the southern half is mainly British in origin.

Nova Scotia, Peninsular Province

Nova Scotia is connected with New Brunswick by the narrow Isthmus of Chignecto; otherwise it is an island, or rather two islands, because Cape Breton Island is separated from the rest of Nova Scotia by the narrow Strait of Canso.

Like New Brunswick, Nova Scotia is also hilly and rugged, with relatively little land that is good for farming. Hills and uplands cut across the province in a northeast and southwest direction. Only rarely are fertile valleys to be found. The largest and best of these is the Annapolis Valley near the Bay of Fundy shore. The southern Atlantic coast of the province is much rockier than the Fundy and gulf shores and is deeply cut with many inlets. These inlets make fine harbors, the largest of which is at Halifax, one of the world's great ports. Yarmouth, at the western end of the province, is the traditional port for trade with the New England states. The southwestern part of the province, under the moderating influence of the ocean, has a milder climate than any other parts of the Atlantic provinces. Much of the interior is barren and supports little population. This is especially true of Cape Breton Island, whose rugged inland is almost uninhabited. This island is cut almost in two by the Bras d'Or Lakes, which are really mighty salt-water inlets.

Prince Edward Island

Across Northumberland Strait from New Brunswick and Nova Scotia lies the crescent-shaped province of Prince Edward Island. At one place its shores are less than ten miles from the New Brunswick coast. There are no striking physical features on the island, which consists of low, rolling hills well suited for agriculture. It is the most uniformly and completely settled portion of the Maritimes and has sometimes been called "the million-acre farm." The one urban center of any importance is the capital, Charlottetown, situated on a well-protected harbor on the south shore. Like those of all the other Atlantic provinces, the coasts of Prince Edward Island are very irregular and provide many good harbors.

Fishing was the earliest economic activity in the maritime region, and it still is among the most important. In former days the favorite craft of Nova Scotia fishermen was a two-masted schooner with auxiliary oil-burning engines. Such a schooner carried several small boats called dories. At the fishing banks the dories, each manned by two men, would leave the schooner and return later to the mother ship with their catch. The most famous of all these schooners was the Bluenose, which for many years was unbeaten in races with ships of its type.

Inshore fishing is usually carried on by motorboats operating within a few miles of the home dock. Its importance has greatly increased in recent years. The Bay of Fundy and the Gulf of St. Lawrence, especially around Prince Edward Island, have been the leading centers of this kind of fishing. The most valuable catch is the lobster, which is caught in wooden traps set in shallow waters near the shore. Lobster has now replaced cod as the leading product of the maritime fishery, for there is a growing market for it in the large cities of the United States and Canada. Oysters and the little herring

known as sardines are also caught by inshore fishing methods.

As we have already seen, the Maritimes are not highly favored for carrying on agriculture, except in some of the river valleys and on Prince Edward Island. The latter grows potatoes and raises hogs, which bring a valuable cash return to its farmers. New Brunswick and Nova Scotia also produce crops for export to other parts of Canada and the world, but in general they import more agricultural products than they sell. New Brunswick's leading farming region is in the St. John Valley, where potatoes are grown on a large scale. The Annapolis Valley in Nova Scotia grows a large part of Canada's commercial apple crop. Dairy farming is important in all the Maritimes except Newfoundland. In general, however, the outlook for agriculture is not as bright as in other parts of Canada.

PAN AMERICAN WORLD AIRWAYS

GANDER, AIR GATEWAY TO CANADA AND THE UNITED STATES

Gander Airport, a fog-free spot in eastern Newfoundland, is one of the busiest airfields in the world. Scores of transatlantic liners, like this Constellation, stop at Gander daily.

The land of New Brunswick and Nova Scotia is much more important for its forests than for its agriculture. In fact, almost as many men are engaged in the forest industries of these two provinces as are employed in their fishing industries. The best-forested areas are found in central and northern New Brunswick, although the trees of Cape Breton Island and western Nova Scotia are also important. For many years fishing and lumbering were closely connected, since a main use of the lumber was in building ships for the fisheries. At the present time the cutting of trees for pulpwood is the most important phase of the forest industries.

The Mines of Cape Breton

Nova Scotia is easily the leading province in mining. Nearly half the coal mined in Canada comes from mines in Cape Breton Island and in the isthmus and north shore region. The Cape Breton mines, which are the most important, are at the ocean shore; indeed, some of them extend outward under the ocean floor for as much as three or four miles and are both dangerous and expensive to work. No other mining in the Maritimes approaches coal in importance, although most of the gypsum produced in Canada comes from Nova Scotia.

These provinces are not an important manufacturing region when we look at Canada as a whole. Nevertheless their production of finished goods has increased considerably in recent years. The coal mines around Sydney, in Cape Breton Island, are responsible for the most important single industry—iron and steel manufacture. Iron ore from Newfoundland is processed in the large mills near the coal mines. Industry has also been built on other local raw materials. Pulp and paper are made in New Brunswick, while many fish canneries and processing plants are to be found throughout the provinces. The two leading ports, Halifax and Saint John, are sites for a wide variety of factories, many of which rely upon imported raw materials, such as petroleum and sugar.

Another feature of the economic picture in the Maritimes is the rapidly growing tourist industry. The relatively cool summer climate of these provinces attracts many people from New England, New York and central Canada. Summer visitors enjoy the yachting, salt-water bathing and fishing as well as the quiet, restful atmosphere. Moreover, the many places of historic interest, such as Annapolis Royal, draw numerous visitors year after year.

Finally, we must note the important place that foreign trade has always played in the life of the Maritimes. Since they have the only ports on Canada's eastern shores which are open all year round, these provinces have built up an extensive trade with many parts of the world, especially Great Britain and the British West Indies. Halifax, a vital naval station, expanded greatly during World War II.

Old Centers of Learning

The visitor to the Maritime Provinces will find an intellectual and cultural tradition of long standing. The first college founded in English-speaking Canada was King's College, which was established at Windsor, Nova Scotia, in 1788. It was later moved to Halifax, where it now shares a common campus with Dalhousie University, the largest institution of higher learning in the Maritimes. Another King's College was established at Fredericton, the capital of New Brunswick, in 1800; this college later became the University of New Brunswick. There are also many other small colleges and universities, both religious and non-denominational, in the provinces. An outstanding example of their contribution to the life of the region is the extension program carried on at St. Francis Xavier University, at Antigonish, Nova Scotia.

Over the years the Maritimes have contributed much to Canada's cultural life. In the 1830's Judge T. C. Haliburton of Nova Scotia began to write his famous sketches of "Sam Slick, the Clockmaker," a landmark in the history of North American humor. Two of Canada's finest poets, Charles G. D. Roberts and Bliss Carman, began their careers in New Brunswick.

By G. M. CRAIG

Facts and Figures are given on page 64.

STATUE OF LONGFELLOW'S EVANGELINE IN NOVA SCOTIA PARK

Evangeline Park in Grand Pré immortalizes the heroine of the well-loved poem. A statue of
Evangeline dominates the park, and a replica of the Acadian church appears in the background.

49

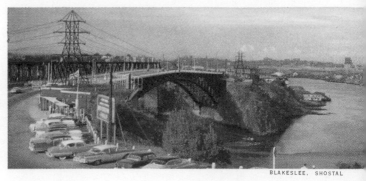

» AT SAINT JOHN, New Brunswick, the high tides of the Bay of Fundy create the Reversing Falls Rapids in the St. John River.

BLAKESLEE, SHOSTAL

LOBSTER TRAPS are loaded on boats tied up at a Prince Edward Island town. Fishing is big business for the province.

MALAK, SHOSTAL

» A SWORDFISH is hauled from Nova Scotia waters.

Life geared to the rhythm of the sea

THE DAY'S CATCH of cod arrives in the hamlet of Ship Cove, Newfoundland.

ST. JOHN'S, Newfoundland. On Signal Hill (background), Marconi received the first transatlantic wireless message.

» FERRYLAND huddles on a "finger" of Newfoundland's Avalon Peninsula, exposed to the Atlantic.

APPLE-PICKING TIME IN ONE OF NOVA SCOTIA'S MANY ORCHARDS

The Annapolis Valley of Nova Scotia is world-famous for its apple orchards. Farming is a major industry of the country, and demonstration farms are maintained in many rural areas.

A FAMILIAR STREET SCENE IN NOVA SCOTIA'S FISHING VILLAGES

Most Nova Scotian villagers who are not engaged in farming earn their living as fishermen. Here stacks of lobster pots, buoys and other fishing equipment line the road along the water's edge.

FREDERIC LEWIS

SHIPBUILDING NEAR SAINT JOHN, A MAJOR CANADIAN SEAPORT

Saint John, New Brunswick, at the mouth of the St. John River, is ice-free the year round. It is a
shipbuilding and repair center, with one of the world's largest drydocks.

53

NOVA SCOTIA LASSIES step out in an energetic Highland fling (folk dance) at a Mod, a Scottish literary and musical festival.

SAILBOATS skim the calm waters of the North West Arm—Halifax, N. S., inlet.

Leisure time in
the outdoors

LOG ROLLING at a sportsmen's meet at Sherbrooke, a Nova Scotia village.

SALMON FISHING in the St. John River at Hartland, N. B.

FORBERT, SHOSTAL

»

A CLAMBAKE—the food redolent of the smell of the sea—brings a happy holiday crowd together at Wedgeport. The town is near Yarmouth, on Nova Scotia's Atlantic coast.

SUNLIT PICNIC in a glade of Cape Breton national park, Nova Scotia.

KUCHIRCHUK, PHOTO RESEARCHERS

EWING GALLOWAY

TODAY'S LOGS ARE TOMORROW'S NEWSPAPERS

One of Newfoundland's major industries is the manufacture of newsprint. Corner Bay Village, above, is one of the centers of the industry, where pulp logs are converted into paper. Newfoundland has about 25,000 square miles of forest lands that feed the numerous pulp and paper mills. Shipbuilding is also quite important, and more than a thousand sawmills are in operation.

A PULP AND PAPER MILL, CORNER BROOK, NEWFOUNDLAND

Second only to its fishing industry in importance is Newfoundland's production of paper. A mountainous island, Newfoundland is covered with rich forests that supply the mills with a plentiful amount of timber. The paper mill at Corner Brook is the larger of two on the island, and it can produce as much as a thousand tons of newsprint a day.

NEWFOUNDLAND FISHERMEN LOADING DRIED COD NEAR ST. JOHN'S

Fishing is the oldest and most important industry in Newfoundland because the island lies only three hundred miles northwest of the Grand Banks, where the world's finest fishing is found. Fleets of fishing vessels come and go at the excellent natural harbor of St. John's, Newfoundland's capital and its center of commerce and manufacturing.

A stream of

THE LOGS will be fed into the huge pulp and paper mills at Corner Brook, Newfoundland.

»

SYDNEY, on Cape Breton Island, Nova Scotia, is a coal-mining and steel-mill center. For the mills, iron ore is brought from Newfoundland.

OIL-REFINERY STACKS outline a section of Halifax Harbour, Nova Scotia.

EVANS, THREE LIONS

«

A HELICOPTER picks up surveyors from a triangulation station in the Labrador-Ungava area—now proved to be an immensely rich source of iron ore.

products from busy mines and plants

JERRY COOKE, PHOTO RESEARCHERS

KOFOD, MONKMEYER PRESS

IN ITS CAGE a prize animal stretches, at one of Nova Scotia's many mink farms. Pelts are being produced in a wide range of colors.

«

IRON ORE is carried up from mine levels that run out under the sea at Bell Island, Newfoundland, the largest submarine iron workings in the world.

MOUNT MORIAH, A FARM SETTLEMENT ON THE BAY OF ISLANDS

Picturesque Mount Moriah is on the hill-rimmed Bay of Islands on Newfoundland's west coast. It is on the Humber River, one of the deep arms of the bay that contains many high islands.

AN UP-TO-DATE SILVER FOX FARM ON PRINCE EDWARD ISLAND

Careful crossbreeding on fox farms, or ranches, results in pelts that are wanted in the fashion marts. In the fall, the fur-growing period, each fox is penned alone to protect its coat.

ATLANTIC PROVINCES: FACTS AND FIGURES

Novia Scotia, New Brunswick, Prince Edward Island and Newfoundland and Labrador, their shores washed by the Atlantic Ocean, are known as the Atlantic Provinces. Total area, 203,971 sq. mi. Population, 1,761,000.

Nova Scotia is composed of the peninsula proper and Cape Breton Island. Total area, 21,068 sq. mi.; population, 683,000.

GOVERNMENT

Government consists of a lieutenant governor appointed by the Federal Government, and a ministry responsible to a House of Assembly of 37 members. Representation in the Canadian Senate, 10; in the House of Commons, 12.

COMMERCE AND INDUSTRIES

Farming, coal mining, fishing and steel manufacturing are the principal industries. Farm products: poultry, dairy goods and fruit. Minerals: coal, gypsum, sand and gravel, barite, salt, stone and silica. Forests include spruce, fir, hemlock and pine. Cod and lobster fisheries.

COMMUNICATIONS

Railway mileage, 1,420; highway mileage, 15,117; several excellent air fields

RELIGION AND EDUCATION

The population is three-fourths Protestant. Education is free, compulsory and nondenominational in primary and secondary schools. There are 10 universities and colleges.

CHIEF TOWNS

Population of chief cities: Halifax (capital), 90,000; Sydney, 31,000; Glace Bay, 27,000; Dartmouth, 16,000.

New Brunswick has a total area of 27,985 sq. mi.; population, 535,000.

GOVERNMENT

Government is vested in a lieutenant governor and a Legislative Assembly of 52 members elected for terms of five years. Representation in Canadian Senate, 10; in House of Commons, 10.

COMMERCE AND INDUSTRIES

Wood and paper processing, food and general manufacturing are the leading industries.

COMMUNICATIONS

Railways, 1,836 mi.; highways, 13,178 mi.; served by Trans-Canada Air Lines.

RELIGION AND EDUCATION

Population is about 50% Protestant. Public education is free and nonsectarian; there are 8 degree-granting institutions.

CHIEF TOWNS

Population of chief towns: Fredericton (capital), 16,018; Saint John, 50,779; Moncton, 27,334; Edmundston, 10,753; Campbellton, 7,754.

Prince Edward Island, the smallest province in all Canada, lies at the mouth of the Gulf of St. Lawrence. It is separated from the mainland of New Brunswick and Nova Scotia by the Northumberland Strait. Area, 2,184 sq. mi.; population, 105,000.

GOVERNMENT

The province is administered by a lieutenant governor appointed by the Federal Government and a ministry responsible to a Legislative Assembly of 30 members. Representation in Canadian Senate, 4; in House of Commons, 4.

COMMERCE AND INDUSTRIES

Fishing and agriculture are important occupations; silver-fox farming extensively carried on.

COMMUNICATIONS

Railway mileage, 286, with ferry connections to the mainland. Roads, 3,180 mi. Air service several times a day to the mainland.

RELIGION AND EDUCATION

The Protestant population is about 55%. Over 20,000 pupils in approximately 500 public and private, primary and secondary schools. There are two colleges in Charlottetown.

CHIEF TOWNS

The population of chief towns: Charlottetown (capital), 15,887, Summerside, 6,547.

Newfoundland is composed of a large island at the mouth of the St. Lawrence River and the eastern portion of the Labrador Peninsula. Total area, 154,734 sq. mi. (area of the island only, 42,734 sq. mi.); total population, 412,000.

GOVERNMENT

Government is under a lieutenant governor, a Cabinet and a General Assembly of 28 elected members. Represented in Canadian Senate by 6 and in the House of Commons by 7 members.

COMMERCE AND INDUSTRIES

Cod, salmon, herring, lobster, haddock, seal and whale fisheries. Crops include hay, potatoes, turnips, cabbage and truck-garden products; livestock numbers about 150,000 head. Chief minerals are zinc, iron ore, lead, copper, fluorspar and limestone. Forest reserves, principally fir and spruce, are considerable; lumber, pulp and paper are the chief items of manufacture. Bell Island is an iron-mining center.

COMMUNICATIONS

Newfoundland has 704 mi. of railways with connections to coastal steamer routes. Motor roads, 5,800 mi. Gander and other airports serve transatlantic airlines. 33,000 telephones.

RELIGION AND EDUCATION

Predominant religions are Roman Catholic, Anglican and United Church of Canada. Education is largely in church schools, aided by provincial government. Newfoundland Memorial University is in St. John's.

CHIEF TOWNS

Approximate population of chief cities: St. John's (capital), 68,000; Bell Island, 10,000; Corner Brook West, 7,000.

Bounteous harvests and prize livestock

»

PLUCKING ripe McIntosh Reds in Nova Scotia's apple-growing Annapolis Valley.

YOKED OXEN are gaily adorned for a parade, Yarmouth County Exhibition, Nova Scotia.

NOVA SCOTIA TRAVEL BUREAU

FORBERT · SHOSTAL

« CULTIVATING a field on the outskirts of New Glasgow, a charming little village on Prince Edward Island.

» CROPLANDS and pastures stretch to the horizon around a well-ordered farm near Clinton, Prince Edward Island.

M. COGNAC, ANNAN PHOTOS

Quebec

...Canada's

largest province

ONCE a slow-paced agricultural province, Quebec is rapidly transforming itself into one of modern Canada's chief manufacturing areas. Between 1939 and 1950 the increase in industrial activity alone was ten times greater than that in the whole nineteenth century. Since 1950 the increase has been stimulated even further by the exploration and development of the immense iron-ore deposits to the north, which Quebec shares with Labrador. As Quebec entered the 1960's it looked forward to an industrial expansion beyond the dreams of its original French settlers. One spokesman predicted that the maze of steel plants springing up on the South Shore opposite Montreal Island would become the "Ruhr Valley of Canada."

The largest proved iron-ore deposit, with an estimated reserve of 400,000,000 tons, lies between Ungava Bay, Quebec, and the Ashuanipi River, in Labrador. In the 1950's a 358-mile railroad was built from the St. Lawrence River at Seven Islands to Schefferville (Knob Lake) to take out the ore. In 1959, plans for a $300,000,000 mining project were

64

announced. It will include a 193-mile railroad, a hydroelectric plant on the Hart Jaune River, a concentrator at Lac Jeannine and two mining villages, one at Lac Barbel, the other at Port Cartier. This unit alone is expected to turn out 8,000,-000 tons of iron concentrates per year.

Meanwhile, survey crews continue to turn up more evidence of mineral wealth beneath northern Quebec's barren, rocky soil. Since World War II, titanium ore has been found on the shores of Allard Lake near Havre St. Pierre, nickel in Quebec's northernmost tip, and copper-zinc deposits are worked at many points in the west.

It is as a world source of iron ore, however, that Quebec expects to achieve its greatest industrial importance. In a recent year, production leaped by almost 90 per cent over the previous year's total. By 1970 the present iron-ore output may be doubled, perhaps even tripled. Most of it is shipped up the St. Lawrence and the Great Lakes to the steel mills in Pennsylvania, Ontario and so on. As production increases, though, more of Quebec's iron ore will be processed at home in the new steel mills near Montreal. It will be a long time before Quebec's mines pull ahead of those of the Mesabi Range in Minnesota, North America's leading source of iron ore, but they have already surpassed Ontario and Newfoundland mines for leadership in Canada.

Rapid industrialization has brought many changes to Quebec's distinctly French way of life. Almost 85 per cent of the population is of French origin. Roughly one million French Canadians have moved from their beloved rural areas to cities in recent years. Education too is changing. Though Quebec schools and universities have not discarded the humanities by any means, the secondary schools are paying more attention to the pure and applied sciences. For two centuries the English-speaking settlers were the commercial and industrial leaders in Canada but no more. Everywhere the hum and bustle of an expanding economy, making, buying and using more products than ever before, strikes the eye in Quebec. "What I can't get accustomed to," said one native Montrealer, returned from years abroad, "is how exciting Montreal has become."

Not all of Quebec's sons and daughters feel this way. They fear that the French Canadians may well lose their group identity in passing from the rural life and agricultural economy that gave form to that identity for so long. Several institutions, among them the Church, also made French Canadian life distinctive, however, and no doubt will continue to do so. In addition the various acts and statutes that make up the national constitution grant each province considerable freedom in local government, above all in Quebec. Canada's Supreme Court has guarded these rights zealously. The provincial governments have sole control over such matters as education, civil and property rights, municipal affairs, licenses and so on. Until fairly recently the provinces also provided for social welfare but that responsibility is now shared, though to a lesser extent in Quebec, by the national Government.

In the 1930's the French Canadians in Quebec set up their own party, the Union Nationale. Growing out of the depression, it originally was formed as a protest against unemployment and economic hardship. It also aimed to safeguard the French tongue and the rights first guaranteed the French Canadians by the Quebec Act of 1774. Though economically radical in the beginning the party has moved far to the right. Though defeated during the war and again in 1960 it has dominated Quebec's legislature most of the time since its inception. The Union Nationale is not a national party. Quebec is represented in Parliament by the Progressive Conservatives and Liberals, the latter in the present century having elected most of the province's members (now seventy-five) to the House of Commons.

Those who love Quebec hope that the prophets of impending uniformity are wrong. The province adds a welcome touch of diversity to the national life and

THE TOWERS support lines carrying power in the Saguenay River area.

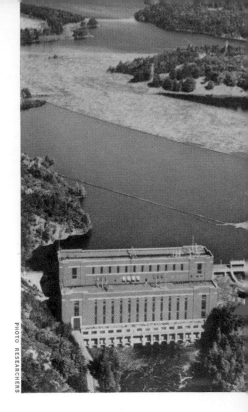

Lumbering and

UNDERGROUND POWERHOUSE of the Chute des Passes installation harnessing the Peribonca River.

"WHITE COAL"—dam spillway of the plant at Chicoutimi.

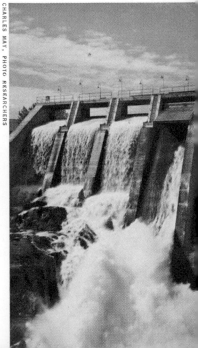

« RESOURCES of wood and water meet in the Gatineau Valley. Vast rafts of logs float in the calm stretch behind a power-generating dam.

SAWMILL at Price, on the Metis River.

hydroelectric power

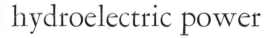

A PAPER MILL is the destination of these logs being poled apart.

LOG BOOM is towed up Ottawa River.

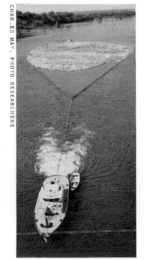

GEORGE HUNTER, ALUMINIUM LTD.

CHARLES MAY, PHOTO RESEARCHERS

PROV. QUE. PUBLICITY BUREAU

its distinctive culture has given Canada many leaders in law, medicine, politics and the arts. In 1959, Queen Elizabeth II added another to the long line of Quebec men who have risen to national prominence when she appointed George P. Vanier the governor general of Canada.

When Canada was united on July 1, 1867, the old province of Canada was divided into the provinces of Quebec and Ontario. These two, together with New Brunswick and Nova Scotia, formed the new Confederation. French Canadians, who had spoken their own language and lived under their own laws for 250 years before the new nation was born, were guaranteed the right to enjoy their traditional civil law and religious privileges in Quebec, as they do to this day.

Waterways and Mountains

Quebec, the largest of the Canadian provinces, covers almost a sixth of the total area of Canada. Most thickly settled of the four major regions of the province is the St. Lawrence Valley. The best farming sections and the most important cities are located on the banks of this great waterway—today a seaway.

North of the St. Lawrence rises the Laurentian Plateau. The mountains here are among the oldest in the world. Some of the peaks in Labrador rise to more than 5,000 feet but the general elevation in Quebec is only 500 to 2,000 feet. This glacier-scoured plateau is part of the Canadian Shield and is dented with numerous hollows and dotted with lakes and streams. Once mere canoe routes, many of the rivers are now sources of mighty electrical energy.

The northern end of the Appalachian Mountain range comes down to the sea at the tip of the Gaspé Peninsula. Along the rugged peninsula nestle the hamlets of fisher folk, dependent for their livelihood on the catches of herring, cod, salmon, mackerel and lobster.

The climate of Quebec along the thickly settled St. Lawrence Valley is pleasant and healthful. Summers are short, but the temperature sometimes rises to 90° F. The long winters are ideal for such winter sports as skating, skiing and tobogganing. The air is dry and bracing. In the far north the climate is sub-Arctic and the thermometer may fall to 30° below zero.

Farmland and Farmers

French Canadians who remain on the land are largely self-sufficient. A farm is often a long, narrow strip, not more than five hundred feet wide, running down to a bit of river front. The typical farmer raises most of the food for his large family, for his hogs supply meat and his cows milk, butter and cheese. He even raises his own tobacco. He cuts fuel from his own wood lot and often makes his own maple sugar and sirup. An occasional family lives today in the same stone or heavy wooden frame house built by an ancestor before the yielding of New France to Britain in 1763.

Many large farms, however, have modern farm machinery and follow modern methods of farming. There are many automobiles in rural Quebec, and its country roads have been greatly improved.

Quebec has English-speaking farmers too, mostly in the Ottawa Valley and in the fertile regions south of the St. Lawrence River. This section, known as the Eastern Townships, along the international boundary, was settled by Loyalists who emigrated from the British colonies south of the border following the American Revolution.

Most English-speaking citizens of Quebec, however, live in the cities and are engaged in business or a profession. Yet Quebec cities, like the countryside, are predominantly French. More than nine out of ten people in the city of Quebec and seven out of ten in Montreal speak French. Next to Paris, Montreal is the largest city in the world where French is the principal tongue. Signs in both languages are everywhere. Telephone operators, street-car conductors, policemen and others in public service speak both languages.

As there are two languages, so there are two religions. As French predominates, so does Roman Catholicism. The doors of the many churches are always open, and a steady stream of worshipers pours in and out from early morning Mass throughout the day. Padres wearing scoop-shaped hats and long, black cassocks, and nuns in their flowing robes are familiar figures on the city streets. Files of children from the schools and convents often walk in pairs along the streets, accompanied by nuns. Many convents are located throughout the province, the largest being in Quebec and Montreal. The convent girls are all dressed alike, in long, black, pleated skirts, black cotton stockings and black hats.

Since both French and English in Quebec wished from the beginning to preserve their identity, they have worked out two separate systems of education. The Roman Catholics have one set of schools, the Protestants another. Each has its own course of instruction, which is supervised by the Roman Catholic or the Protestant committee. Because there is no minister of education, the schools are kept out of politics. A superintendent in charge of the Department of Education is assisted by two deputy ministers, one of whom is the director of Protestant education. From top to bottom the two school systems are distinct and different. Almost all non-Catholics attend Protestant schools.

In the rural parts of the province, which are largely French and Catholic, the language used in the schools is French. Roman Catholic children are usually taught in French, and Protestant children in English. Montreal has 227 Roman Catholic public schools with more than 100,000 pupils, and 47 Protestant schools with about 30,000 pupils. But each language is taught in the schools of both types. Because English is so widely spoken on this continent, however, French children usually adapt themselves to English better than the English do to French.

High schools, classical colleges and even the universities are similarly divided along linguistic or religious lines. In certain technical and trade schools, however, both French- and English-speaking students are frequently taught in the same institution.

In Protestant high schools the course of study is much the same as that in any of the English-speaking provinces; and graduates are prepared for McGill University, Bishop's University and other institutions of higher learning. Graduates of the Roman Catholic high schools may enter either Laval or Montreal University or a normal school. A colorful sight years ago was the Laval uniform for boys—blue coat piped with white and bound with green *ceintures*. For three centuries students wore this dress.

Though English is taught in the French schools, and vice versa, recent census returns indicate that more than 70 per cent of the total French population speak only French. Yet the majority of city-born and educated French Canadians understand English and use it for everyday business in office, shop or factory. On the other hand, a large percentage of English-speaking people, even in the large cities, neither understand French movies nor use the French language in shopping or for business.

Montreal publishes daily and weekly newspapers in both languages, and these are on a par with newspapers in most

JACKSTRAWS FOR A GIANT

These logs, cut to uniform size, are raw material for Quebec's vast paper industry.

NATIONAL FILM BOARD

SCOFIELD, SHOSTAL

IN THE LAURENTIANS—visitors to Sainte Adèle bask in winter sun.

ON A CRISP AFTERNOON, on the slopes of Mount Royal,
ice skaters throng a frozen pond in the heart of Montreal.

SAM TATA

HOCKEY—the Montreal Canadiens play the Detroit Redwings.

The pleasures
of wintertime

»
MAKING the snow fly a Montreal resident clears a path in the drifts with a power snowplow.

SAM TATA

TOBOGGANS FLASH down slide toward Château Frontenac, Quebec.

other American cities. Private radio stations broadcast in either French or English, or both, and Radio Canada in Montreal is consistently bilingual.

Montreal is the great metropolis of the province. Though located a thousand miles inland from the sea, it is one of the most important ports in the world. For a time in the nineteenth century, it was the capital of the United Province of Canada. No longer the political capital, it is still the commercial heart of the nation. Enormous grain elevators, wharves and docks store and ship more grain than those of any other port in the world. In Montreal East great oil tanks and refineries have been built where millions of gallons of crude oil are processed daily.

Like Manhattan, Montreal is an island city. It is about 30 miles long and 7 to 10 miles across. Here was the Indian encampment of Hochelaga, which Jacques Cartier discovered on his second voyage to Canada in 1535. From the commanding heights of Mount Royal, for which Montreal is named, Cartier marveled at the windings of the mighty river which had brought his frail sailing ships so far inland from the sea and promised to lead him still farther toward the golden west.

Mount Royal remains the leading landmark of the city, which has grown from an important fur-trading station in the days of New France into the financial center and metropolis of Canada. Gradually the growing city has climbed up the sides of the mountain to higher and higher levels, but the view from the summit is still worth the effort. The only way to reach the top is to walk, ride up in an open carriage or go part way by automobile or street car, for no motor cars are allowed on the final stretch of the winding road leading to the Lookout.

Downtown Montreal is a great center of shipping, by land and by sea. From the time the last ice goes out in springtime at the Strait of Belle Isle to admit the first ship of the season, the water front is filled with passenger ships and freighters from many countries. Last to clear port in the fall, before ice closes the river to navigation, are the grain ships heavily laden with

PATTERN OF POWER
Part of a plant that harnesses water power at Beauharnois, up river from Montreal.

Canadian wheat, many bound for Europe.

The capital of the province is its namesake city of Quebec. For 150 years Quebec was the capital of France in America, and it remained the capital of Canada for 30 years after New France passed under British rule. This "city on a rock" is the most picturesque city in North America and is the only walled city on the continent. Quebec lies north of the river at the foot of the beautiful Laurentian Mountains, and its ancient citadel towers 350 feet above the quay.

Fringing the water front and on the lower slopes of the rocky bluff are the narrow steps, stone churches, steep-roofed houses and shops of the quaint old Lower Town. At the top of the bluff, separated from the Lower Town by massive walls, is the more modern Upper Town, the fashionable residential quarter. Here are the fine buildings of the provincial parliament and government departments, as well as spacious parks, fine old churches and convents. The Basilica, or French Cathedral, is famous. Begun in 1647, and destroyed by fire in 1759 and 1922, it has since been rebuilt. In the nave of the Ursuline Convent chapel are enshrined the remains of the Marquis de Montcalm. The Seminary of Quebec has buildings dating from the late seventeenth century, and, with Laval University, is the oldest seat of French learning and culture in the New World.

Dominating the Upper Town is the magnificent Château Frontenac, one of the most famous hotels in America. Built to resemble a medieval French castle, it is named for the great Governor of New France. Near the hotel is Dufferin Terrace, a famous promenade 1,800 feet long and 600 feet wide. Here hundreds of people stroll on summer evenings or coast on winter afternoons. The view from the terrace is magnificent. Directly below are the jumbled roofs of the old town, and beyond them flows the broad St. Lawrence. The St. Charles River empties into the St. Lawrence here and, in midstream, lies the island of Orléans.

The city of Levis is situated on the bank of the St. Lawrence opposite to Quebec, and on the east the Beauport shore stretches as far as Cap Tourmente, while the Laurentian Mountains extend to the east, west and north. Along the bank of the St. Charles River and in the new industrial center of St. Malo are numerous thriving factories operated by electric power from Shawinigan Falls. Quebec is the tourist center of eastern Canada, and, next to Montreal, is the largest and most prosperous city of the province.

When Samuel de Champlain first saw this incomparable site in 1608, he recognized it at once as the ideal location for a colony. Here on the north bank of the river he built his habitation of logs, fortified by a moat and stockade, not far from the present Levis ferry slip. That was twelve years before the Pilgrims landed at Plymouth. It marked the first permanent settlement by white men on Canadian soil. The Company of New France, under Champlain's leadership, was a group of Frenchmen to whom their King granted the right to colonize the new land, control its fur trade and convert the Indians.

As long as Champlain lived, his faith and enthusiasm held the pioneers together in spite of raids by the hostile Iroquois, whom he had unfortunately antagonized. After his death, in 1635, the Company of

STOREHOUSE OF ENERGY ON THE SAGUENAY RIVER

Generating power house at Shipshaw, center of a thriving aluminum industry. It requires tremendous amounts of electricity, which is produced by the rushing river waters.

Bounty from the soil and the sea

»

GREEDY GULLS, anticipating a meal, hover above Gaspé fishermen who are skillfully cleaning an ocean-fresh catch of cod.

HERBERT LANKS, SHOSTAL

AS ANGELUS BELLS ring out, a farm family on the Isle of Orleans pauses for noon prayer. The islanders cling to old French customs.

J. JULIUS FANTA, PHOTO RESEARCHERS

G. LUNNEY, NATIONAL FILM BOARD, OTTAWA

FISHERMEN'S HUTS line the St. Anne River. There, during the cold winters, fish are caught through the ice.

KOFOD, MONKMEYER PRESS PHOTO

DRYING COD at Cap Chat, on the St. Lawrence coast of the Gaspé Peninsula.

AN OLD WINDMILL—reminder of New France.

TOBACCO flourishes in the vicinity of Joliette, northeast of Montreal.

KOFOD, MONKMEYER PRESS PHOTO

KOFOD, MONKMEYER PRESS PHOTO

WHAT WILL THE FIGURE BE?

The gentle art of wood carving came to Quebec with the first settlers and still flourishes.

New France was disbanded. Seven years later, the Sieur de Maisonneuve founded Ville Marie de l'Isle de Montréal, and Montreal later outstripped the older colony, though Quebec remained the capital of New France.

The other principal cities of the Province of Quebec are Sherbrooke, a manufacturing and distributing center called the "garden of the Eastern Townships"; Three Rivers, one of the greatest centers of pulp and paper manufacture in the world; Hull and Valleyfield, both well known for their textile mills; St. Hyacinthe, famed for the manufacture of organs as well as for boots and shoes; and Drummondville, noted for its celanese, or artificial silk, industry. Westmount, Outremont and Verdun are large suburbs of the rapidly expanding city of Montreal.

The province supports some 12,000 manufacturing enterprises and produces annually goods worth $4,000,000,000. These manufactures run from pins to Die-

AN OPEN-AIR ARTIST ON THE ISLAND OF ORLEANS

Many Quebec farm wives are gifted at making the gay kinds of hooked rugs you see here. They may take their subjects from the life about them or design bright flower patterns.

sel locomotives for streamlined trains.

Quebec's forests cover a huge area, and pulp and paper making is a valuable industry. The best timber in the province is red pine and spruce. There are 220,-772 square miles of forest in the province, most of which is provincial crown land. The Quebec government closely controls the exploitation of the forests and is now pushing forward a dynamic reforestation program. To patrol the forests and give warning of fires, the government engages many forest rangers and aircraft.

In water-power development Quebec leads the Canadian provinces, its total installation producing almost ten million horsepower.

Reminders of French Canada's proud history appear everywhere in Quebec. Facing the City Hall in Quebec City, near the site where the first farmhouse stood, stands a splendid stone figure of Louis Hébert, the first farmer of New France, designed by Louis Philippe Hébert, one of his descendants. An even more famous monument stands in the Governor's Garden, commemorating the British General Wolfe and the French General Montcalm, who were both killed in 1759 as a result of the decisive battle for New France on the Plains of Abraham. Wolfe and Montcalm were enemies but each is honored as a gallant soldier. When the British won, they brought to an end the French colonial empire in North America.

The residents of New France continued to occupy the land they loved after France yielded, and the new government helped them to adjust themselves and to maintain their homes by its recognition of their cultural and religious traditions. Though English settlers came to the new country in increasing numbers, especially after the American Revolution, the French remained the great majority in Quebec. Difficulties have naturally arisen from time to time between the two peoples, yet French and English have come to know and to respect each other more and more as the years have passed. Today Quebec is a striking example of two peoples living together in friendship as fellow citizens of one country.   By W. P. PERCIVAL

QUEBEC: FACTS AND FIGURES

THE PROVINCE

Includes the island of Anticosti, Bird Islands and Magdalen Islands in the Gulf of St. Lawrence. The total area (as amended by the Labrador Boundary Award) is 594,860 sq. mi. (including Ungava, 351,780); land area, 523,-860 sq. mi. Total population, 4,650,000.

GOVERNMENT

Administered by a lieutenant-governor, appointed by the Federal Government, a responsible ministry, a Legislative Council of 24 members (appointed for life) and an elected Legislative Assembly of 93 members. Representation in Canadian Senate, 24; in House of Commons, 75.

COMMERCE AND INDUSTRIES

Agriculture is the basic industry; wheat, oats, barley, rye, peas, buckwheat, tobacco, mixed grains, flaxseed, corn, potatoes, turnips, hay, clover and alfalfa are grown. Fox-farming and fishing are important occupations and the province leads Canada in pulpwood production. Chief minerals: asbestos (about 75% of the world's supply), iron ore, gold, copper, zinc, silver, feldspar, graphite, magnesite, mica, molybdenite, phosphate, hematite and lead. Leading manufactures: pulp and paper, ferrous and nonferrous metal smelting and refining, cotton and its products, clothing, cigars and cigarettes, dairy products, flour and its products, railway rolling stock, synthetic textiles and silk, boots and shoes, furniture, sawmills, electric light and power, feeds, meat packing and breweries.

COMMUNICATIONS

Railway mileage, 5,081; roads, 43,750; almost 1,000,000 motor cars and over 1,000,000 telephones.

RELIGION AND EDUCATION

Population about six sevenths Roman Catholic. Schools are sectarian; more than a million pupils attend the nearly 11,000 schools of all kinds. There are 5 universities.

CITIES

Population: Quebec, capital, 175,000; Montreal (second-largest French-speaking city in the world), 1,110,000; Verdun, 80,500; Sherbrooke, 58,000; Trois Rivières, 55,000; Hull, 48,000.

AN ASBESTOS MINE at Thetford Mines, which is the center of a rich mineral area.

Products of mining and manufacturing

DRUMS OF OIL, piped from the West, are shipped from Montreal.

« A VAST HEAP of reddish iron ore awaits shipment at Sept Iles (Seven Islands). The ore has come from mines in northern Quebec.

KOFOD, MONKMEYER PRESS PHOTO

RACKS OF FRANKFURTERS await packaging in a co-op slaughterhouse at Princeville.

MAKING SNOWSHOES at Loretteville, which specializes in Huron Indian crafts.

D. FORBERT, SHOSTAL

Ontario
... central province

ONTARIO is in many ways the leader among Canadian provinces. Though settled relatively late, it ranks first in population, with nearly six million people (it is second in total area). Ottawa, located near the southeastern corner of the province, is the national capital. Farther south, Toronto, with its excellent television and radio programs, its many publishing houses, and music and theater organizations, is a cultural center for English-speaking Canadians. Ontario also ranks first in mineral production, first in total manufactured goods and boasts by far the most varied economy. The long-awaited St. Lawrence Seaway, opened in 1959, which provides easy access from the Atlantic Ocean to the Great Lakes region, is stimulating further economic growth.

The need for a seaway runs back to the sixteenth century, when the French explorer Jacques Cartier was turned back by the rushing waters of the Lachine Rapids, just west of Montreal. During the next four centuries, canals and locks were constructed around the barriers to navigation in the St. Lawrence and the waters connecting the Great Lakes. The first improvement dates back to 1700 when a canal deep enough only for canoes was built to bypass the Lachine Rapids. In contrast is the vast Seaway. Strictly speaking the name applies only to the stretch between Kingston and Montreal. Work was begun in 1954, to cost about a billion dollars.

The Seaway opens up the heart of North America to ocean-going trade. Now grain can be loaded at a Lake Superior port and carried abroad in the same ship. The ultimate advantages for both Canada and the United States are enormous. For Canada it means being able to ship iron ore cheaply from northern Quebec and northern Ontario to inland mills, and a much larger volume of trade between Europe and inland ports. Toronto especially is expected to expand commercially from the increased ship traffic. The city has already extended its port facilities substantially. The United States gains easy access to the Atlantic for its Midwest mining and industrial products.

Farsighted planners in both Canada and the United States were already talking of such a project at the end of the 1800's. Work did not begin until 1954, partly because Congress was reluctant to grant the necessary funds. Nevertheless, by 1959 the International Rapids section

CURVED STREETS and circles are features of Toronto's growing suburban developments. Such housing is in part an answer to Ontario's rapidly increasing population.

was finished. At impressive inauguration ceremonies in June, Queen Elizabeth II and President Eisenhower joined Prime Minister Diefenbaker in opening the Seaway.

Ontario is also setting a cultural pace. Every summer an increasing number of visitors, foreigners as well as Canadians, are drawn to the Shakespeare Festival Theater at Stratford, Ontario. The festival was founded by a committee of drama lovers at Stratford. As their town is a namesake of William Shakespeare's birthplace, Stratford-on-Avon, in England, they determined to establish a summer theater featuring his plays. The committee made appeals for funds throughout North America. Eventually the generosity of thousands of Canadians enabled the project to get on its feet.

Moreover, the Stratford committee did not skimp but hired the best talent it could find. The well-known Shakespearean director Tyrone Guthrie was lured from England to launch the first productions—in a tent. With the growing flood of visitors the festival is today on a sound financial footing. In the late 1950's, grants from the Canadian Government and various foundations underwrote the building of a permanent playhouse.

Though foreign stars may be imported, the regular members of the repertory company are all Canadian. Year after year the productions win high critical praise. Stratford is today broadening its activities to include music and film festivals, exhibitions of painting, sculpture and ceramics, a drama school and a French Canadian company specializing

ANNAN PHOTOS

GRAIN CAN BE SHIPPED abroad directly from elevators at Port Arthur, Lake Superior.

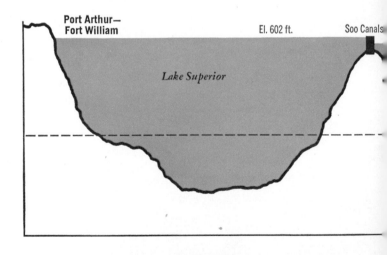

»

STRADDLING the river between Barnhart Island and the New York shore, the Long Sault Spillway Dam is the chief means of controlling the downstream flow.

Continental artery—
the St. Lawrence Seaway

DEPT. OF TRAVEL & PUBLICITY, ONTARIO

NIAGARA FALLS glow orange in the powerful lights turned on at dusk.

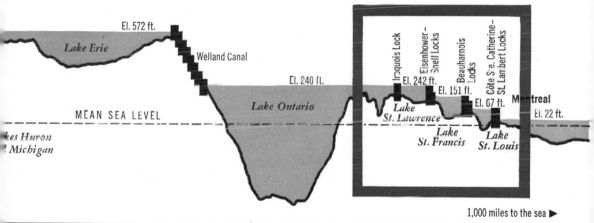

1,000 miles to the sea ▶

WATER-LEVEL PROFILE. Sailing from the Atlantic Ocean to the head of Lake Superior through the Seaway, a ship rises 602 feet. This great lift is accomplished largely by means of sixteen locks. The locks of the Welland Canal, which bypasses Niagara Falls and the Niagara River, alone raise a ship 326 feet. Within the square is the old International Rapids section. There a new lake, St. Lawrence, has appeared as the water is now held back by huge control (Long Sault) and power (Moses-Saunders) dams. In the rapids section, seven new locks were built.

in the brilliant comedies of Molière.

Though the people of Ontario most frequently lean toward the Conservative Party, the province has given the Liberal Party some of its greatest statesmen, including Mackenzie King and Lester B. Pearson. In the Liberal Government of Louis St. Laurent, Pearson was foreign minister and brought Canada international fame for his work in the UN. He made his name in the UN Relief and Rehabilitation Administration and as president of the General Assembly. He was awarded the Nobel Peace Prize in 1957. Since 1957, when the Conservatives came to power, Pearson has been national leader of the Liberal Party.

Since 1912 the northern boundary of Ontario has been Hudson Bay. Another water line forms the southern boundary —from Lake of the Woods and Rainy River through Lakes Superior, Huron, Erie and Ontario. The lakes moderate the climate of Ontario.

Ontario has two distinct sections. The northern part, about 330,000 square miles, has been opened up only in recent years. The southern is an older-settled region, about 77,000 square miles. All the larger cities and most of the manufacturing and farming districts are here.

Across the surface of the province runs a ridge of Archaean rocks forming a watershed which turns some rivers north to Hudson Bay and others south to the St. Lawrence system. In general the surface is undulating, veined by rivers and small lakes, whose infinite number, especially on the northern slope, accounts for the epithet "land of little lakes." Lake Nipigon (70 miles by 50 miles), the largest, is a beautiful body of water some 250 feet above Lake Superior. From the southeast end of the latter St. Marys River leads into Lake Huron by the falls at Sault Ste. Marie. The northeastern shore of Lake Huron is broken by large inlets and fringed into innumerable islands. Most of these are small but Manitoulin, the largest island, is 80 miles long and up to 32 broad. Into Georgian Bay flows the French River from Lake Nipissing, Severn River from Lake Simcoe.

Both Lake Superior and Lake Huron are very deep but St. Clair, the next in the series, is shallow and marshy, and Lake Erie is comparatively shallow. From Lake Erie the water is carried over the Niagara escarpment and down the precipitous gorge into Lake Ontario, which is only 247 feet above sea level. Today the Welland Canal, built in 1932, through which shipping enters Lake Ontario from Lake Erie, is part of the Seaway system.

Below Kingston, at the northeast end of Lake Ontario, the St. Lawrence flows through the Thousand Islands, then on past Montreal and Quebec City to the broad gulf of the St. Lawrence. Next in size of the south-flowing rivers in Ontario are the Ottawa and the Trent.

To the east of Georgian Bay lie the highlands of Ontario, before white settlement the hunting grounds of the Hurons. Here no less than eight hundred waterways, lakes, rivers, streams are to be found. It is to this region, with its many government parks and game reserves, that city dwellers flock at vacation time.

The vast area of northern Ontario was formerly a part of the territory of Keewatin but in 1912 the Federal Parliament extended the boundaries of Manitoba and Ontario north to Hudson Bay and gave eight great districts to Ontario. Four times as large as south Ontario, it is a region of forests, rocks, rivers, lakes. While the mineral areas are beginning to yield richly, much is still unexplored. Nipissing, named for its great lake, is a sportsman's paradise and includes Algonquin Park and part of Timagami. Timiskaming, stretching to Hudson Bay, was the hunting ground of the earlier French and English fur trappers. Prospectors of a later day discovered the rich deposits at Cobalt, Elk Lake City and Gowganda, and railway scouts prospecting for good lands for settlement came upon the immense stretch of fertile country known as the great clay belt, stretching through Algoma and Timiskaming. Algoma, a vast territory extending 360 miles north from the vicinity of the Soo Canals to the Albany River, is a true land of lakes and rivers.

A CLOVERLEAF INTERSECTION ON THE QUEEN ELIZABETH WAY

The Queen Elizabeth Way, the four-lane expressway from Toronto to Niagara Falls, forms a cloverleaf intersection outside Toronto with Highway No. 10, another four-lane road. The loops and ramps are designed so that a motorist may enter or leave either road safely without having to cross a lane where there is traffic moving in the opposite direction.

In its 200 miles of coast-land on Lakes Huron and Superior the largest town is the historic little Sault Ste. Marie named by French *voyageurs* of the seventeenth century from the falls in the St. Mary's River. Thunder Bay has a grim frontage on Lake Superior and a forested region lake-studded to the north. Fort William and Port Arthur, twin cities with immense docks and elevators stand to-day where formerly stood the rude lodges of the North-West Company of fur-traders.

Rainy River, so called from the perpendicular fall between lake and river which gave forth spray like rain, was discovered by the French and ministered to by the Jesuits. Kenora, an early Hudson's Bay Company's fort under the name of Rat Portage, is the boundary district between Ontario and Manitoba and has been the site of boundary disputes. To-day its many lakes form a playground for the citizens of Winnipeg. Patricia, eighth and last district of New Ontario, is the largest of all, adding fifty-six per cent to the area of Ontario. It has a shoreline of six hundred miles on the James and Hudson bays, but as yet has not been fully explored.

But the history of New Ontario is still in the making, while that of Old Ontario has inscribed many a crowded page in its brief 160 years of life. The wooded wilderness lying to the south of the Laurentian rocks was known only by the fur-trapper and the explorer at the end of the eighteenth century. Champlain had penetrated from Quebec as far as Georgian Bay, the Récollets and the Jesuits had labored for the Hurons, LaSalle had seen the country as he made toward the Mississippi; but the Hurons had been exterminated and the English fur-trappers had only a few fortified posts on Hudson Bay, and the French at Fort Frontenac and Michilimackimac and Sault Ste. Marie. When the French lost Quebec in 1763 what was known as "Upper Canada" lay a wilderness for twenty years. In 1782 bands of United Empire Loyalists began to come in. Surveyors sent by General Haldimand chose lands in four districts for the loyal exiles: along the St. Lawrence opposite Fort Oswegatchie, around the Bay of Quinte above Fort Cataraqui, in the Niagara Peninsula opposite Fort Niagara, and in the southwest section within reach of Fort Detroit. The settlers were of varied origin—Highland Scots, German, Dutch, Irish, Eng-

The flourishing state of the arts

DEPT. OF TRAVEL & PUBLICITY, ONTARIO

SINGER-ACTORS rehearse for a production of Gilbert and Sullivan's ever delightful *Mikado* to be telecast over a network from a studio in Toronto.

CANADIAN BROADCASTING CORP.

« ON DISPLAY in Toronto's Art Gallery are Lawren Harris' *Country North of Lake Superior* (left of door) and Tom Thomson's *The West Wind* (right).

CHARLES MAY, PHOTO RESEARCHERS

DRAMA-LOVERS' MECCA—the eye-catching structure that is the home of the noted Shakespeare Festival Theatre in Stratford.

GRACE AND COLOR—an act from the enchanting *Nutcracker* as danced by the National Ballet Company of Canada.

KEN BELL

lish. Most of them had already gone through the pioneer stage in settling new lands and brought valuable experience to bear upon their problems. The government allotted them lands, gave them implements, seed-grain and at first even food. To the forest succeeded small cleared areas, which in turn bore grain and food for man and beast. As well as lumberman and farmer, the settler of those days must be a trapper also to supply his family with food and clothing. Slowly the settlements grew and the trails widened, though the waterways long continued the chief avenues of communication.

Until the end of the century the Loyalists continued to come, and there were besides the loyal Indians of the Six Nations. For these land was purchased, a tract six miles wide on each side of the Grand River in western Ontario, and

here under the Mohawk chief, Joseph Brant, many settled.

To thirty years of struggle with the wilderness succeeded a struggle with their neighbors across the line. In the War of 1812, the Loyalists bore heroic part, fighting as they were to defend the homes so hardly won. When the war began the population of Upper Canada numbered about eighty thousand, for Simcoe the first governor had done all in his power to encourage immigration; and many besides the Loyalists had come in from the United States.

Three years' fighting was a serious setback to the work in field and homestead but the pioneer women were cast in heroic mold and the work was not stayed. At the close of the Napoleonic Wars many British veterans began to pour into Upper Canada and were given lands in townships to the rear of those

NATIONAL FILM BOARD

WHERE PEACETIME USES OF ATOMIC ENERGY ARE EXPLORED

At Chalk River, Ontario, the Canadian Government maintains a pilot plant that produces materials for the release of atomic power. No war weapons are produced here; scientists are studying possible ways in which the atom's energy can make man's life easier and better. Workers at the plant live in the near-by town of Deep River, built for them by the Government.

LABORATORY TECHNICIANS at the government's Polymer Corporation near Sarnia, Ontario, test a sample of buna S rubber. Canadian synthetic rubber must meet rigid standards.

settled by the Loyalists, or in unoccupied ones lying between. By 1826 the population had increased to 166,000; by 1836 it was 374,000 and in 1841 it was 456,000. People lived on their own land, towns were comparatively small. Kingston was the largest; then came York (later Toronto), London, Hamilton, Brockville.

The British settlers brought in good livestock and a knowledge of breeding which placed agriculture on a firmer basis. Oxen were as yet more numerous than horses for they were hardier. But now to skins were added homespun garments from the wool of the sheep, and coarse linen fabrics from the homegrown flax. Roads pierced the forests and broke down the isolation of frontier settlements. Mills, schools, churches acted as magnets to draw people together. The Loyalists had sacrificed their first homes on the altar of freedom; they were

not content until the Constitutional Act of 1791 separated their province from Quebec or Lower Canada, and gave them English civil and criminal law, a legislative assembly and council and a lieutenant-governor. The Ottawa River was chosen as a boundary, but the two seigniories of New Longueil and Vaudreuil were still kept by Quebec although on the western side of the river.

In 1841 the two provinces were united and given responsible government. For twenty-seven years the neighbors were yoked together but the equality of representation granted to them became unfair to Upper Canada as her population first equaled and then surpassed that of Lower Canada. Separate schools conceded to the Roman Catholics in 1863 contributed another grievance. When federation of the provinces was mooted Upper Canada was strongly in favor of

A FOUNDRY and steel plant, one of the largest in Canada, covers acres of ground at Hamilton, the thriving city that stands at the head of Lake Ontario.

THE PLANT of a gold-mining concern at Kirkland Lake, center of one of the chief areas of gold mining in North America.

PROSPECTING by plane for uranium in the Kapuskasing River district.

From mines and mills

» THE DAY'S WORK is done and workers leave one of the giant steel mills that cluster in Hamilton.

ASSEMBLY LINE of an automotive plant. The gleaming body is being lowered on the chassis. »

AT SAULT STE. MARIE—logs destined for paper.

CHARLES MAY, PHOTO RESEARCHERS

MALAK, SHOSTAL

SEAGRAM'S LTD.

» NICKEL SMELTER at Sudbury. Much of the Western world's supply of the valuable metal comes from Sudbury.

91

it, for it meant her freedom again from her uneasy yoke fellow. Since Federation (1867) she has been known as Ontario, and Lower Canada as Quebec.

The racial origin of the present population of Ontario is reported by the census as predominantly of the "British Races," chiefly English, Irish and Scotch in the order named. There were over eight hundred thousand of "other" European origin, chiefly French and German, though almost every people in Europe is represented. There are a few Asiatics, and over thirty thousand Indians.

The Cities of Ontario

Great cities and flourishing towns have sprung up in Ontario. There is one city of over half a million—Toronto—two others larger than 200,000—Hamilton and Ottawa—and two more over 90,000—Windsor and London. We tell about these and other Canadian cities in the chapter that begins on page 121.

After the American Civil War large tracts of land were opened to farmers in the Middle West, and this not only attracted men from Ontario but the better conditions for growing wheat destroyed the crop in the older east. Then with the development of the Canadian Northwest —the real wheat belt—consequent upon the completion of the Canadian Pacific Railway in 1885, farmers in Ontario suffered from genuine depression. Readjustment of crops took time, but the process developed the fruit-growing and dairy-farming to a very considerable degree.

Ontario today is a leading fruit-growing province of the Dominion. She has an abundant rainfall, a suitable soil, plenty of warm sunshine. The Prairie Provinces to the west, the United States to the south, Europe to the east furnish good markets which her facilities by rail, canal and river can easily supply.

Where the Fruit Grows

The St. Lawrence fruit belt extends from the eastern end of the province to the city of Kingston and grows many of Canada's famous apples. In the Ottawa Valley between l'Original and Pembroke, the Yellow Transparent, Duchess, Wealthy and McIntosh flourish. Prince Edward County on the Bay of Quinte is a notable fruit area, and the orchards continue west through the counties of Northumberland, Durham and Ontario. Toronto provides a great market for central Ontario.

At Port Credit a new small fruit and vegetable country begins stretching along the lake shore to Hamilton. From the base of the ridge or mountain at Hamilton, a great fruit market, a level floor runs to the shore of Lake Ontario. This floor—once a lake bed—forms the far-famed peach belt of Ontario. Grapes grow here too in profusion—the Concord, Worden, Champion, Niagara and Delaware. The sweet cherry is cultivated only in the Niagara region, though the sour cherry is widely grown as well over that part of the province west of Toronto to Georgian Bay. The Lake Erie district is a home of successful fruit-growing, and in the Georgian Bay fruit belt large crops of winter apples, plums and pears are shipped from Owen Sound.

Great Mineral Production

Ontario leads all the other provinces in mineral production. Over the ten-year period ending in 1950, the average worth of the annual mineral output was $260,-870,000. Ontario's output, approaching a value of $400,000,000 a year, now accounts for a third of Canada's total mineral production. Though northern Ontario has not yet been fully explored, what little is known gives zest to further development. There is no richer mineralized area than that of Sudbury to the north of Superior with its vast known reserves of base and precious metals in the ore bodies of the nickel ridge and the copper-zinc-lead deposits of the basin which the ridge encloses.

Farther north is the famous Cobalt camp where the silver-cobalt mines for many years turned out some of the most profitable ores the world has seen. Farther north still are the gold mines of Porcupine which has produced gold worth hundreds of millions and is still one of the largest gold-producing camps in Canada.

In the north of Ontario there is a large tract of forests. The Georgian Bay district contains the largest area of white pine in the world and sufficient to supply the trade for a number of years. Ontario has a considerable amount of hardwood and an inestimable supply of spruce. In the north the characteristic trees are maple, beech, birch, elm, ash, oak, hickory, pine, cedar, spruce and hemlock. The forest growth of south Ontario is different and the predominant trees are oak, hickory, chestnut and buttonwood.

Another Loyalist settlement in the Niagara Peninsula is but a short boat's journey from Toronto. After crossing Lake Ontario and entering the Niagara River the steamer passes by densely wooded banks, where stands Niagara-on-the-Lake, formerly Newark, the first capital of Upper Canada. Here again, as in Kingston, Loyalists succeeded Indians and Frenchmen. Farther up the Niagara River rise Queenston Heights where in 1812 was fought a memorable battle. Here in heroic resistance fell the British general Sir Isaac Brock and in his honor a tall monument rises today. From Queenston or Lewiston it is a short journey through a precipitous gorge toward the thundering Falls of Niagara.

Through the garden of Ontario from Niagara to Hamilton, orchards and vineyards stretch their ranks, spreading in spring a lovely panoply of pink and white and in autumn a luscious wealth of fruits. St. Catherines, high-set upon its hill, has healing waters in its wells, and a fine boys' school. Hamilton, at the head of Lake Ontario, has many industries, which include the manufacture of automobiles, guns, buttons, brass, jewelry.

On Grand River, where once the Indians forded, stands the modern city of Brantford. Not far away is the burial place of Joseph Brant—Thayendanegea —famous Indian chief. St. Thomas, one of the most important railway centers of the country, and London on the Thames with its University of Western Ontario, are situated in the fertile stretch of country bordering on Lake Erie. Sarnia on Lake Huron is a starting point of navigation on the upper Great Lakes; the little town of Sault Ste. Marie on the canal between Lakes Huron and Superior has iron and steel works, pulp and water mills, dry docks and shipbuilding plants. Port Arthur, at the head of the Seaway project 1,217 miles from Montreal, has a large number of lumber companies as well as water-power plants, pulp and paper mills and various other industries. Nearby is the city of Fort William, where grain is stored. These two cities form a link between the Prairie and the Atlantic provinces.

ONTARIO: FACTS AND FIGURES

THE PROVINCE. Central province of Canada with a total area of 412,582 sq. mi.; land area 363,282 sq. mi. Population about 5,405,000.

GOVERNMENT. Administered by a lieutenant governor appointed by Federal Government and a ministry responsible to a Legislative Assembly of 98 members. Representation in Canadian Senate, 24; in House of Commons, 85.

COMMERCE AND INDUSTRIES. The province is rich in agricultural and mineral resources. Chief farm products are milk, hay and clover, oats, eggs, tobacco and wheat. Valuable timber resources include spruce, pine and poplar. Leading minerals are nickel (world's principal source), gold, copper, platinum, sand and gravel, iron ore and cement. Leading industrial province with over 13,500 manufacturing establishments. The chief manufactures are automobiles and parts, electrical equipment, pulp and paper, nonferrous metals, prepared meats and flour.

COMMUNICATIONS. Heavy shipping on Great Lakes, most bordering on Ontario, several canals and the principal rivers. Railways, 10,385 mi.; highways, 80,892 mi.; 167 licensed airports; nearly 1,507,000 telephones.

RELIGION AND EDUCATION. Population more than three fourths Protestant; no discriminatory laws. Complete state system of elementary and secondary schools with more than a million pupils. Seven universities, several colleges and professional schools, and one military college.

CITIES. Populations: Toronto, provincial capital, 1,400,000 (metropolitan area); Hamilton, 285,000; Ottawa (national capital), 233,000; Windsor, 120,000; London, 98,700.

IN THE SPRING the parkways and lawns blaze with tulip blossoms. Royal Canadian Mounted Police, in work uniforms, patrol the parkways.

»

IN THE CENTER of Confederation Square stands the imposing National Memorial to the Canadians who fought in the first World War.

THE SKYLINE as seen from across the Ottawa River, in Hull, Quebec Province.

Ottawa, beautiful capital of the whole nation

A LOCK on the Rideau Canal, which winds through many lovely city parks.

A PARADE OF GUARDS stands at attention in front of the Parliament Buildings. The superb cliff site seems made to order for a national legislature.

The Western Provinces ...prairies, mountains and forests

THE western provinces are really two groups, geographically speaking. The Prairie Provinces—Manitoba, Saskatchewan and Alberta—are similar, although the land gradually rises, in a series of steps, to the grand climax of the Rockies in western Alberta. British Columbia, on the other side of the continental watershed, receives much more rain. So amid its mountains and plateaus there are lush river valleys. British Columbia is also different from the other three in having a much used seacoast, deeply indented and protected by hundreds of islands.

All four provinces have one characteristic in common, a growing economy. Though this is true of most of Canada, it is especially noticeable in the west.

Though agriculture is still the main source of income in the Prairie Provinces, the trend is toward greater economic variety. Mining and manufacturing are taking on new importance. They leaped ahead in Manitoba during the 1940's and 1950's. Manufacturing output, together with construction, tripled during this period. Today manufacturing and construction account for two thirds of the value of Manitoba's total production.

Alberta is blessed with one of the world's largest known oil deposits. It lies in the Athabaska oil sands, 165 miles northeast of Edmonton. Extraction of oil from the sands has not yet proved commercially feasible, but there are other huge deposits exploited by wells in the southern parts of the province. Since 1947 production has soared. The province now turns out 80 to 90 per cent of Canada's oil production per year, yet only a small part of

its resources have been tapped thus far. Construction of refineries and the like has kept pace with the tremendous output of the wells. In a recent year, bolstered by a thriving meat-packing industry, Alberta's manufacturing production equaled agricultural production in value for the first time.

Neighboring Saskatchewan is enjoying a similar kind of advance. Though leaning heavily on agriculture, its economy has been much strengthened by an upturn in mineral production, particularly of uranium. It was on August 4, 1952, that the Government opened twenty-three square miles of the Beaverlodge fields to public claims. About 300 claims were filed in twenty-four hours, 18,316 in 1953. The years following saw a number of private firms set up plants to process uranium. In 1959 the value of uranium mined in Saskatchewan reached $58,705,000. The value of mineral production as a whole increased more than 400 per cent between 1953 and 1960.

For many decades the economy of British Columbia depended on the sale of raw materials. In recent years the province has become a leading manufacturer of wood products, pulp and paper, aluminum, iron and steel products, chemicals, petroleum products and transportation equipment. In the late 1950's the manufacture of such secondary products accounted for almost half of British Columbia's gross output.

Enthusiasm for public-works construction has also marked the western provinces since World War II. Manitoba is at work on a $32,000,000 highway construction program. Part of this is a section of the Trans-Canada Highway, spanning the continent. Saskatchewan is building a 500-mile highway from La Ronge to Uranium City in the north. Ultimately this highway will join a road system in the Northwest Territories, giving Canada a land link with the Arctic. Both Saskatchewan and British Columbia are engaged in extensive dam projects which will provide irrigation for thousands of acres. In addition, British Columbia's project, in the northwest, is taking advantage of that region's tremendous water-power resources to provide power.

Since 1958 the government of Alberta has had a five-year public-works plan under way to build new hospitals, schools and roads. The main purpose of the plan is to guard against recession. Other features of the plan include guaranteed loans for farm-home improvement and leadership training in cultural and recreational programs.

The western provinces are as bold in politics as in business. Though they have sent many Progressive Conservatives to represent them in Ottawa from time to time, the western provinces are given to political experiment at home.

The Social Credit Party is strong in Alberta and British Columbia, the Co-operative Commonwealth Federation in Saskatchewan. The theories of Social

ALUMINUM INGOTS being maneuvered from pier to ship at Kitimat, British Columbia. Hydroelectric power has made Kitimat a western center of aluminum production.

ANNAN PHOTOS

PRAIRIE SYMBOL—a grain elevator. There wheat is collected from farms for shipment to eastern Canada and to countries across the sea.

KOFOD, MONKMEYER

GEORGE HUNTER, FPG

Resources—oil wells and vast farms and ranches

AUTUMN FOLIAGE frames a drilling rig in Alberta at the foot of the Rocky Mountains.

J. ALEX LANGLEY, TEXACO, INC.

HUNTING for oil in the Liard River district, which is partly in northern British Columbia.

IMPERIAL OIL LTD.

A PIPELINE PUMPING STATION is dwarfed in the broad expanses of the prairie near the historic Qu'Appelle Valley, in Saskatchewan Province, once a route for traders of the Hudson's Bay Company.

UNTAMED HORSES about to cross the Red Deer River, in Alberta. They have been rounded up to take part in the Calgary Stampede.

«

Credit were developed by Major C. H. Douglas (1879–1952), an English engineer. He was inclined to be suspicious of international bankers and his platform was largely one of monetary reform. By "social credit" he meant annual dividends, based on the amount of national wealth, to be distributed by the government among its citizens. His followers have held political power in Alberta since 1935 and in British Columbia since 1952.

The CCF is devoted to a fairly orthodox brand of socialism. Like the British Labor Party, it is a member of the Socialist International, closely allied with trade unions. The CCF proposes widespread public ownership of banks, transportation, communications and the like. Manitoba has been a stronghold of the Liberal Progressives, a farm party in origin, throughout most of this century.

Fur Traders and Colonists

The history of western Canada is a long and colorful one. Three events decided the destiny of the Prairie Provinces: in 1670 Charles II issued a charter to the Hudson's Bay Company; in 1783 Montreal fur merchants abandoned their rivalries to form the North-West Company; in 1811 Lord Selkirk received from the Hudson's Bay Company a grant of 113,000 square miles on the Red and Assiniboine rivers. Selkirk immediately opened up his land to needy Scottish crofters, an act that neither the North-West nor Hudson's Bay Company fur traders welcomed. The Nor'Westers feared the threat to their monopoly of fur routes. When in 1814 Governor Macdonell prohibited the unlicensed export of provisions from the colony, the traders lured away many of the colonists to Upper Canada. Selkirk retaliated by importing Swiss mercenaries to protect the little colony, but he was fined for resorting to arms. Bitterly disappointed and dispirited, Selkirk retired to England and died two years later, but his Red River Settlement persisted.

In 1869 the Canadian Government took over the territory owned by the Hudson's Bay Company, which then included Selkirk's old colony. Red River and the other western settlements had at this time a population of twelve thousand of whom about five sixths were of mixed Indian and French or Scottish descent, the métis. The Government did not consult the settlers about the transfer of their territory and seemed in its new surveys to be contemplating forfeiture of land. The métis rose under Louis Riel and set up a provisional government. But Riel's extreme position aroused such opposition that arrangements were finally made to permit the Red River Settlement to enter the Dominion as the Province of Manitoba, in 1870.

The way was now opened for the extension of the Dominion to the Pacific Coast where a colony had already been established. Terms of union were settled upon wherein the Government promised to begin within two years and complete within ten a railway to the Pacific Coast. British Columbia entered the Dominion in 1871.

At first few settlers were attracted to the prairies. Then, at the end of the 1800's, Clifford Sifton, minister of the interior, by an intensive campaign of advertising in newspapers and pamphlets in Britain, Europe and the United States, induced a great tide. The total immigration into Canada in 1897 was 21,000; in 1902 it was 67,000; in the following year 125,000; and by 1913 it reached nearly 400,000. During this period of rapid expansion nearly as many settlers came from the United States as from Britain, while just over a quarter of the total immigration came from Continental Europe. Not only did people arrive from across the seas and from the south but the people of the eastern provinces moved westward into the new lands.

The Railway Network Spreads

With the new settlement and increased crops further transportation seemed necessary. Sir Wilfrid Laurier's Government in 1903 agreed with the Grand Trunk Railway Company for another transcontinental railway, the Government itself building the part from Moncton to

OIL REFINERY AND LABORATORIES IN TURNER VALLEY, ALBERTA

Alberta is the heart of Canada's rich oil fields, which are making the country an important one in the world petroleum market. The Canadian oil industry first developed in Turner Valley.

A SALMON-FISHING FLEET at Port Renfrew, British Columbia.

The shape of western industry

LUMBER MILLS along Lake Cowichan's shore, Vancouver Island, British Columbia.

FLIN FLON, Manitoba, is a complex of mines and smelters, from which there is an endless flow of needed metals—copper, zinc, gold, silver, cadmium.

A WELDER at work on a Kitimat, British Columbia, dock. The port serves the aluminum industry. »

ALUMINIUM, LTD.

MODERN METHODS SPEED THE HARVESTING IN WESTERN CANADA

A caterpillar-type tractor pulls a large combine that harvests and threshes the grain while moving over the field. Canada ranks high among the great wheat-producing countries of the world.

Winnipeg. Thence the railway company went on to Edmonton and through the Yellowhead Pass to the Pacific. A branch was made from the main line to Fort William so as to give an outlet for grain by way of the Great Lakes. A third system, the Canadian Northern, under William Mackenzie and Donald Mann, by construction and purchase had in 1902 nearly 1,300 miles of road in operation between Lake Superior and Saskatchewan and by 1915 the links of a third transcontinental railway system had been welded together. Both the Grand Trunk Pacific and the Canadian Northern found the cost of construction beyond their estimates and were forced to obtain loans from the government, which in turn sought means to recover its investment. Finding none, after the war, it took over the companies altogether under the name of the Canadian National Railways.

What of the problems connected with transfer to the government, with settlement and railway development? First it was necessary to secure title to lands from the Indians. This was done by a series of wise treaties, in which the rights of the aborigines were protected. In subdividing the land for settlement, a plan similar to that in use in the United States was adopted. An area one mile square was employed as the unit of division and this area, known as a section and containing 640 acres, was divided into quarter-sections of 160 acres. Townships were of uniform size, six miles square and divided into thirty-six sections. At first settlement followed the streams and at Battleford, Prince Albert, Duck Lake, St. Albert and Edmonton colonies were formed, but with the construction of the Canadian Pacific Railway, lands along the railway became most valuable. Order was kept on the plains by the organization of that famous body, the Northwest Mounted Police. At first these police were a police of the wilderness looking after the Indians and criminal whites; as villages and towns sprang up and farmers grew crops they had to "maintain the law" in town and country. When the western towns grew larger they set up their own police forces leaving the Mounted Police as a rural constabulary. In 1905 the "Mounties" received the title of Royal from King Edward VII. During the first World War two squadrons of "Mounties" saw active service overseas. In 1920 the Royal Northwest Mounted Police were combined with another police force, the Dominion Police, to form the Royal Canadian Mounted Police.

The Force rendered yeoman service in World War II, guarding vulnerable points throughout all of Canada. It is the sole police force operating in the Yukon Territory and the Northwest Territories, and performs a variety of services in all provinces and both Territories for the Canadian Government.

When the provinces entered Confederation they received annual grants from the Canadian Government. A persistent effort was made by Manitoba to get better terms and in 1912 not only was its annual grant increased but the province was enlarged to more than double its size by the extension of the northern boundary to 60° N. and by the addition of a large triangle extending to Hudson Bay, thus giving the province a seacoast.

Sixty years ago the great plain stretching from the Red River to the Rockies, the abode of over a million and a half of people and forming the provinces of Saskatchewan and Alberta, was inhabited only by wandering bands of Indians, by herds of buffalo and a few intrepid fur-trappers. Agriculture has been the chief source of the wealth of both provinces; manufacturing has steadily increased; and the coal production of Alberta surpasses that of Nova Scotia. The farmers, mainly occupied in grain-growing, early formed co-operative organizations to care for the storing and selling of their crop. Thus the wheat-pool has gradually emerged as the medium for the sale of western grain. Owning large elevators at Fort William and Vancouver the pool handles the grain from the local railway to the purchaser. The opening of the Panama Canal has made it possible to send grain to Europe throughout the year without so long a train haul as the eastern ship-

NATIONAL FILM BOARD

WRESTING ATOMIC FUEL FROM THE EARTH—BEAVER LODGE MINE
New proof of the wealth to be unearthed in Saskatchewan is the uranium mine (above) at Beaver Lodge. As a source of uranium-bearing ore, Canada is second only to the Belgian Congo.

CANADIAN PACIFIC AIRLINES

A TURBOJET-POWERED PLANE, which flies the polar route to Europe, is serviced in a hangar at Vancouver International Airport.

Meeting transportation

ISOLATED FARMING FAMILIES rely on automobiles and good roads to reach such

J. ALEX LANGLEY, TEXACO, INC.

HOLLYMAN, PHOTO RESEARCHERS

FREIGHT TRAINS stretch as far as the eye can see in the yards at Winnipeg, Manitoba, distributing center for the whole West.

DEFROSTING the treads of a bull-dozer, in the Peace River area, Alberta.

A TUG pushes a barge, laden with a mixed cargo, down the Saskatchewan.

needs of long distance

large cities as Calgary (shown at dusk), Alberta, which are themselves long distances apart.

«
SCHOOL IS OUT and these true children of the plains gallop home (which is Castle Creek, near Calgary, Alberta) on horseback.

TRUCKLOADS OF SUGAR-BEETS ROLL INTO A CANADIAN FACTORY

Sugar-beets grow well in cool countries, and Canada's crops have increased enormously during recent years. The sugar-beet is usually larger than the table vegetable and yellow or white in color. When the sugar has been extracted, the pulp can be fed to animals. Another important product that is made from sugar-beets is molasses.

ping entails. In the year 1931, the Hudson Bay Railway was finally completed; it offers for a brief summer period a sea-haul shorter by a thousand miles.

The citizens of the Prairie Provinces are very varied in origin—and for this reason education is of vital importance. As early as 1877 the University of Manitoba was established, and it has become the center of the provincial educational system. The University of Alberta at Edmonton was established in 1905 and the University of Saskatchewan in 1907. In all of these universities agricultural education is an important side of the curriculum.

A map of Saskatchewan would be easy to draw as its north and south boundaries are parallels of latitude (49°—60° N.) and its eastern and western boundaries are meridians of longitude (109°—104° W.). The area of the province is 251,700 square miles—slightly less than that of Manitoba and greater by 5,000 square miles than the combined areas of Great Britain, Ireland and Norway. The country is for the most part open rolling prairie at an average altitude of 1,500 feet above sea level. In the north it is more broken and as yet but slightly developed. The climate is continental, the summer temperatures almost tropical but with cool nights. The winter temperature occasionally reaches 40° below zero but it is tolerable on account of the dryness and absence of high winds. Light rains fall in summer and only a moderate snow in winter. This dry vigorous climate is healthful for stock. Wonderful lakes are to be found in the northern part of the province, forest-set and rock-framed. The population (1951 census) is 831,728, about three-fifths of which is agricultural and lives on the land. Their produce constitutes a large part of the provincial income. Acreage value of field crops in Saskatchewan is enormous; the wheat, oats and barley grown are of very fine quality. The wheat is hard and heavy, the oats plump and hard. Rich grasses cover the land in parts not cultivated and upon the grazing lands vast herds of cattle and sheep feed. The only cities of any size are Regina, the capital, Saskatoon and Moosejaw, which will be mentioned elsewhere.

Lying between Saskatchewan on the east and the Rocky Mountains and the 120th meridian on the west, and bounded on the north and south by the Northwest Territories and the United States respectively, is the province of Alberta. Its area, 255,285 square miles, is the greatest of the Prairie Provinces. Formerly almost exclusively a ranching country, it has now become a great wheat-producing region, the frontier of the grain-growing area. In the southwest, considerable coal and oil-mining are carried on; lumbering is important in the more mountainous western parts and in the north, while some ranching is still pursued in the less populous sections. Rainfall is somewhat scanty in southern Alberta but extensive irrigation areas have been formed east and north of Lethbridge and along the Canadian Pacific Railway from Calgary to Medicine Hat. Central Alberta is the best settled area in the province with a rich soil and sufficient rainfall. Northern Alberta is sparsely populated, but well watered. Nearness to coastal influence and the prevalence of the chinook wind modify the climate considerably. The great divide in the Rockies forms the western boundary line of Alberta leaving much beautiful mountain scenery within her borders. The important cities are Edmonton, the capital, and Calgary, which are described elsewhere.

Manitoba, the most easterly of the Prairie Provinces and also the oldest in point of settlement, extends roughly from a line joining the west coast of Hudson Bay and the Lake of the Woods to a line approximately the 102nd meridian west. On the north and south it is bounded by the 60th and 49th parallels of latitude respectively. The total area of Manitoba is 246,512 square miles, of which a large part is rolling prairie land, the home of the buffalo in the days of Indian and fur-trader. These prairies are now wheat fields, and instead of Indian and trapper we have the farmer and manufacturer. About 775,000 people live in the province. Those of British descent make up about 50 per cent of the population. There are many of French descent in and around St. Boniface and a number of other nationalities throughout the province. About 16,000 Indians still live in Manitoba, most of them engaged in farming, herding cattle, trapping and fishing on reserves. We tell about them in another chapter. Win-

A SEAPLANE ARRIVES AT WEST TAHTSA CAMP ON BURNS LAKE

A small plane, equipped with pontoons, lands on Burns Lake, British Columbia. The plane is delivering mail and supplies to people whom other forms of transportation cannot reach.

CANADIAN PACIFIC RAILWAY

OUTFITTING for big-game hunting at Telegraph Creek, in the north British Columbia wilds.

»

BISON (AMERICAN BUFFALO) graze safe from human enemies in an Alberta sanctuary.

A CREVASSE yawns in the path of mountain climbers on the Columbia Icefield, Alberta.

« A CRACK TRAIN speeds past Cathedral Mountain, in the Yoho park vicinity, British Columbia.

The call of the outdoors in a majestic landscape

TOTEM-POLE CARVING remains an active art in Thunderbird Park, Victoria, B. C.

nipeg is by far the largest city, but Brandon and St. Boniface are growing.

The soil of Manitoba is very rich, yielding wheat, oats, rye and barley abundantly. In the north are great forests of white spruce and jack pine, and from the north too comes a rich harvest of furs, and a promising return of minerals from the famous Flin Flon copper ore and the rich Mandy copper claim in The Pas. Although the winter climate is severe yet there is a great amount of bright sunshine and but little cloudy weather. Rain falls in June and July.

The Climate of the Province

British Columbia is in some respects the most favored part of Canada. Within its boundaries are reproduced all the varied climates of the Dominion and almost every natural feature, while some of its climatic and geographical conditions are peculiar to the province. Extending from the Rockies to the Pacific and from the 49th to the 60th parallel of latitude, it has an area of 366,255 square miles, about three times the size of Italy. The many islands of the Pacific Coast, notably Vancouver Island (area 12,408 square miles) and the Queen Charlotte group, are included in the province. They are noted for their temperate climate and abundant natural resources. The mines, timber areas, fisheries and agricultural resources of the province are remarkable for their quality and extent.

Mountains and Valleys

British Columbia is essentially a mountainous country, comprising practically the entire width of the Cordilleran belt of North America. The chief system in this belt are the Rocky Mountains proper on the northeast side, and the Coast Range on the southwest or Pacific side. Between these are lower ranges running southeast and northwest. Vancouver Island and the Queen Charlotte group are remnants of still another range now almost entirely submerged in the Pacific. The highest peak in the Canadian Rockies is Mount Robson; Mount Fairweather on the International Boundary is the highest peak in the province. Other high peaks include Columbia, Forbes, Assiniboine, Bryce. Passes over the Rockies are many: the South Kootenay, Crow's Nest, Kicking Horse (traversed by the main line of the Canadian Pacific), the Yellow Head Pass (used by the Canadian National) and the Peace River Pass. The Coast Range renders the coastline of British Columbia remarkable not only for its extent (7,000 miles) caused by deep fjord-like indentations, but also for its great beauty as the mountains rise from the water's edge to a height of 5,000 to 8,000 feet.

Mountains imply valleys and it is in these valleys that the agricultural wealth of the province of British Columbia is produced. The Okanagan Valley, stretching for eighty miles north and south, is famed for its apples, cherries, apricots and peaches. The Fraser Valley floored with rich alluvial soil brought down by the Fraser River grows immense crops of hay and grain and supports a large dairy industry. The benchland on its borders is well adapted for the growing of berries and other small fruits, and here the Japanese have entrenched themselves very strongly.

Great Mineral Wealth

Mountains often contain minerals, and the settlement on the mainland of British Columbia was due largely to a "gold rush" of the early sixties up the Fraser Canyon to the Cariboo country. On Howe Sound rich copper is worked by the Britannia Company; at Stewart on the Alaskan border is the Premier mine, one of the richest small mines known, producing both gold and silver; at Anyox near Prince Rupert more copper is to be found; near the southeastern corner of the province is the greatest zinc-lead mine in the world, the Sullivan mine, and not many miles away at Trail is a great smelter where very pure zinc and lead are made from Sullivan ore.

British Columbia has the largest area of salable timber of any country. Three-quarters of her area is covered with valuable timber and the forests include yellow pine, Douglas fir, red cedar, hem-

PROSPECTING with Geiger counters in the uranium-rich area of northern Saskatchewan.

STAKING A CLAIM near Uranium City, center of the Saskatchewan development.

POWER-HOUSE SITE at Kemano, British Columbia. It is part of the vast Kitimat project under which water-power resources are being developed to supply the aluminum industry.

113

lock, balsam and spruce. Most majestic of all the western forest trees is the Douglas fir, which grows at times to a height of nearly two hundred feet, has a girth exceeding thirty feet and a finished lumber which almost equals oak in beauty.

A large part of the commerce of British Columbia is derived from the sea. The chief product is salmon caught along the coast and in the rivers and inlets. Large canneries are in operation employing many fishermen, white, Indian and Japanese. The headquarters of the halibut fishery are at Prince Rupert and from this point hundreds of boats set out.

Early in the nineteenth century four nations, Spain, Russia, Great Britain and the United States, claimed the "Oregon Country." Spain surrendered her claims to any land north of the present California to the United States and Russia withdrew within the present Alaska, leaving only two claimants for the vast region. Both based their claims chiefly upon ex-

ploration, Captain Cook (1778) and Captain George Vancouver (1792–94) had explored the coast. Alexander Mackenzie, Simon Fraser and David Thompson, all of the North-West Fur Company, had reached the Pacific overland. On the other hand, Captain Robert Gray of Boston had entered and named the Columbia River in 1792, and Lewis and Clark had floated down the Columbia. In addition the United States had succeeded to whatever claim Spain had had. Both nations established fur-trading posts, and finally, in 1846, the region was divided by prolonging the 49th parallel, leaving, however, all of Vancouver Island to Great Britain. The island's southern tip is below the parallel.

Vancouver Island was proclaimed a British colony in 1849, and, in 1858, following a gold rush, the territory on the mainland was proclaimed as British Columbia. Eight years later the two districts were joined in administration. In

SASKATCHEWAN GOVERNMENT

THE DAY'S WORK IS DONE and both cowboys and horses turn happily homeward on a Saskatchewan ranch. The weathered log bunkhouse, in the grove of trees, is still in use.

EXPERT INSPECTION OF PELTS BEFORE A FUR AUCTION BEGINS

Buyers look closely at muskrat skins at an auction room in Winnipeg. They are permitted to do so until the sale begins. Only registered individuals and representatives of firms known to be members of the fur industry may offer bids at a raw fur auction. Auctions, which speed up the trade in pelts, date back to the early days of the Hudson's Bay Company.

LUMBERJACKS stand on springboards wedged in the trunk to help them cut a spruce.

AN A-FRAME DERRICK lowers two hundred tons of logs into the booming ground.

CANADIAN LUMBER lies on the docks of a port in British Columbia before being shipped all over the world. The lumber industry provides Canada with one of her largest exports.

1871 British Columbia entered Confederation on condition that the government would bring a railway through the mountains, and also introduced responsible government. At that time her population was only 36,000, but with the coming of the railway the increase was rapid. In 1951, according to the census that year, it was 1,165,210. The percentage of British born (over thirty) is larger in this province than in any other.

The development of her rich natural resources has led British Columbia into a difficulty. Facing eastward, she looked to the Orient to supply her labor. By 1884 nearly 10,000 Chinese were in the Province working cheaply and sending their savings back to China. In 1902 the head tax on Chinese was raised to $500, reducing immigration from China. However, people from Japan and India continued to come and make their homes. Many of them went into such occupations as gardening, lumbering and fish-canning.

The chief cities of the province are Victoria, the capital, on Vancouver Island, Vancouver on the mainland, New Westminister on the Fraser and Nanaimo in Vancouver Island. At Point Grey the growing University of British Columbia occupies a magnificent site, which was chosen for it after much discussion.

NATIONAL FILM BOARD

AN AUTOMATIC DRILL makes blasting holes for dynamite, in the great open-pit mines at Flin Flon, Manitoba. The ore is rich in such metals as zinc, copper, gold and silver.

FEDERAL GOVERNMENT GRADERS in the Winnipeg stockyards stamp beef carcasses according to structure, age and weight. About 500,000 cattle a year go through the stockyards.

BRITISH COLUMBIA AND THE PRAIRIE PROVINCES: FACTS AND FIGURES

This chapter includes the three prairie provinces of Manitoba, Saskatchewan and Alberta and the coastal province of British Columbia.

BRITISH COLUMBIA has a total area of 366,255 square miles; land area, 359,279 square miles, including Vancouver Island (12,408 square miles). The total population is 1,305,000. A bill to annex the Yukon Territory to British Columbia has been considered. Administered by a lieutenant governor and a ministry responsible to a Legislative Assembly of 48 members. Representation in Canadian Senate, 6; in House of Commons, 22. Manufacturing, forestry, mining and agriculture are important occupations. Forests include fir, cedar, hemlock, spruce and pine. Leading minerals are lead, zinc, gold, coal, copper and uranium; province ranks third in value

COURTESY CANADIAN NATIONAL RAILWAYS

POCAHONTAS POST OFFICE, ALBERTA

In rural communities and in new sections the post office is the center of community life.

of mineral production. There are 3,526 manufacturing establishments; leading products—lumber pulp and paper, fish, ships and ship repairs, fertilizers, plywood, beverages, fruits and vegetables. Population about four-fifths Protestant. Provincial public education is compulsory for ages 7 to 15. There are 1,027 public schools and several private schools, 2 normal schools, 1 vocational school, a junior college, and the University of British Columbia at Vancouver. Railways, 5,775 miles; roads, 22,797 miles; telephones, 363,032; air transportation; and steamship service. Populations of chief cities: Victoria (capital), 51,350; Vancouver, 344,850; New Westminster, 28,650; North Vancouver, 15,700; Trail, 11,450.

MANITOBA has a total area of 246,512 square miles; land area, 219,723 square miles.

Population is 849,000. Province is administered by a lieutenant governor appointed by the Federal Government and a ministry responsible to a Legislative Assembly of 57 members. Representation in Canadian Senate, 6; in House of Commons, 14. Agriculture and stock-raising important; chief farm products are wheat, oats, barley and milk. The leading minerals are copper, zinc, cement and gold. Fresh water fisheries are extensive. There are 1,650 manufacturing establishments, devoted chiefly to slaughtering and meat-packing, railway equipment repairs, butter- and cheese-making, printing and brewing. Railways, 5,048 miles; all-weather roads, 9,765 miles; telephones, 199,338. The province has 1,722 schools with 145,222 pupils, and 6 colleges are affiliated with the University of Manitoba. The populations of chief cities: Winnipeg (capital), 243,300; St. Boniface, 26,350; Brandon, 20,500; Flin Flon, 9,900; and Portage la Prairie, 8,550.

SASKATCHEWAN has a total area of 251,700 square miles; land area, 237,975 square miles. Population of province is 889,000. Administered by a lieutenant governor appointed by the Federal Government and a ministry responsible to a Legislative Assembly of 52 members. Representation in Canadian Senate, 6; in House of Commons, 17. Agriculture, manufacturing and mining are the chief industries. Leads Canada in the production of wheat, oats and rye. Copper, zinc, gold, coal and sodium sulfate are the chief minerals. There are 1,200 manufacturing establishments producing chiefly meats, flour and feed, beverages, butter and cheese and printed material. Railways, 7,011 miles; surfaced roads, 8,280 miles; telephones, 164,404. In public schools, 173,390 pupils. There are 2 normal schools and 1 university. Populations of chief cities: Regina (capital), 71,350; Saskatoon, 53,300; Moose Jaw, 24,400; Prince Albert, 17,150; North Battleford, 7,500.

ALBERTA has a total area of 255,285 square miles; land area, 248,800 square miles. Population is about 1,050,000. Administered by a lieutenant governor appointed by the Federal Government and a ministry responsible to the Legislative Assembly of 61 members. Representation in Canadian Senate, 6; in House of Commons, 17. Agriculture, manufacturing and mining are chief industries. Chief farm products are wheat, milk, barley and oats. Coal, crude oil (95% of the country's production) and natural gas are the chief mineral products. There are 1,685 manufacturing establishments producing chiefly meats, beverages, flour and feed and lumber. Railways, 5,085 miles; surfaced roads, 29,860; Edmonton is terminal for air flights to the north and across the Pacific; telephone-wire mileage, 341,781; 113,000 telephones. In public schools, 210,000 pupils; correspondence-school students, 8,000; in addition to provincial university and technological institute there are private colleges and normal schools. Populations of chief cities: Edmonton (capital), 209,400; Calgary, 168,900; Lethbridge, 28,300; Medicine Hat, 20,000.

Canadian Cities ... *variety and striking contrasts*

CANADA'S cities display vividly the story of the country. Their architecture reflects its rugged history; their size proclaims its present prosperity; their location, like the rings in a tree, records the stages of its growth. For there is a logic in their development which underlies the ethnic and economic patchwork of modern Canada. True, many towns were created almost by accident: the establishment of a police post, as at Medicine Hat; the arrival of an Indian chief, as at Brantford; the settlement of Pennsylvania Germans, as at Kitchener, or of United Empire Loyalists, as at Fredericton. But by and large, Canadian cities were born and grew in response to three things: shipping, commerce and industry.

In the sixteenth century the first, the maritime, phase of the growth of Canada's cities began. Shipping towns appeared, like St. John's, Newfoundland; Halifax, Nova Scotia; Saint John, New Brunswick. Nestling in the indentations of the Atlantic coast, these little ports gave refuge to the storm-driven sailor and provided a market or processing center for his cargo. The sea, via the St. Lawrence River, nudged the voyager into the heart of the continent, where the Great Lakes and the network of rivers that feed them made water the key to settlement. Trading posts sprang up at river junctions and portages: Montreal, for instance, at Lachine Rapids, which was then head of ocean navigation. They would not have become cities so early but for the struggle between the French and English. Fortresses were built on the sites of trading posts: at Toronto, for instance, in 1749; and at Windsor, Nova

Scotia, in 1750. There the hunter and pioneer gave way to the soldier and administrator. Increased dependence on the sea for food, arms and men left its mark on the map in the form of dense settlement on the lower St. Lawrence. After the British conquest, commerce dominated the scene. New maritime communities continued to appear, sometimes in response to trade, like Sarnia, and sometimes to discovery, like New Westminster. Doubtless the St. Lawrence Seaway will strengthen this trend, producing new cities on the Great Lakes.

The sites of such places largely depended on natural water routes. In the next, the commercial, phase the settlements depended on man-made routes, the railroads. Saskatoon, established in 1883, got a rail connection in 1890. The railroad itself created new towns, a by-product of the over-all economic thrust of the nineteenth century. This made cities like Winnipeg, Edmonton and Galt, and expanded old ones, like Halifax and Quebec.

The last stage of Canadian city development, the industrial third phase, has occasionally been spectacular. Thus Dawson City was created and swollen by the Klondike gold rush into a community of about 20,000 people in 1898. Today it has little over a thousand and is just plain Dawson, though it has become a prospecting center again, this time for oil. Some of the new mining communities, like Port Radium, live under the threat of Dawson's post-gold rush fate. Less dramatic but more permanent are cities like Lethbridge and Sudbury, also the products of the mining industry. Industry expanded commercial towns in the same way as commerce had expanded the maritime ones. Calgary, Regina and Moose Jaw gained oil refineries, Hamilton and Stratford became hives of industry, Medicine Hat became a center for the extraction of natural gas, coal and clay. Toronto expanded its commercial facilities to handle a new surge of business.

Despite great progress the industrial phase is far from finished. It will probably populate the Pacific coast and the north; it will build new cities away from the rivers, railways and frontiers. As for the existing cities, they are spreading fast as the population mounts and the automobile becomes universal. Clusters of suburban communities are multiplying accordingly, as in Montreal, Toronto and Quebec. Whatever happens they will remain the pride of the nation. Could any other country of such small population and vast area match the vigor and variety of Canada's cities?

When Newfoundland became a British colony in 1583, St. John's was well established. It was already a fishing center with a bustling harbor. It became known far and wide as the commercial and processing headquarters for the great Atlantic cod fisheries and as a major shipping point. In 1949, when Newfoundland joined Canada, St. John's became the capital of the new province.

Among the city's notable buildings is the Anglican Cathedral, a fine Gothic structure designed by Sir Gilbert Scott, famous nineteenth-century English architect. Another is the Roman Catholic Cathedral, which stands in a commanding position on a hill. Government House is a replica of Admiralty House in Plymouth, England. Memorial University and the Newfoundland Hotel are more modern buildings.

The way from the ocean to St. John's harbor passes between beetling cliffs 500 feet high, known as the Narrows. From Cabot Tower, on the north side of the Narrows, Marconi received the first transatlantic wireless message, forerunner of radio, in 1901.

Five hundred miles away lies Halifax, founded in 1749. It is the capital of Nova Scotia, Atlantic headquarters of the Royal Canadian Navy and eastern Canada's chief winter port. From the old stone citadel on a dome-shaped hill there is a superb view of the city and the magnificent harbor, protected by powerful forts and batteries. Halifax has been an important naval and military base for two centuries. One of the largest bridges in the British Commonwealth connects the city with the town of Dartmouth.

The city's two cathedrals, the new public library, Dalhousie University, the oldest Protestant church in Canada and many other fine buildings help to give Halifax dignity and charm. The public gardens and parks are delightful, and an arm of the sea that reaches behind the city, known as North-West Arm, is one of the finest aquatic playgrounds to be found anywhere.

Prince Edward Island's only city is a small and attractive one, Charlottetown, founded as Port La Joie before 1750. Its picturesque old Colonial Building was the scene of the historic meeting in 1864 that led to the Confederation of Canada three years later. Charlottetown has lob-

GARDINER EXPRESSWAY, on the outskirts of Toronto, is a dramatic example of the highways being constructed to connect the major cities of Canada and their rapidly expanding suburbs.

HUNTING SURVEY, ANNAN

ster and oyster fisheries; and with several delightful seaside resorts only a short distance away, it attracts a great many summer tourists.

Although Fredericton is the capital of New Brunswick, Saint John is the largest city in the province. It is also the oldest incorporated city in Canada, with a Royal Charter dated 1785. Originally built as a fortress on solid rock at the mouth of the Saint John River, it was the landing place of ten thousand United Empire Loyalists who left the United States during the War of Independence in order to remain under British rule. Because of serious fires which swept the city in recent times, Saint John today consists mostly of modern buildings. Its harbor is notable not only for its varied trade but also for the Reversing Falls, which produce surging torrents at each change of the tide.

The motto of the province of Quebec is *Je me souviens,* "I remember." That is what the ancient stones of Quebec City seem to murmur as one explores the narrow, crooked streets and the old buildings of the lower town, huddled at the base of the great rock upon which the city stands. To reach the upper town, one can climb flights of steps or winding roads cut out of the rock, or ride in huge elevators. Here in the upper town are Laval University and the Grand Seminary, the Château Frontenac, and Dufferin Terrace, a famous boardwalk set out from the side of the cliff. Here are the Wolfe-Montcalm monument and the monument to Champlain, who established a trading post at Quebec in 1608, making it the first permanent settlement in Canada. And dominating all, high above the river, crowning what is surely the most dramatic city site on the continent, is the Citadel. From the battlements one looks below to the roofs of the lower town and across the broad and busy St. Lawrence to the Isle of Orleans and the city of Lévis on the farther shore. Beyond are range upon range of mountains, the summits rounded

THE PROTECTED HARBOR of St. John's is a haven for the Newfoundland fishing fleet as well as for other kinds of vessels. Around the harbor the city is spread out on hills.

THE TOWN CLOCK crowns Citadel Hill, the highest point in Halifax. From this vantage point there is a sweeping view of the city's business section and the sheltered bay.

by time, fading into the blue distance.

Quebec City is such a fascinating place in which to wander, so full of the echoes of times past, that the casual visitor is likely to overlook its day-to-day activity as a provincial capital, as a religious and educational center, as the home of many industries and as a port. But it is all of these things as well as a tourist resort, and its people live amid a mixture of past and present.

The same is largely true of Canada's biggest city, Montreal, which lies 180 miles farther into the heart of the continent along the St. Lawrence. Called Hochelaga by the Indians and Ville-Marie by the early French settlers, it takes its present name from Mont Réal (Mount Royal), a volcanic hill rising about 800 feet from the island of Montreal. The city is built on a series of terraces on the hill's lower slopes. Above the harbor comes the business district, with the Bank of Montreal as the most stately of many impressive buildings. Nearby, in the Place d'Armes, is Hébert's striking

EDWARD CORNWALLIS, English soldier, still looks over Halifax, which he founded.

123

MARKET SLIP at Saint John, New Brunswick, where a variety of supplies reach the city. It is a major Canadian port, ice-free the year round, with one of the world's largest dry docks.

bronze figure of Maisonneuve, founder of the city. The principal stores and hotels are halfway up the slope; the main residential districts are higher still. The topmost part of the mountain has been left more or less in its natural state. It forms a public park commanding lovely views.

Four centuries ago Jacques Cartier planted a crude wooden cross on the summit of Mont Réal. Today the chief landmark by night is a great illuminated cross at the same spot. No symbol could be more fitting, for Montreal is a city of religions. Nearly all beliefs have a place there. However, scores of buildings—ancient shrines, convents, churches, hospitals, seminaries—show that here is a bastion of the Roman Catholic Church. Outstanding among the religious buildings are St. James Cathedral, modeled on St. Peter's in Rome; the parish church of Notre Dame, which seats ten thousand; the Anglican Cathedral, Christ Church, St. James United Church and the quaint

Bonsecours Church. The hospital of the Hôtel Dieu has existed for over three hundred years, but not in its present building. The city's most interesting older buildings are perhaps the Seminary of St. Sulpice and the Château de Ramezay, once the home of the French governors and now a museum. McGill University and the University of Montreal are centers of higher education and research.

Montreal has grown from a settlement relying mainly on the fur trade into an industrial, commercial and financial metropolis of over a million people. It serves a huge area and has world-wide connections. It is the headquarters of Canada's two transcontinental railway systems. Many banks, industrial corporations and other national enterprises have their head offices there. However, it is shipping in all its branches that is the most important industry. Montreal's unique position as a sheltered seaport, a thousand miles from the open sea, makes it the chief link between the world's ocean trade, the vast water-borne trade of the Great Lakes, and the wealth of the West. When the St. Lawrence Seaway is completed, the harbor and docks of Montreal will probably be even busier than they are today.

Verdun, Outremont, Westmount, Laprairie and Lachine, neighboring cities and towns forming the suburbs of Montreal, are delightful, with many attractive homes and gardens. As in the city itself, their people of different national origins and creeds mingle in harmony and work together for the common good.

About a hundred miles west of Montreal, just inside the province of Ontario where it borders Quebec Province, is Ottawa, the nation's capital. It occupies a magnificent site on the Ottawa River, chief tributary of the St. Lawrence. Once known as Bytown, after Colonel John By of the Royal Engineers who built the Rideau Canal in the 1820's, this former lumbering center became the city

of Ottawa in 1854. Three years later, much to the dismay of the hopeful rival cities of Montreal, Quebec and Toronto, Queen Victoria selected it as the capital. Although Ottawa is first and foremost a seat of government and a city of imposing official buildings, it is also a place of rivers and rocks, of bridges and locks and canals, streams and cascades. The Parliament Buildings stand on a high bluff above the Ottawa River, with the distant ranges of the Laurentian Mountains as a backdrop for their graceful towers and buttresses. Almost as familiar to visiting statesmen and diplomats are the towers of the nearby Château Laurier Hotel, a gem of period architecture. Rideau Hall, the governor general's residence, is a large, rambling building surrounded by attractive grounds.

Near the center of the city are the seething Chaudière Rapids; elsewhere the Gatineau River and the Rideau Canal wind past sections of well kept lawns and multihued flower beds. Ottawa is perhaps at its best on a fine May morning.

THE PROVINCE BUILDING in Charlottetown, home of the Prince Edward Island legislature. When the present city was laid out in 1768, it was named Charlotte(town) for George III's wife.

THE CHATEAU FRONTENAC, one of the landmarks of the upper town of Quebec City. Dufferin Terrace, the famous railed boardwalk, runs along the cliff top beside the hotel.

Then the tulips which are an annual gift from Queen Juliana of the Netherlands are in full bloom around Ottawa's buildings and along its waterways; the sun glints on the swirling river and its rocky banks, and the city's elm-lined streets are vistas of tender green.

Connected with Ottawa by the Rideau Canal is the old city of Kingston. At first it was a French fort; later it became a British one. Fort Henry, built during the War of 1812 to protect the naval dockyard which had recently been established there, is now a national historic site. The city's many fine old buildings include the City Hall, St. George's Cathedral and the Royal Military College, which corresponds to Sandhurst in England and West Point in the United States. Queen's University is noted for the quality of its teaching and the harmonious beauty of its gray limestone buildings.

A "Forest" City

On his first visit to Toronto, a well-known British diplomat looked out of his window high up in a big hotel and said, "Why, it's not a city at all; it's a million people living in a forest!" All kinds of trees are to be found in Toronto's downtown streets and in its many parks and beautiful residential sections and suburbs, such as Rosedale, Forest Hill Village, Alexandra Wood and the Kingsway. Canada's second largest city is growing at such a pace that some of its many trees have made way for expressways, factories, office buildings and blocks of apartments. However, those that remain are a lovely natural asset.

Toronto is the largest unit in a confederation of thirteen neighboring municipalities. It is the political and financial capital of Ontario, a leading industrial and commercial center and a lake port with a good harbor and several miles of docks and wharves on Lake Ontario. Its citizens can name a long list of outstanding local features that include the only subway in Canada; the largest university, the largest hotel (the Royal York), and the highest building (the Canadian Bank of Commerce) in the British Common-

PHILIP GENDREAU

CHAMPLAIN MONUMENT in Quebec, the city founded by the French explorer-soldier.

wealth; the busiest mining-stock exchange in the world; the largest annual fair in the world (the Canadian National Exhibition); and more telephones per person than any other city of the Commonwealth.

Toronto is a sprawling, bustling, go-

127

OLD-FASHIONED VICTORIAS carry sight-seers to the park at the top of Mount Royal. The bustling metropolis of Montreal is spread out below, girdled by the St. Lawrence River.

ST. JOSEPH'S ORATORY, Montreal, founded in 1904 by a humble lay brother, André.

getting business city. But at the same time it is a cultural center of note. It prides itself on its fine museums, art galleries and libraries, supports its own symphony orchestra, and appreciates the opera, the ballet and the theater. It also is proud of its historical heritage. Old Fort York, built by Governor Simcoe in 1794 and recently restored, is an interesting relic of colonial days. Another historic spot is the homestead of William Lyon Mackenzie, first mayor of the city and leader of the Upper Canada Rebellion of 1837. However, the leading tourist attraction is a storybook "castle" named Casa Loma. This enormous, fantastic structure was built as a residence by the late Sir Henry Pellatt at a cost of nearly $3,000,000. It is now operated as a showplace and ballroom for charitable purposes.

Hamilton, at the western end of Lake Ontario, is sometimes called "the Pittsburgh of Canada" because it is the coun-

128

IN DOWNTOWN MONTREAL the Laurentien Hotel displays one of Canada's great products, aluminum. The walls are faced with more than 70,000 square feet of the silvery metal.

try's foremost center of the iron and steel industry. By night the chimneys and blast furnaces light up the surrounding sky. Hamilton is also an attractive place by day. It has good public buildings and residential districts, and its celebrated open-air market handles much of the luscious output of the Niagara fruit belt. McMaster University, on the city's outskirts, enjoys a reputation that is all out of proportion to its small size. The exquisite rock gardens on Hamilton "Mountain" attract visitors from far and wide.

Another city of southwestern Ontario with lovely surroundings is London, an old pioneer settlement. Governor Simcoe wanted to make it the capital of Upper Canada in 1792, but he was overruled in favor of Toronto. The locomotive on the civic coat of arms is no mere figurehead, for modern London is an important railway center. This delightful and compact city is big enough to be interesting in most of the ways that matter, but it is

OUTSIDE STAIRCASES along an old Montreal street. It is illegal to erect them today.

PARLIAMENTARY LIBRARY in Ottawa. It is a circular structure in the Gothic style.

small enough to have a particular charm of its own. Its natural beauties are numerous. It would be difficult, for instance, to find a more beautiful campus than that surrounding the University of Western Ontario.

Like Hamilton, the city of Windsor is a hive of industry dominated by huge plants and shops. This great automobile-manufacturing center lies along the Detroit River opposite Detroit, Michigan, to which it is connected by bridges, tunnels and ferries. Windsor has an assured place in history, for here is the Bâby House which was used as a headquarters by General William Hull when he invaded Canada from the United States in the War of 1812. It is said to be the oldest brick house in Upper Canada. Before the American Civil War, Windsor spelled freedom for many of the slaves using the "underground" escape routes from the South to Canada.

Ontario has more cities than any other Canadian province, and all are interesting in one way or another—Brantford and Brockville; Guelph and Galt; Peterborough with its tremendous lift lock on the

BOTH PHOTOS, NATIONAL FILM BOARD

SUPREME COURT BUILDING in Ottawa. Like most of the other federal government buildings, this one has a magnificent location on the bluffs above the Ottawa River.

NATIONAL FILM BOARD

LADY GREY DRIVE in Ottawa guides visitors along a wandering route following the Ottawa River and past the Royal Canadian Mint (right) where the country's coins are made.

Trent Canal; St. Catherine's and its mineral springs; Stratford, famed for its annual Shakespeare festival; Sarnia, city of oil refineries; Sudbury and Timmins, the mining cities of the north; Kitchener, once called Berlin; the twin lake-head cities of Fort William and Port Arthur, marked by rows of enormous elevators crammed with grain from the west awaiting shipment overseas. These twin cities form a vital link between eastern and western Canada. In western Canada our first important stop is Winnipeg, capital of Manitoba. This largest city of the prairies and the fourth largest in Canada is at the junction of the Assiniboine River and the Red River of the North, in the center of Canada's richest farmlands. Winnipeg began as a small Hudson's Bay Company post called Fort Garry, about 1820. Its early days were marked by the bitter struggle between rival companies for control of the rich fur trade. The city grew very slowly; in 1871 the population was under 250. Then the Canadian Pacific Railway arrived in 1881, followed by a rush of settlers, and the population began to soar.

Into the railway yards of Winnipeg come great trainloads of wheat, oats, barley, rye and flax; the turbulent but orderly Grain Exchange buys and sells them. Early settlers planned the city on a generous scale. Its wide, airy streets are in agreeable contrast to the congested streets of most other great cities. The buildings, both public and private, are admirable. Outstanding are the beautiful Legislative Building, opened in 1920, and the Hudson's Bay Company's department store, which occupies a whole block. The company has landscaped and presented to the city the ivy-covered tower of the old fort, last reminder of earlier, stormier days.

Though founded in 1882, Regina, the capital of Saskatchewan, is thoroughly modern in appearance, for the original

131

LAKE FRONT, TORONTO. Docks and warehouses stretch along the water's edge. On the skyline are the Royal York Hotel (left rear) and (right of hotel) the tower of the Bank of Commerce.

SEMICIRCULAR SECTIONS with Ionic columns emphasize the Greek style of Convocation Hall, Toronto University. The institution has an especially beautiful and spacious campus.

A RECONSTRUCTION OF FORT YORK on the old site in present-day Toronto. The French built the fort in 1749 and the British captured and destroyed it ten years later.

A GREAT LAKES FREIGHTER takes on grain from the huge elevators at Fort William, Ontario. On Thunder Bay on the northwest shore of Lake Superior, the city has a fine natural harbor.

BLAST FURNACES in busy steel mills make the night sky glow over Hamilton, Ontario. The attractive city at the head of Lake Ontario is the center of Canada's iron and steel industry.

city has disappeared. On a June day in 1912, it was laid in ruins by the most devastating tornado ever to hit Canada. After the storm, ungainly temporary buildings were put up. Gradually these were replaced, until the city became a bright, thriving place with excellent buildings, large park areas and a profusion of trees. This pleasant city is the distributing and marketing center for a huge prairie region and is the home of several flourishing industries, such as woodworking, oil refining and printing.

Northwest of Regina, in the heart of the hard-wheat belt, is Saskatchewan's second largest city, Saskatoon. It also is a roomy, modern city which has grown steadily from small beginnings into a prominent trading center for farm products. There are extensive flour mills and a few other manufacturing plants. Spread along both banks of the South Saskatchewan River, the city is linked together by several large bridges. Near the river are tree-shaded parks and the attractive campus of the University of Saskatchewan.

The main line of each of Canada's great transcontinental railway systems serves one of the two major cities of Alberta. From Regina, the Canadian Pacific Railway goes by way of Moose Jaw and Medicine Hat to Calgary. Farther north, the Canadian National Railway connects Saskatoon with Edmonton, the capital of Alberta. Like many other Canadian cities, Edmonton's early fame developed from the fur trade. The city takes its name from Fort Edmonton, a Hudson's Bay Company trading post set up in 1795 on the North Saskatchewan River. The city has always been prosperous because it lies near good farm country and deposits of coal, gold and pitchblende. Its extraordinary growth lately is due to the discovery and development of oil fields in Alberta. Chemical production is a leading industry, and the presence of great quantities of natural gas is another industrial asset.

For good reasons, Edmonton has been called "the gateway to the north" and "the crossroads of the world" because it is a transportation hub of the first importance. No less than thirteen lines of railway enter the city. Here, too, is the chief junction for the air routes to the great tracts of country being opened up in the north.

On the western edge of the Alberta prairies, not far from the Rocky Mountains, the foothill city of Calgary is the commercial center of the oil boom. Calgary was first settled as a Royal North West Mounted Police post in 1875. It soon became the local capital of the ranching country surrounding it and carried on a huge trade in cattle, sheep and horses. Standing 3,500 feet above sea level, where the Bow and Elbow rivers meet, the city is only 80 miles east of the

Rockies. The westerly view at sunset is almost unbelievably beautiful.

Calgary is rich in parks and public gardens. In Dinosaur Park can be seen life-sized models of the fearsome reptiles that roamed Alberta millions of years ago. The domain of the ancient dinosaurs is today the home of the wild horses which snort and plummet into the ring at the annual Calgary Stampede. This world-famous show is a colorful mixture of agricultural fair and thrilling competition. There are parades of cowboys and Indians, chuck-wagon races, and steer-roping and riding contests. Most exciting of all are the competitions between three-man teams attempting to rope, halter and ride unbroken horses.

Smaller Alberta cities on the route west are the industrial center of Medicine Hat and Lethbridge. The latter is an impor-

THE SHAKESPEAREAN FESTIVAL held every year has made Stratford, Ontario, a Mecca for lovers of the theater from all over North America. Performances are of high professional caliber.

tant air-line junction which took its name from William Lethbridge. He was the head of a company operating local coal mines and a narrow-gauge railway nicknamed "The Turkey Trail."

Few cities in the world can boast a natural setting to equal that of Vancouver, British Columbia, Canada's third largest city and her greatest seaport. Vancouver lies on the Gulf of Georgia, just north of the Canada-United States border. The lofty mountains of the Coast Range rise behind the city and from practically every point there are lovely vistas of sea and mountain. Originally a small mill town named Granville, Vancouver took its present name in 1886. That same year it was wiped out by fire. It was speedily rebuilt and has been growing at a great pace ever since. Today it is the western terminal of the Canadian Pacific and Canadian National railways. Its great harbor handles a higher tonnage of shipping than any other port in Canada.

STANDARD OIL CO. (N. J.)

LIFELINES OF INDUSTRY flow through Winnipeg, Manitoba, one of the largest railroad centers on the continent. There are 270 miles of track in the Canadian Pacific freight yards.

A TIME-WORN GATE—the remains of old Fort Garry. There Hudson's Bay Company traders once met. Today the spot is a national historic site, standing in the midst of downtown Winnipeg.

BROADWAY BRIDGE, one of several spans that link Saskatoon, Saskatchewan. Spread out along both banks of the South Saskatchewan River, the city is spacious and modern.

BOTH PHOTOS, NATIONAL FILM BOARD

SASKATCHEWAN'S BEAUTIFUL CAPITAL. Regina is on Waskana Creek, which here forms a pretty lake. The large building with a cupola houses the legislature of the province.

AN ATTRACTIVE ROW of comfortable modern homes in Lethbridge, Alberta. The city is well planned. Streets are wide and lined with trees; and householders take pride in their gardens.

DOWNTOWN IN BUSY EDMONTON. In the central part of Alberta, at the southern end of the Alaska Highway, the city serves an area rich in mineral resources—coal, oil, gas.

DINOSAUR IN CONCRETE in the Fossil Gardens of St. George's Island Park in Calgary, Alberta. Remains of such beasts have been found not far away, in the Deer River valley.

CALGARY, the city where the Bow and Elbow rivers meet. Long famous as the center of a stock-raising area, its prosperity has been further increased by the rich oil fields near by.

THE CITY HALL of Vancouver, British Columbia, is a spacious structure in modern setback style, with a clock on each side of the top. Shrubs are massed near the entrance.

Immense cargoes of wheat, lumber and other commodities are shipped to the Orient, to the United States and South America, and to Europe by way of the Panama Canal. Besides being a major center of trade, industry and transportation, Vancouver is one of the chief pleasure resorts and residential cities of the northwest Pacific area, with numerous beaches and delightful suburbs. The climate is mild and the grass stays green all the year round.

Thousand-acre Stanley Park is the best known of Vancouver's many fine parks and open spaces. Perhaps the most striking building in the city is the Hotel Vancouver, opened in 1939 and now a leading social and business center. The city's Chinese quarter houses many thousands of Chinese people and in North America is second only to the Chinese quarter of San Francisco. A splendid feature that arrests the eye of a visitor is the Lions Gate Bridge over the harbor mouth. Over 1,500 feet long, it is the longest and largest suspension span in the British Com-

monwealth. The University of British Columbia occupies a beautiful site on Vancouver's outskirts.

Twelve miles from Vancouver is the city and port of New Westminster, a distributing center for the fruit of the Fraser Valley. It was founded in 1859 by the Royal Engineers and was for a time the capital of British Columbia. Fish processing is the main industry at Prince Rupert on Kaien Island, five hundred miles northwest of Vancouver. Each year millions of pounds of fish are processed in its colossal plants.

When Vancouver Island became a crown colony, Victoria was selected as its capital. It remained the capital when the island united with the mainland colony of British Columbia. Today it is a beautiful, quiet, well-kept city with few echoes of its boisterous past. However, at the time of the Cariboo gold rush, about a century ago, it was a lusty tent town of ten thousand people, most of them gold-crazy and many of them violent. This hardly sounds like the place of which

BASKING ON THE BEACH at Stanley Park, in Vancouver. The well-tended park covers nine hundred acres. Besides the wide beach there are a zoo and extensive gardens.

THE GRACIOUS CAPITAL of British Columbia—Victoria—viewed from the top of the Parliament Building. Its many parks—Beacon Hill, Gorge—are beautifully landscaped.

Rudyard Kipling said, "I tried honestly to render something of the color, the gaiety, and the graciousness of the town and the Island, but only found myself piling up unbelievable adjectives."

Victoria—with its flowers and gardens and magnificent views, its Empress Hotel and attractive Parliament Building set amid velvety lawns, its Scottish tweeds to wear and its English crumpets for tea—is sometimes called "a bit of old England in new Canada." There is some truth in this, but not very much. Victoria is essentially a Pacific coast city with its interests and connections centered in the Pacific coast. This charming residential city is important both as the capital of its province and as one of Canada's busiest ports.

The census of 1956 showed that Canada had 50 cities with a population of 25,000 or more. This does not include many suburban areas around the bigger cities, which have large populations but are not themselves incorporated as cities. One city, Montreal, had over 1,000,000 people. Toronto had over 600,000, Vancouver over 300,000. There were four cities with more than 200,000 inhabitants—Edmonton, Hamilton, Ottawa and Winnipeg. Four others had more than 100,000—Calgary, London, Quebec and Windsor. Halifax, Kitchener, Regina, Saint John (New Brunswick), St. John's (Newfoundland), Trois Rivières, Brantford, Oshawa, Saskatoon, Sherbrooke, Verdun and Victoria each claimed between 50,000 and 100,000 people. The populations of twenty-seven cities ranged from 25,000 to 50,000. Forty-three cities had from 15,000 to 25,000 persons. About a third of the people of Canada live in cities with more than 25,000 inhabitants. This proportion will no doubt increase because the cities attract both Canadians and the many new immigrants who have come from Europe in recent years.

By R. D. HILTON SMITH

143

OIL PROSPECTORS take off in a helicopter from a dusty street in Dawson, Yukon. 'Copters have special value in prospecting as they can land despite lack of roads or water.

The Yukon and Northwest Territories

... the roof of North America

THE Yukon and the Northwest Territories extend Canada's domain far into the Arctic. Part of each territory lies within the Arctic Circle. The Yukon, in Canada's extreme northwestern corner, borders Alaska. The Northwest Territories are administered as three districts, Mackenzie, Keewatin and Franklin. They make up one third of Canada's total land area. Spreading from the Yukon to Davis Strait the Northwest Territories include not only mainland but many islands, which extend northward like steppingstones. Alert, a weather station on Ellesmere Island, is only five hundred miles from the North Pole.

The severe climate, especially in the eastern section, has long hindered both settlement and economic development. But a change is in the air. The stimulants are the area's vast mineral wealth—oil and base metals—and its strategic importance in the cold war. "Never in the history of Canada," a government official remarked, "has there been such a concentration of men and machines engaged in an investigation to advance the economic strength of our Northland." The manager of the airport at Norman Wells, a busy hub of the activity in the Mackenzie District, put it in a more striking way:

"This is the great tomorrow country."

As a territorial area, and not provincial, the "tomorrow country" has largely been governed from Ottawa. Local government is limited. The Yukon has a resident commissioner appointed on the advice of a five-member elected legislative council. Powers of the council are more limited than those of a provincial government. The Yukon and the Northwest Territories send one representative apiece to the House of Commons. Like the Yukon, the Northwest Territories are governed by a commissioner and legislative council. Here, though, five of the nine-member council are appointed; the four elected members are chosen in the Mackenzie District only. The council must sit in Ottawa for one of its two annual meetings.

The Federal Government is building a new town, however, that will bring some branches of the territorial government north. Inuvik, 150 miles north of the Arctic Circle, is in the Mackenzie District. The town will one day serve as an administrative, educational and welfare center for the western Arctic. *Inuvik* is an Eskimo word meaning "the place of man." Construction began in 1956. It is the first such major project in the far

144

north to employ a force of Eskimo and Indian workmen. An airport and more than a hundred houses had already been built in 1960, with schools, hospitals and other federal structures to follow soon. In 1956 the Legislative Council held one of its annual meetings there—the first time the council had ever met so far north.

Nevertheless the people of the two territories feel that progress toward self-government is too slow. In the late 1950's and early 1960's demands for more self-government increased. It is argued that Ottawa governs by remote control—that it is too far away to understand local problems. Further, there is the matter of taxes. Many territorials feel that for the dollars sent eastward to Ottawa there is too little return in the form of capital investments. A Dawson newspaper editor complained: "This one-sided flow of the area's resources is a classic example of a country being bled for an outsider's benefit. It is about time this was stopped." Nonetheless most authorities feel that a provincial form of government must wait on population growth.

The far north might still be an unknown wilderness were it not for the airplane. Air service provides transportation between towns in the territories and, even

more important, is the supply lifeline from the south. But it is extremely expensive. For large-scale settlement and development, the territories need roads. Construction in such country is enormously difficult. In spite of this, the Government has stepped up road-building programs in the area. A 450-mile stretch was begun in 1960 between Dawson in the Yukon to Port Brabant, an Arctic harbor. Another road will soon veer northward 150 miles from Dawson to the Yukon's first productive oil well, at remote Eagle Plains. Farther east, the town of Yellowknife is being connected with Coppermine, a port on Coronation Gulf. Yellowknife itself is linked to the Mackenzie Highway by a 276-mile road circling the west end of Great Slave Lake. Nor are new roads the only concern of planners in the North. In 1960, reconstruction projects on the Canol Road and the Whitehorse-Mayo Highway in the Yukon were almost completed.

Other possibilities are in the wind. To provide heat and power, tons of fuel must be brought into the towns. Nuclear reactors may supply heat and power on the spot in the not too distant future. For permanent housing, ice and snow may provide the basic material. It has been found in experiments that ice can be strengthened by the addition of small quantities of glass fibers, and can be made to fit together more easily by treatment with alcohol. Another idea is to build roads in a sort of tunnel construction, roofed over and so protected from the weather, instead of above ground.

Adventure and Exploration

For more than three centuries the history of the territories was a story of gallant adventure. Soon after North America was discovered, bold mariners began seeking a route—the elusive Northwest Passage—through the unknown icy seas at the "top" of the continent. Between 1576 and 1587 English explorers discovered Davis Strait southwest of Greenland, and in 1610 Henry Hudson entered the bay named for him. For twenty years thereafter a series of expeditions sought vainly to get through from Hudson Bay to the Pacific Ocean. Brave attempts also were made to find the Northeast Passage—the route eastward from the Pacific Ocean.

After 1860, however, the attention of explorers turned to the conquest of the North Pole. A number of American and British parties, under such leaders as Hayes, Hall, Nares and Greely, explored Ellesmere and other northern Arctic islands before Peary reached the North Pole in 1909 from a base on Ellesmere Island.

Exploration of the mainland of the territories was begun by Samuel Hearne, an employee of the Hudson's Bay Company stationed at Fort Prince of Wales. He crossed the Barrens—the far northern tundra—and reached the mouth of the Coppermine River in 1771–72, the first white man to reach the Canadian Arctic coast. Not long afterward North-West Company fur traders arrived at the Athabaska River (in present-day Alberta) and in 1789 Alexander Mackenzie descended the river named for him to the Arctic Ocean, returning to his base at Fort Chipewyan after a journey of 102 days.

Trading posts were soon established along the newly discovered waterways, and for a time there was bitter rivalry between the North-West Company and the Hudson's Bay Company. The latter won out in 1821, and thereafter sent men to explore the Liard River and other tributaries of the Mackenzie system. They reached the Yukon River in the 1840's by way of both the Liard River (from the south) and the lower Mackenzie and Porcupine rivers (from the north). The coast line of the mainland was mapped between 1821 and 1853.

Whalers from Europe and the United States were among the first white men to penetrate the Arctic in search of a livelihood there. In fact, Herschel Island, at the entrance to Mackenzie Bay, was not only a fur-trading center but was also a favorite wintering place for whalers from 1890 until the decline of the whaling industry after 1906.

Originally the Northwest Territories included not only their present area but also the Yukon and northern parts of present-day provinces. The territories were under the British Crown; they did not become a part of Canada until 1870. It was even later, in 1912, that some of the area was surrendered to the provinces. Today the dividing line between the provinces and all the territories is the 60th parallel, stretching between Hudson Bay and the Alaska boundary.

The Klondike Gold Rush

To go back a bit, in 1896 the discovery of gold in the gravel bars of the Klondike River (a branch of the Yukon) started a feverish rush to the Klondike. Some 100,000 persons set out for the Yukon and perhaps half that number actually reached the district. Many of them were ill-equipped and perished from the hardships suffered on the way.

In 1898 the Yukon Territory was organized, with its eastern boundary marked off by the Mackenzie Mountains. On the map the territory has the shape of a triangle, wedged in between Alaska, British Columbia and the Northwest Territories. It has only a narrow strip of coast, on the Arctic Ocean. In 1899 Dawson City, then boasting 25,000 inhabitants, became

THE ELDORADO MINES OF PORT RADIUM ON GREAT BEAR LAKE
Neat white buildings, tanks and stilted sheds vary the bleak rock shore of Great Bear Lake.
Pitchblende from Eldorado supplies great quantities of uranium for atomic research.

the capital of the new territory. Agriculture and lumbering prospered, and a railway was built from Skagway, Alaska, to Whitehorse. More than $100,000,000 worth of gold was found in the first seven years after the Klondike rush. However, no new discoveries followed, most prospectors departed and the territory declined in importance. In 1921 barely four thousand people remained.

Before we consider what has been happening to the territories in recent years, let us see what the land itself is like. East of Great Slave and Great Bear lakes, the miles-wide Canadian Shield sweeps in an enormous semicircle, from the Arctic islands down to the Great Lakes and up around Hudson Bay. It is an exposed formation of Precambrian rock. In the hollows of the rolling surface lie thousands of lakes, many of them drained by the Kazan, Dubawnt, Thelon, Back, Coppermine and Anderson rivers. Steep cliffs, one thousand feet or more in height, occur where it edges water and at the western end. To the east, on Baffin and Ellesmere islands, it forms high mountain ranges. The thin soils of the Shield support only grasses, mosses, Arctic flowers, shrubs and dwarf trees, the trees becoming larger and more numerous as one nears the Mackenzie Lowland.

The Mackenzie Lowland is the northern portion of the great central plain of Canada and the United States. It is 600 miles wide at the sixtieth parallel but tapers to less than 100 miles at the Arctic Ocean. In the southern part are ranges of hills; and farther north, a mountain chain—the Franklin Mountains—lies between the Mackenzie River and Great Bear Lake. Most of the lowland is drained by the Mackenzie system which enters the territories at Fort Smith, as the Slave River, and after passing through Great Slave Lake emerges as the Mackenzie River. In places the Mackenzie is two to three miles wide, though before it reaches the Arctic it breaks up into many streams to form the Mackenzie delta. This mighty river of the north is fed by the Hay, Liard, Great Bear, Peel and Arctic Red rivers, and the system also drains two of the world's largest freshwater lakes, Great Bear and Great Slave. The most typical plants of the region (except in the delta) are poplar, spruce and birch trees.

West of the Mackenzie Lowland and extending to the Alaska border is the

147

PORTRAIT OF A THRIVING TOWN IN THE PIONEER NORTHLAND

Covering the promontory at the head of Yellowknife Bay and stretching into the lowlands beyond, Yellowknife has grown with the fast pace of industry in the Great Slave Lake region.

northward range of the Cordilleras, the backbone of North and South America. The Mackenzie, Selwyn, Ogilvie and Coast mountains continue the ranges of British Columbia, while the St. Elias Mountains extend into Canada southeast from Alaska. In these latter mountains is Mount Logan, 19,850 feet, the second highest peak in North America. The ranges stand on a high plateau which covers most of the Yukon Territory. Cut deep into the plateau are wide valleys in which flow the main tributaries of the Yukon River—the Lewes, Pelly, White and Stewart rivers—which drain most of the territory. The high altitude of the plateau makes it a grassland, but the valleys are well forested with spruce, poplar and birch.

In the Yukon Territory and the Mackenzie Valley, on the average, winters are long and cold but the short summers are surprisingly warm. However, the climate is erratic and may be mild or severe depending on whether gentle west winds

blow from the Pacific or bitter winds blow from the Arctic or the interior of the continent. Snow covers the ground from October to March and frosts may occur in the summer months. Nevertheless the summers are long enough to allow some agriculture near Dawson City and along the Mackenzie, as the long hours of sunlight help to offset the briefness of the season.

The Arctic islands and the eastern mainland are always at the mercy of cold polar winds, which bring bitter winters and very short, cool summers. In fact, the Franklin District, or Eastern Arctic, lives up to the popular idea of the frozen north. In winter the temperature may remain below 20 or 30 degrees for weeks on end. Summer temperatures may go up as high as 70, and then hordes of flies and mosquitoes come out. The climate here is very dry. Rainfall averages only from nine to thirteen inches a year in the western part and from six to nine inches in the east and north.

White people form the majority of Yukon settlers; and Eskimos, 80 per cent of the population of Keewatin and Franklin districts. About half the inhabitants of the Mackenzie District (clustered chiefly along the Mackenzie waterway) are Indians, one-third are white and the rest are Eskimos.

The fur trade has continued to flourish in the territories, though on somewhat more prosaic lines. The more recent history of these lands centers about the growth of settlement, improvements in transportation and the gradual development of other natural resources besides furs. In the Yukon the growth of aviation and the building of the Alaska Highway during the war years revived settlement, though Dawson City has never recovered.

In the Northwest Territories the fur trade has expanded to include strings of posts along the west shore of Hudson Bay, along the Arctic coast of the mainland and among the northern islands. A number of mineral discoveries since 1920 have resulted in the development of an

FRONTIER BANK, YELLOWKNIFE

Bank of Toronto's log-walled branch serves the brisk financial needs of Yellowknife industry.

oil field at Norman Wells (the main source of petroleum for the Mackenzie District), one of the world's largest sources of uranium and radium at Port Radium on the eastern shore of Great Bear Lake, and a number of productive gold mines along the North Arm of Great Slave Lake. Here the town of Yellowknife has grown into the largest settlement in the Northwest Territories.

The war years increased the amount of shipping and improved transportation facilities along the Mackenzie waterway. Airports and weather stations were built. A six-hundred-mile pipeline—the Canol project—was constructed from Norman Wells to Whitehorse, though this was later abandoned. Since the war a highway has been laid from the Peace River area (of northern Alberta) to Great Slave Lake. There is now a commercial fishery on this lake as well.

Silky Pelts from the North

Many of the world's finest furs come from the territories, particularly Arctic fox, which provides almost the whole income of the Franklin District Eskimos, and muskrat, caught chiefly in the Mackenzie delta. Other fur-bearing animals abound—weasel, mink, red and cross fox, marten, lynx, wolf and beaver.

The trapping season for all except muskrat and beaver is the winter, when

PETROLEUM FROM THE SOUTH

Tanks lashed to a barge from Alberta contain Yellowknife's gas and oil for the coming winter.

AT POND INLET, BAFFIN ISLAND

An Eskimo and a hooded lad discuss the important business of hunting for seal and fishing.

equipment, a few luxuries and some articles of food and clothing. In good years the income from furs has been large enough to enable some trappers to buy schooners and motorboats. Yet it is an uncertain livelihood. The trapper can never tell in advance how big his catch will be or what he will receive for it, as the price of furs fluctuates considerably. In bad years, traders, missions and the Government come to the rescue.

Fortunately, the trappers are able to obtain much of their food and clothing from hunting and fishing. Great quantities of fish are caught each year just to feed the sled dogs. Meat and clothing for the hunter and his family are provided by moose, bears, seals, white whales and, especially, the herds of caribou that migrate each year from the Arctic islands to the southern limits of the territories. Reindeer herds have been introduced and are established along the Arctic coast.

the furs are at their prime. Snares are set along courses through the woods, and the trappers inspect them regularly. In the spring the trappers make their way to the trading posts to exchange the pelts for

While most natives fish, hunt and trap, mining is the main employment of white settlers. In the Yukon Territory gold is still extracted from the gravel beds of streams. Copper, silver, lead and coal are mined, especially around Mayo and Keno Hill. The most exciting mining activity,

ON THE BARE NORTHERN TUNDRA—A FOREST OF ANTLERS

Reindeer, their fur molting but antlers in full glory, gather in a great herd at a government station, one of several in the territories reserved for native herdsmen and hunters.

however, centers about the riches of the Northwest Territories, which we mentioned earlier. Finally, this little-known land is yielding its secrets. Modern prospectors armed with all the latest scientific equipment are finding treasures far more valuable than gold—radium, uranium, lead, zinc, even oil. The oil strikes have been so promising, in fact, that some experts believe northern Canada may well become one of the world's great oil- and gas-producing areas.

Because of the climate and the distance from large markets, little agriculture is carried on in the territories, considering their vast size. Nevertheless, a number of farmers in the Yukon raise feed, live-

stock and vegetables and sell their produce and dairy products in the towns. Along the Slave, Liard and Mackenzie rivers large mission farms and many family truck gardens are cultivated.

All settlers benefit from the work of many small Royal Canadian Mounted Police detachments, who patrol the most remote districts. Government radio stations supply a link with the outside world, and travel is helped by weather reports broadcast from observation posts.

Undoubtedly more mineral wealth will be discovered. Certainly the 25,000 people who live there today represent only a fraction of possible settlement.

By Morris Zaslow

CANADIAN TERRITORIES: FACTS AND FIGURES

THE YUKON

Located north of British Columbia, this area, which was made a separate political unit in 1898, covers 207,076 sq. mi. of land, but has a population of only about 12,000.

GOVERNMENT

The Yukon is administered by a commissioner (appointed by the Federal Government) and a legislative council of five members who are elected and serve for three years.

INDUSTRIES

Mining is the main occupation of the people; gold, silver and lead are the chief minerals. The region, however, is gradually increasing its production of timber, manufactured goods and fur pelts. Monetary unit (in all of Canada including both territories), the Canadian dollar.

COMMUNICATIONS

The territory has less than 60 miles of railway as most of its traffic is carried on the Yukon River and nearly 2,000 miles of road, including the Alaska Highway. Several commercial airlines provide passenger and freight services to Canadian and Alaskan cities.

EDUCATION

Eighteen schools for white and half-breed children under territorial government; schools for Indians conducted by Federal Government or missionaries. British Columbia curriculum followed; resident superintendent at Whitehorse.

CHIEF TOWNS

Whitehorse (capital), population, 2,600; Dawson (former capital), 850; Mayo, 250.

THE NORTHWEST TERRITORIES

These territories include numerous islands and comprise 1,304,903 sq. mi. They have only about 16,000 inhabitants, most of whom are whites and Eskimos.

GOVERNMENT

The region is divided into three districts; Mackenzie, Keewatin and Franklin; and their administration is vested in a commissioner and a nine-member council, one of whom is the deputy commissioner. Numerous Canada-U. S. meteorological stations and air bases have been established on the most northern islands.

INDUSTRIES

Fishing and fur trading were the principal industries until recent years when gold, oil, pitchblende (ore of uranium and radium) and other minerals were discovered.

COMMUNICATIONS

Despite the all-weather Mackenzie Highway, boats and planes are the chief means of transportation, owing to the few vehicles and the long distances between the communities.

EDUCATION

Schools are operated in the main villages by the Federal Government and missionary organizations; and correspondence courses are prepared for children living too far away to attend the classes.

CHIEF TOWN

The area has only one town of any size: Yellowknife, in the Mackenzie District, with a population of 3,500.

The United States

...present and past

TODAY most Americans enjoy a standard of living such as the world has never seen before. Practically every family has at least one car and one television set. Though prices are high, so in general are wages and salaries. Americans can afford to buy a multitude of labor-saving devices and to furnish their homes in what earlier generations would have considered luxury. Working hours are short, in many cases only thirty-five hours a week. Paid vacations, often of three weeks, the automobile and the airplane give rein to the yearning of thousands of Americans to poke into almost every corner of the globe. Catering to the almost universal increase in income and leisure time, many once small businesses, such as travel agencies, are skyrocketing.

Backing the material prosperity is a giant industrial plant. It accounted in large part for a Gross National Product (the value of everything produced) in 1960 of about $500,000,000,000, which is expected to increase to at least $750,-000,000,000 by 1970. These enormous sums represent a yearly economic growth of about 3 to 4 per cent. Many economists think this rate should be higher. Though in 1960 the industrial production of the United States was still more than double that of the U.S.S.R., estimates of the latter's yearly growth run as high as 9 or 10 per cent.

In any case, American living standards, industry, farming, transportation, communications—all are being affected by the technological revolution of our time, the application of science to production of every kind. Automation, for example, means that a handful of technicians can tend a whole plant, as an oil refinery. Computers are taking over the drudgery of clerical work. Thus, because the market for unskilled workers is dwindling, a serious amount of unemployment remains in the midst of prosperity. With farm technology, fewer hands are producing ever larger yields. Warehouses bulge with surplus crops. Supermarkets display a dazzling abundance and variety of foods. Yet the problem of distribution is so complex that farm income has been shrinking.

In spite of its over-all material riches the United States today is faced with the most towering problems since the Civil War. The gravest domestic problem is related to that war, the status of Negro citizens. But coloring all other issues is the contest with the Soviet Union.

As the two most powerful nations on earth the United States and the Soviet Union are the leaders in an awesome, world-wide struggle for nothing less than men's minds. The United States stands for belief in individual freedom and government by consent; the Soviet Union, for control of the individual by the state, and for rule by a small group. The Soviet system is actually far more a form of totalitarianism than the classless communist society that Karl Marx envisioned.

The United States has allies; the Soviet Union, satellite states and close association with Communist China. What each side does—above all, what each side accomplishes—is watched by the millions

of people in the uncommitted, or neutral, nations, many of them newly independent and inexperienced in government. Some of their leaders have been inspired in part by the ringing words of the Declaration of Independence. The United States Constitution is copied. Unhappily, often as the word "freedom" is invoked there is seldom full understanding of the responsibilities it entails. Rather, the people are most impressed by the West's standard of living. This is what they want and they want it in a hurry. And because the Soviet Union has advanced from backwardness to industrial might in less than a half century its methods have the appeal of speed. The lack of real freedom there is much less obvious to people just emerging from hated colonialism.

This places a further burden on United States foreign relations as the Western alliance includes old colonial powers. To complete the vicious circle the Soviet Union harps on colonialism to keep distrust of the West alive, the while it pretends that its satellites are free nations.

Rivalry appears in foreign aid. This is not just a matter of wooing the allegiance of underdeveloped lands. The globe has been so shrunk by modern transportation and communications that widely different standards of living come face to face. The well-being of advanced nations can never be completely secure while want and misery shadow the underdeveloped areas. United States foreign aid, economic and military, has been running to some $4,500,000,000 a year.

The above, in brief, is why international issues seem to loom above domestic ones in the nation's political life. They are, in fact, intermingled. In appealing to the colored peoples of Asia and Africa the Soviet Union distorts and magnifies such matters as the resistance in some of the southern states to attendance of Negro and white children at the same schools. Certainly discrimination still exists against the Negro in housing and employment as well as in education, and not only in the South. But progress cannot be denied either, and it is beginning to move faster.

Education in general is affected. The achievements (space vehicles, nuclear energy and so on) of Soviet scientists, engineers and technicians and the numbers of them being turned out by Soviet schools have sparked intense discussion of the American systems. Critics claim that basic skills such as writing and reading have been neglected, that gifted children are wasted in a sea of conformity. Nevertheless the tide seems to be turning in the direction of increased emphasis on subject matter and the "quality of excellence." Also, against the criticism of American education must be placed such indications of cultural maturity as the enormous demands for serious music, "live" and on records, and huge sales of serious literature in paperback form.

Aggravating the education issue and

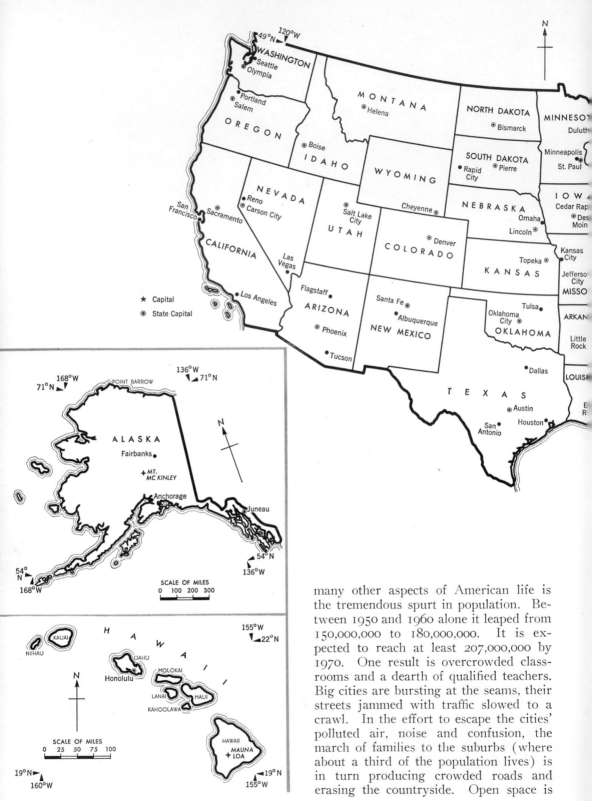

many other aspects of American life is the tremendous spurt in population. Between 1950 and 1960 alone it leaped from 150,000,000 to 180,000,000. It is expected to reach at least 207,000,000 by 1970. One result is overcrowded classrooms and a dearth of qualified teachers. Big cities are bursting at the seams, their streets jammed with traffic slowed to a crawl. In the effort to escape the cities' polluted air, noise and confusion, the march of families to the suburbs (where about a third of the population lives) is in turn producing crowded roads and erasing the countryside. Open space is

154

revenues are devoted to defense. Some economists suggest that Americans spend less on comforts and pleasure. Others believe that the costs, which will no doubt increase, can be met by increasing the rate of economic growth, mentioned earlier.

The Spanning of a Continent

How has the United States come to occupy its present world position? The story is long and complicated but one of its brightest threads can be traced in the movement west. The early settlers left their homelands in western Europe for a variety of reasons, but once in the New World their first and all-important consideration was to establish homes. So, one after another, the little colonies were planted along the Atlantic seaboard.

The newcomers found no roads but only narrow trails worn by Indians, or by wild animals in search of salt licks. No journey was undertaken except for urgent reasons, and then it had to be on foot or on horseback or by canoe. For plodding through the thick woods, the pioneers quickly adopted the Indian moccasin. Snowshoes also came into use during the northern winters. Poles with wooden disks at the bottom—similar to ski poles—gave the traveler on snowshoes extra support. Even so, winter journeys were preferred. Then frost hardened the trails and ice covered the streams, and it was easier to slip through the woods.

Early canoes were more like dugouts. A log was hollowed out by burning and chiseling with crude tools. The more typical canoe was made of birch, spruce or elm bark. Its frame, however, was of cedar or spruce; and the bark was attached to the frame by tough, slender larch or balsam roots. To prevent leaking, the seams were sealed with melted balsam or spruce pitch. The canoe was another idea borrowed from the Indians.

The early settlers made practically everything they needed at home—tools, soap, candles, homespun cloth dyed with homemade vegetable dyes. Money was extremely scarce, and the few things that

at a premium in the northeast and on the west coast. Shortages of water and power are developing in many areas.

Another factor in the expanding population is that the proportion of people over age sixty-five is rising steadily. Yet some 60 per cent of senior citizens have incomes of less than $1,000 a year. How to provide decent living conditions for these people is a major domestic problem.

There is no argument about the urgent need for city renewal, new schools, highways and the like. Debate is over how they are to be paid for, at a time moreover when about half the Government's

155

THE PURCHASE of Manhattan Island, carved on the base of a flag pole in New York.

dering over the country on foot and carrying his pack on his back. If he was fairly prosperous, however, he might have a pack horse. The animal was fitted out with a packsaddle and a pair of hobbles made of flexible twigs. Around its neck was a bell, silenced while traveling. At night the horse was hobbled and then the bell was unmuffled so that the horse could be located in the morning.

The First Highways

Road-making began when the Indian paths were broadened by hauling wider loads over them. Very early there were crude highways of this sort connecting neighboring villages. The first long stretch, however, was not opened until 1654. This was the Common Road between Boston and Providence, Rhode Island. Most famous of the colonial highways was the Boston Post Road, between Boston and New York.

The first road laws provided that they be ten feet wide with all trees cut close to the ground. As old accounts often speak of stumps in roads, the law seems to have been honored more in the breach than in the observance. In marshy or swampy places, corduroy roads were common— logs laid close together, crosswise over the highway. They made a solid but extremely bumpy surface.

had to be bought—needles and pins, nails —were precious. To supply these articles, especially to isolated farms in the clearings, peddlers soon appeared. The peddler was a welcome visitor, not only for his stocks but also for the news he brought of the outside world. Though the Puritans of New England and the Quakers of Pennsylvania might frown on ribbons and trinkets, the peddler was more than willing to cater to the vanity of girls in other colonies. By the time of the Revolution, his stock was likely to consist of "Yankee notions"—tinware and brassware besides nails and pins—made largely in Connecticut.

The peddler was a solitary figure, wan-

Some dirt roads were of clay one to two feet deep. If it was wet, every time a struggling horse or ox pulled a foot out, there was a "pop" like the sound of a gun. Animals might become so deeply mired in the clay that they died there. The Bull-skin Road, for instance, which lay between Pickaway, Ohio, and Detroit, Michigan, was so named because of the many oxen that perished on it.

Vehicles did most of the actual work of leveling roads. First came clumsy two-wheeled carts. The wheels were cross sections of tree trunks, often six feet in diameter and six or more inches wide. Such wide wheels naturally helped to smooth a highway, and laws encouraged their use. If a man drove a cart with wheels six or more inches wide, he was exempt from road tax, and he did not

CAPTAIN JOHN SMITH is remembered in a monument that looks out over the James River, Virginia. Near this spot he established the first permanent English colony in the New World.

FORT RALEIGH, on Roanoke Island, is today a national historic site. The blockhouses are reconstructions of those erected to defend the colony that disappeared so mysteriously.

SCENE from *The Lost Colony*, an outdoor drama given every summer on Roanoke Island, off the North Carolina coast. It re-enacts the story of Sir Walter Raleigh's ill-fated settlement.

ELIHU COLEMAN HOUSE on Nantucket Island, south of Cape Cod, built in 1722. By that time prosperous New Englanders were erecting spacious though often austere-looking homes.

have to turn out when he met a cart with narrower wheels. Two-wheeled carts, however, were in general use but a few years.

The four-wheeled wagon is more typical of colonial days. Each of its two axles was a different length so that the front and back wheels would pass over a different part of the road. The tops of these wagons were covered with linsey-woolsey, a mixture of linen and wool cloth, or sometimes a mixture of nettle fiber and milkweed down. Under these tops women and children huddled in bad weather. The men usually walked.

Along frontier roads there were stations, or stores, only at long intervals, so food had to be carried for both human beings and animals. Bags of feed might be dropped along the way to provide food for the horses on the return trip. Human travelers carried large wallets filled with bread, jerked meat, boiled ham and cheese. The stations supplied mainly salt and sometimes a few nails, which were paid for in furs. Salt sold for $5.00 a

bushel, and nails, from 15 to 25 cents a pound.

Until after 1776 practically no one traveled on Sunday. Indeed, in the Puritan settlements, no one might even walk in the streets on Sunday unless he was going to church. The law defined "Sunday" as from sunset on Saturday to sunset on Sunday. More than one traveler started on a journey Sunday evening, believing that the sun was down, only to have it appear from behind a cloud after he was on his way. For such a miscalculation, which seldom went unobserved, the traveler was fined.

The Puritans were no less strict in other matters. There was no place in their stern lives for play, even for the children. Football was to them "nothynge but beastlye furie and exstreme violence." Elsewhere in the colonies, however, social life was more relaxed. As anyone who has read *Rip Van Winkle* knows, the Dutch of New Netherlands loved bowling. The southern colonies, once they were well established, were gay. There was

PHILIP GENDREAU

A MINUTEMAN still stands in Lexington, Massachusetts, where the first shot of the Revolution rang out in 1775. Patriots were pledged to take arms "at a minute's notice."

FRAUNCES TAVERN, in New York City. It was a gathering place for prominent men during the Revolutionary period. Washington bade farewell to his officers here in 1783.

FANEUIL HALL, in Boston. Originally a public market, it was given to the city by a merchant, Peter Faneuil, in 1742. It served as headquarters of New England Revolutionaries.

WITH A FIRE crackling on the hearth, the well-kept tavern was a comforting haven for travelers in wintry weather. The room is in the old Munroe Tavern, Lexington, Massachusetts.

much visiting among the plantations, and dancing was popular—minuets, qua drilles, reels. Christmas was celebrated joyously until Twelfth Night.

Children had a sweet tooth then as now, and it was amply satisfied in the seaports after trade began with the West Indies. Ships brought in not only sugar and molasses but also chocolate and ginger. One colonial shop sign read:

> I have Sucket, Surrip, Grene Ginger
> and Marmalade
> Bisket, Cumfet, and Carraways as
> fine as can be made.

Children living in the woods of New England feasted on maple sugar and syrup.

To the colonists the land seemed inexhaustible, and it was often used so carelessly that yields grew less. Even if they had known better how to conserve the soil, it seemed cheaper to move into new territory. They were not in the least daunted by the fact that backbreaking labor would be required to win another clearing in the forest. Thus settlement

spread inland, and the frontier was pushed back to the foothills of the Appalachians.

For a long time rivers were the best highways, even though boats had to be propelled upstream against the current. A variety of craft were rigged with sails —pinks, pinnaces, ketches, schooners, lighters, shallops and pirogues. The pirogue, for instance, was really a very large canoe, often equipped with sails; it was sometimes forty to fifty feet long and six to eight feet deep. It could carry tons of household goods. If hostile Indians were encountered, however, a sailboat was practically defenseless.

As the colonies prospered and trade increased among them, a better means of hauling goods overland was needed than the clumsy wagons we have mentioned. The answer was the Conestoga, or Pennsylvania, wagon. It first appeared in 1755, although the name Conestoga was not bestowed on it until later. In that year, General Braddock used such a wagon on his expedition to Fort Duquesne

(Pittsburgh) in western Pennsylvania.

The Conestoga had a boat-shaped body that fitted it for mountain trails. No matter how the wagon was tilted, the cargo stayed in place. For feeding the horses there was a trough attached to the rear end. A Conestoga had six or seven bows —narrow, arch-shaped pieces—those in the center being a little lower than the end ones. These bows supported a covering of white canvas. The wagon was capable of carrying up to eight tons, though for each ton a horse had to be added to the team.

A wagoner was always proud of his fine-toned hame bells. In case he had trouble on rough or slippery roads and another driver helped him, it was the custom to give the hame bells to the rescuer. Sometimes a wagoner in trouble deliberately broke the tongue of his vehicle so that a passing driver could not help and, therefore, could not claim the bells. After the Revolution, paint made the Conestoga almost flauntingly patriotic. In contrast to the white of the canvas, wheels and sideboards were red, and the running gear and under part were blue.

The need for overnight stopping places brought about the establishment of inns or taverns. In fact, a Connecticut law of 1644 required each town in the colony to keep one. Americans used the word "tavern" more often than "inn," although the term "ordinary" was common in the South. Taverns were licensed, which gave a community some control in the selection of a keeper. Beer and wine were sold, and it would seem that the flavor of the wine left something to be desired, for it was the custom to spice it with nutmeg. Nutmegs were a luxury, and travelers carried their own in nutmeg holders made of wrought silver or Battersea enamel. A holder was just large enough to hold one nutmeg, and a pierced or corrugated surface on the inside of the cover served as a grater.

Taverns were often named for patriots, and above many a tavern door swung a crude portrait of Washington, Franklin, Pitt or Lafayette. Philadelphia had a

BLACK STAR

IN CRUDE HUTS such as these, the bedraggled Continental Army spent the bitter winter of 1777–78 at Valley Forge. Then the fate of the new nation was "suspended by a thread."

Four Alls Tavern before the Revolution. Its signboard read:

1. King—I govern all.
2. General—I fight for all.
3. Minister—I pray for all.
4. Laborer—I pay for all.

Even as restaurants do today, taverns frequently specialized in the food served. One tavern advertised fresh trout dinners; another served smoked ham that the owner himself had cured; still another served his own chickens. The waitresses were often the proprietor's daughters, and perhaps his wife—whose age had not "effaced the agreeableness of her features." Nor was the owner himself above giving service.

Early taverns took the place of newspapers or might have the only copy in a town. People went to the tavern to get information; and the proprietor himself was likely to be as inquisitive as any reporter. The story goes that when Ben-

PHILIP GENDREAU

BLACK STAR

BENJAMIN FRANKLIN arriving in Philadelphia—a famous statue by R. Tait McKenzie.

BETSY ROSS HOUSE, Philadelphia, where Mrs. Ross supposedly made the first flag.

THE LIBERTY BELL. From the steeple of Independence Hall, Philadelphia, July 1776, it rang out to proclaim the Declaration of Independence. The precious relic is inside the hall today.

THE HUDSON RIVER, one of the routes by which the early Americans first worked their way inland. A number of bridges span it now—here the Bear Mountain Bridge, near New York.

VAN DEUSEN HOUSE, in Kingston, New York, is a charming example of the stone dwellings erected in the Catskill Mountains by refugee Huguenots from France, during the 1600's.

166

jamin Franklin entered a tavern, he would say:

> My name is Benjamin Franklin. I was born in Boston. I am a printer by profession, and am traveling to Philadelphia, shall have to return by ...... and have no news. Now what can you give me for dinner?

Any newspaper available was read until it was almost in shreds. A sign on a mantelpiece in one tavern read: "Gentlemen learning to spell are requested to use last week's newsletter." Before the Revolution, almost any kind of reading matter was at a premium. The few newspapers themselves were small and poorly printed, and books were scarce and dear.

The tavern was usually the social center of a town. On occasion, town meetings, religious services or theatrical performances might be held in it. If low-spreading trees grew nearby, the proprietor might build platforms connecting one tree with another. They made wonderful playhouses for children.

Outside of New England the theater began to flourish in the 1700's. The first colonial theater was built at Williamsburg, Virginia, in 1716; and by 1750 there were a number of Shakespearean companies. In 1766, the Southwark Theater in Philadelphia, said to be the first permanent theater erected in the colonies, opened with *Katharine and Petruchio*. (Evidently this title was preferred to *The Taming of the Shrew.*)

It was many years before Americans undertook lightly the hazards of an ocean voyage. Even in fair weather, it took a sailing vessel a month to cross the Atlantic by the northern route and two months by the southern. The experience of the famous Adams family gives us a glimpse of what a trip to Europe meant in the late 1700's. On one of his several diplomatic missions overseas, this time to Holland, John Adams took along his young sons, John Quincy and Charles. They sailed on November 13, 1779. The Atlantic was stormy, and the vessel leaked so badly that two pumps operated twenty-four hours a day to keep it from sinking. The ship was forced to land at Ferrol, Spain, and Adams and the children had to cross the Pyrenees Mountains in a carriage in wintertime. That part of the journey was perilous indeed, but they reached Holland without mishap.

A few years later, while Adams was still in Europe, his wife Abigail and daughter "Nabby" made the crossing. They sailed with two servants, John Brisler and Esther—who soon became Mrs. Brisler. The ship carried oil, which leaked, and potash, which smoked and fermented. Sleeping quarters were cramped, windowless and almost lacking in privacy. All four of the party were seasick. Moreover, the vessel was dirty, and this aroused the strong-minded Abigail's ire. She ordered brushes, mops and vinegar, and set Brisler to work. In a short time the ship was transformed, and the captain had the grace to thank Mrs. Adams.

Stagecoach Stations

As roads improved, stagecoaches became popular, especially after 1700. To accommodate them, there were stations every twelve or fifteen miles. At what was called a "swing" station, the stage stopped only long enough to change horses. At a "home" station, meals and lodgings might be obtained. A stage usually halted about ten o'clock in the evening and departed at three o'clock in the morning.

Stagecoaches were splashes of color—vivid red, blue, yellow or green. From four to six good, well-matched horses drew them. This was especially true of horses used on stages in the West. The stage driver was proud of his skill, independent and inclined to look down on other occupations. Stage driving, in fact, was such a good business that the same families furnished several generations of drivers.

Imagine what it must have been like to drive a team of spirited horses and a burdened coach over a deeply rutted road. If a stage approached a rut on the left, the driver would cry out, "To the right, gentlemen!" Then the passengers would lean to the right, sticking halfway out the stage windows. A moment later there might be a cry, "To the left, gentlemen!" So the stagecoach was right side up most of the time. On exceptionally bad roads, however, a stage might tip over or it might get stuck in the mud. Then the male passengers would generally get out and help the driver pull the vehicle out of the mudhole or set it upright.

One day, when a stage got stuck in the mud, the passengers were reluctant to help. Whereupon the driver sat down on a stone by the side of the road. After a few minutes a passenger asked the driver what he was waiting for. To which the driver retorted that he was waiting for the road to dry out!

Streams were always a problem to stagecoach drivers. Though some ferries could take a whole stage across, others could carry only the coach and the passengers. The horses had to swim.

To Charles Dickens, stagecoach travel in America was an ordeal, even though he experienced it at a later period. He wrote that the drivers chattered to each other at the stations like so many monkeys; and he detested their habit of chewing tobacco. Dickens was also displeased with the "chirping" of frogs and the grunting of pigs along the highway. As for the horses, he was quite sure that some of them were wild animals that had never been broken. Furthermore, he feared that riding over the corduroy roads would dislocate his bones. Of the few good features that Dickens admitted, one was that no driver could go to sleep because of the number of stumps in the roads. Nor could the horses run because the mud was so deep, and they did not have enough room to shy.

For all Dickens' strictures, stagecoaches were far superior to travel by post. The average person dressed well for a stagecoach trip, and he could usually count on arriving at his destination in a

VIRGINIA STATE CHAMBER OF COMMERCE

AN OLD-TIME CARRIAGE before the Governor's Palace in Williamsburg, Virginia. The palace was begun in 1705, burned in 1781 and restored in our century amid lovely gardens.

A CHARMING WAYSIDE INN—the Swan Tavern in historic Yorktown, Virginia. On either side of the door are hitching posts where guests once tied up their horses.

reasonably clean and tidy state.

During the colonial period, the "West" simply meant unsettled land, the habitat of Indians and wild beasts. By the time of the Revolution, however, the term meant the country between the Appalachians and the Mississippi River. Most famous, though not the first, of the frontiersmen who ventured across the mountains was Daniel Boone. Over the route that he blazed through the Cumberland Gap (later known as the Wilderness Road), settlers began to pass even before the roar of the Revolutionary battles had died away. So many new homes were established in the eastern half of the Mississippi Basin within the next few years that states were soon carved out of it: Kentucky, 1792; Tennessee, 1796; Ohio, 1803.

Life in the backwoods was rough, and out of it grew a special brand of American humor—the tall tale. Stories like the following were always told with an absolutely straight face. One day a man was riding by a swamp and noticed a large beaver hat lying on the surface with the crown upward. As he looked at it, the hat moved. So he touched it with his whip and underneath was a smiling head, which said, "Hello, stranger." The man asked if he could be of any help, but the head said, "No, thank you—I've a good horse under me."

No one could tell such tales better than Davy Crockett, who was elected to the Tennessee legislature largely on the strength of his storytelling skill. There is a host of hilarious legends associated with him, many of which he no doubt helped along. This man of racy wit was to die in the defense of the Alamo, in 1836.

When the United States purchased the Louisiana Territory in 1803, Americans knew little of the great tract beyond the Mississippi that they had bought. Nevertheless, there were some few white men already in the Far West. They were fur traders, trappers, hunters—a strange,

CUMBERLAND GAP. Through the break in the Appalachians, Daniel Boone blazed the Wilderness Road into Kentucky, in 1775. After the Revolution, it became a well-beaten highway.

wild breed called the "mountain men." Like Daniel Boone, they never had enough elbow room; and for the sweet sake of their solitary freedom they endured incredible hardships—sometimes almost starving or freezing to death. They abhorred and fled the civilizing influences brought by the advancing tide of settlement that began after the War of 1812. Most of them died unmourned and unsung. Yet it was they who made known the passes through the mountains and in many cases led the explorers and pioneers on the way west.

Lewis and Clark Expedition

When President Jefferson urged that the Louisiana Purchase be explored, Meriwether Lewis and William Clark were chosen to lead an expedition. Both of these young Virginians had been army officers and—a big asset—they were used to dealing with Indians. The expedition was ordered to go up the Missouri River as far as possible and to search out a route to the Pacific. It was also to report on the Indians of the region, animals, plants, minerals and trade possibilities. (Both Lewis and Clark wrote detailed journals, justly famous today, even with all their erratic spelling.) The permanent party consisted of the leaders, 23 soldiers (9 of these, skilled hunters), 2 interpreters and Clark's Negro servant.

On May 14, 1804, the group started up the Missouri River from St. Louis, in a keelboat and two pirogues. To promote friendly relations with the Indians, the explorers carried gifts—trinkets, medals, flags, red coats, paint and tobacco. The passage up the river was far from easy. A swift current had to be battled, there were snags and falling banks, and during the summer the men were plagued with "ticks, musquiters and knats" day and night. At the end of October, the party made camp for the winter in the Mandan Indian country (near present Bismarck, North Dakota).

Here the expedition secured the services of a Shoshone Indian girl as a guide for the coming trip through the Rockies. Sacajawea (the name means "bird woman") was the wife of a French Canadian trader, Toussaint Charbonneau, who also acted as a guide. (On February 11, 1805, Sacajawea gave birth to a son. The baby went along on the expedition all the way to the Pacific and back. Later Clark paid for the boy's education and he became one of the best interpreters in the West.)

In April 1805 the expedition pushed on. As it traveled west, it saw an abun-

MONKMEYER

THE HOMESTEAD near Reading, Pennsylvania, where Daniel Boone lived in his youth.

dance of wild game—buffalo, elk, deer, antelope, turkeys, magpies, prairie chickens, "barking squerrels," beaver, trout, mountain rams, badgers and bears. Bears seemed to be especially troublesome. "These," Lewis wrote, "being so hard to die reather intimeadates us all; I must confess that I do not like the gentlemen and had rather fight two Indians than one bear."

The Great Falls in the Missouri River (in the present state of Montana) presented one of the worst obstacles. To make the portage around the falls and the rapids beyond, the men made rude carts, using the cross sections of tree trunks for wheels. On these carts the heavy canoes were piled, and horses hauled them. Though the portage was only eighteen miles long, it took a month.

PHILIP GENDREAU

PENNSYLVANIA "DUTCH" LANDSCAPE
—barn built by descendants of German settlers.

All along the way the Indians were friendly, and this was probably due to the influence of Sacajawea. Through her efforts, the explorers were able to secure about thirty horses from the Shoshone Indians. Their chief was a brother of hers, whom she had not seen for five years. More horses were obtained from the Flathead Indians; and the Arikaras contributed corn, beans and dried squashes from their own precious stores.

In spite of this help, food became scarce. A long spell of rain hindered both exploring and hunting. For a time the men were forced to live on fish, dog meat and roots. Frequently they had to eat "portable soup" made from horse and dog meat.

At length they came to a river that proved to be the Columbia. They followed it to its mouth, and on November 7, 1805, Clark wrote: "Great joy in camp, we are in view of the Ocian." The expedition had achieved its main object. Win-

ter was approaching again—a season of blinding blizzards and arctic cold in the mountains—so the party camped on the coast for several months.

Sea water was boiled to obtain salt; and a whale that the tide had washed ashore yielded meat and oil. One soldier wrote: "We mix it [whale] with our poor elk and find it eats well." During their stay the men killed 150 elk and 25 deer for the meat and skins. The elk skins were used to make 338 moccasins for the return trip.

On March 23, 1806, the group started on the long journey back home. It made good time and reached St. Louis on September 23. As many people had given the expedition up for lost, the men were welcomed with joy.

Venture into the Southwest

In the same year another army officer, Zebulon Montgomery Pike, led a party to locate the sources of the Arkansas and Red rivers. The explorers traveled as far west as Pueblo, Colorado, and gathered considerable information about the Southwest. On November 15, 1807, Pike sighted but did not succeed in climbing the mountain later named for him, Pikes Peak.

Although of less importance than the two expeditions we have just discussed, the one led by Major Stephen H. Long is in curious contrast. On June 6, 1820, the Long party started west from the Missouri River into Nebraska, on horseback. As it was summer, the explorers saw the thriving fields of corn, beans and pumpkins cultivated by Pawnee Indian squaws. Along the Platte River, large herds of buffalo and occasional bands of wild horses appeared. On June 13, the summit near Estes Park, Colorado, now named Longs Peak, loomed up. The odd part about this expedition is that Long, after exploring a considerable region, reported to the Government that the area between the Missouri River and the Rocky Mountains was unsuitable for farming. In his opinion its future value would be to keep the population of the United States from moving too far west!

A **"WIDOW'S WALK"** surmounts an old house on Martha's Vineyard, an island off Cape Cod. In days of sail, a sea captain's wife kept watch for her husband's ship from the lookout.

173

THE PILLARED ENTRANCE to a lovely pre-Civil War home—Choctaw—in Natchez, Mississippi. In this city the chivalry and graciousness of the old South reached their fullest flower.

On his map, Long labeled the high-plains region the "Great American Desert." Thus it appeared in school geographies for half a century. Today the "Great American Desert" contains the largest irrigated area in the world and is one of the wealthiest agricultural and stock-raising regions in the United States.

Following in the wake of the government explorers, privately financed parties went west. Unfortunately, they were often less well equipped and suffered even greater hardship.

Between the years 1824 and 1830 Sylvester Pattie and his son, James Ohio, led a group of 116 men through the Southwest (most of which still belonged to Mexico). It was a record six years of endurance. Their horses' feet became so tender from being cut by sharp grass that they had to be shod with buffalo-skin moccasins. At one time the air was so hot that it seemed to burn the lungs, and the men could hardly talk because their tongues were swollen from thirst. To relieve it, they rolled bullets in their mouths, which would cause a little saliva to flow. When they finally reached water and began to drink, they became very ill. On another occasion, food was so short that they had to eat the horses. By 1827, only sixteen men remained with the company.

On their journey, the Pattie party stopped now and then to mine or to trap. A copper, gold, or silver mine could be rented from the Indians for five years for $1,000 a year. In copper mining, the Patties were fairly successful. As for trapping, once in a single morning thirty-seven beavers were caught. The company arrived in Santa Fe (New Mexico) with a valuable collection of furs, but the Mexican Governor seized them because

PHILIP GENDREAU

NEAR NEW ORLEANS, Louisiana, a typical Mississippi River ferryboat churns across the wide expanse. The great stream was, and still is, the chief gateway to the fertile Midwest.

THE PENNSYLVANIA MEMORIAL at Gettysburg. The terrible battle that occurred here on July 1–3, 1863, halted the Confederate forces and was the turning point of the Civil War.

GENERAL LEE'S HEADQUARTERS at Gettysburg. Though his army met defeat on the field, with dreadful loss of life, and continued to be harassed, it managed to make an orderly retreat.

the men had no trapping license from him.

From Santa Fe, the Patties continued westward, though it meant crossing the desert and Sylvester was ill. Eventually they reached San Diego, California, confident that they could secure food and water at one of the missions. Instead, the Mexican authorities arrested the Patties as spies and clapped them into prison. There Sylvester died. James gained his freedom some time later because he had been foresighted enough to carry smallpox vaccine with him. While he was in prison, a smallpox epidemic broke out in California; and he was released to give vaccinations. After all his years of effort, he got back to the United States a penniless man.

In 1834, Nathaniel J. Wyeth led twenty-one men, mostly farmers and artisans, to the Northwest. The journey began at Independence, Missouri, which was to become one of the assembly points for the emigrant trains taking the Oregon Trail. The Wyeth party followed the Platte River Valley, and the going proved so hard that about half of the men became discouraged and turned back. Only Wyeth and eleven others continued on to Fort Vancouver on the Columbia River. Among them was an ornithologist, John K. Townsend, who published his *Narrative of a Journey across the Rocky Mountains to the Columbia River* in 1839. The picture this book painted helped to fan the "Oregon fever" that now spread through the Midwest. Thousands started out from Independence, often to the tune of Stephen Foster's *O, Susanna*—"don't you cry for me"—played on a banjo.

On a later trip, Wyeth built Fort Hall in southeastern Idaho, which served as a gathering place and an outfitting point for emigrants for many years.

Ordeal of the Donner Party

The most tragic story of the western migration is that of the Donner party, which was among the first to include women and children. Two of the families were named Donner. In 1846 the group started for California, with high ideals of what it might accomplish. Mrs.

George Donner carried books and paints along with which she hoped to start a girls' school. During the winter of 1846–47, the emigrants were trapped by snow in the Sierra Nevada, near Lake Truckee; and their sufferings were indescribably horrible. Valuable cattle were shot to end the beasts' misery and also to secure food—thirty-six of the animals had been left in the desert, some dead, some lost. When the last of their meat gave out, they ate the bark and twigs of trees, field mice and even their moccasins. When a stray deer was slain, they first drank the blood as it flowed from the wound and then ate the meat. Before rescue came, famine had reduced the company from eighty-one to forty-five; and the survivors were driven to cannibalism.

The Great Mormon Trek

Among the most successful treks westward was that of the Mormons. Their religious beliefs, especially the practice of polygamy, had aroused violent hostility in Illinois, and they hoped to find peace somewhere in the Far West. In the spring of 1847, under the leadership of Brigham Young, a mass migration began. It is estimated that altogether in that year 12,000 Mormons moved west, in companies of about 3,000 each. The march was brilliantly organized, with provision made for every possibility that could be imagined. A few leaders went ahead and established camps. They built log cabins, dug wells, plowed land and planted crops so that those who followed could depend on finding shelter and food. The last permanent camp was Winter Quarters, on the present site of Florence, Nebraska, just north of Omaha.

The route chosen lay along the North Platte River and through South Pass and Fort Bridger, both in Wyoming. In places, buffalo were so thick that the men had to drive them away to make room for the wagons to pass. With a device called an odometer, the leaders kept track of the number of miles traveled each day.

Eventually the advance party selected the Great Salt Lake area in Utah for a permanent home. When Brigham Young

A CONESTOGA WAGON, first designed for transportation over the Alleghenies. Its boat-shaped body was fitted for mountain roads. No matter how it tilted, cargo stayed in place.

178

saw the beautiful valley, he said, "This is the place."

Though the opening of the Far West was one of the most thrilling episodes in United States history, it must not be forgotten that during the same period the East was becoming ever more thickly populated. To provide easier transportation between markets on the Atlantic seaboard and the farms of the Great Lakes region, the Erie Canal was opened in 1825. It gave Midwestern agriculture a tremendous boost; and as other canals were built, traffic on all the waterways of the East increased enormously. Larger vessels were built, and travel by boat became popular. Then the Ohio and Mississippi rivers came into their own.

There was a great variety of river and canal craft—arks, barges, flatboats, keelboats and skiffs. Arks and flatboats were built of heavy timbers and often served as living quarters for the family of the boatman. Part of the upper deck was fenced off to provide play space for the children. Everything the family owned was carried along—furniture, farm implements, horses, pigs, cows, chickens, dogs, cats, kegs of powder, boxes filled with provisions. The boat was a floating log cabin, fort, barnyard and grocery store. The boat was laden with extra provisions to sell to settlements along the river.

The voyage downstream, in fair weather at least, was carefree. A boat anchored at whatever spot the family fancied. Toward evening someone usually played a fiddle so that the young people could dance. Who could resist a jig to *Turkey in the Straw?* Storytelling and singing also helped to pass the time on a trip that might last for months. To go from the mouth of the Ohio River to New Orleans took about six weeks; but a return journey, if it were made, required four and a half months.

Practically all the boats could be propelled upstream, but it took so much time and energy that most owners broke

PRAIRIE PIONEERS often lived in sod houses at first. There were no trees to provide logs, so turf was dug up and cut in the shape of bricks. Glass windows were a rare luxury.

THE PIONEER MOTHER, a statue in Kansas City, Missouri. The words around the base are from the Bible—Ruth's beautiful declaration to Naomi—"Whither thou goest, I will go . . ."

up their boats when they reached New Orleans or some other southern town. The timber might be sold or else the boatman would build himself a house with it. This practice was an important factor in the growth of settlement in the lower Mississippi Valley.

The bullboat was a western version of river craft. It was about 30 feet long, 20 feet wide and 12 feet deep, and had the shape of a brimless hat turned upside down. The frame was of willow, and this was covered with buffalo hides. A mixture of tallow and ashes calked the seams. Though a bullboat could carry six thousand pounds, it was so light that it could be taken to shore, turned upside down and used as a shelter. Lightness gave it another advantage because of the frequent portages that had to be made around the falls and rapids of western waterways.

Frontier boatmen had a stamp all their own. Usually tall, slender and sinewy, they wore a picturesque costume that set off their splendid physique—a bright red

flannel shirt, a loose blue jerkin that extended to the hips, and coarse brown linsey-woolsey trousers. The boatman's hat was of untanned skins with the fur side out, and he was shod in moccasins. Attached to his belt was a hunting knife and a tobacco pouch.

A boatman's speech was no less colorful than his costume—an "iridescent vocabulary." Of a sudden occurrence, he said that it happened "quicker nor an alligator can chew a puppy." If he wanted a person to act quickly, he commanded, "Start yer trotters." Of a difficult task he proclaimed that it was "harder nor climbin' a saplin' heels uppard." To silence a long-winded individual, the phrase was "Shut off your chin music" or "Shut your mouth before you sunburn your teeth."

River navigation called for extreme alertness and skill. Often a rock large enough to wreck a boat lurked hidden beneath the water. A sawyer—a sunken tree bobbing up and down with the movement of the current—was another danger. Even worse was the sleeping (hidden) sawyer. Another hazard was the planter—a log firmly buried in a stream. As such obstructions were very difficult to remove, boatmen sometimes cut canals through islands.

As early as 1785, John Fitch believed that steam could be applied to navigation, and he invented a steamboat. However, the steamboat was a gradual development, and most authorities give Robert Fulton credit for the invention. At any rate, in 1807, his Clermont made the first successful trip in America, up the Hudson River.

Most early engines on steamboats

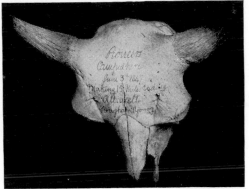

BUFFALO SKULL with an inscription by Brigham Young, leaving word of a camp.

A TRAIN OF MORMONS in the Utah territory. The picture is an early photograph, taken on July 10, 1878. Mormons continued to move west after the great migration of the 1840's.

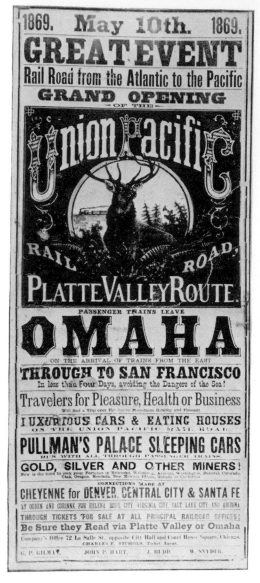

passion for racing each other. Then the steam pressure would be allowed to mount dangerously. Boiler metal was likely to be of poor quality, and it would burst under high pressure or from lack of water. In a race, a man might sit on the safety valve to keep up the pressure of the steam. So when the boiler exploded, he, and the passengers too, went up with it. Another perilous practice was to add pitch, oil, turpentine or lard to the fire to make it hotter and thus get more steam. Moreover, as the early steamboats were usually made of wood, they caught fire easily from sparks.

Life on the River Steamers

Accidents seem to have been an accepted hazard, for the river boats never lacked passengers; and they were often as colorful and oddly mixed a lot as might be found on an ocean liner—immigrants, migratory workers, patent-medicine vendors, theatrical troops, gamblers and preachers. On a boat, a preacher was sure of an audience, and he was equally certain that many of the passengers needed his services.

The Mississippi River pilots are immortalized in the works of Mark Twain, who was himself a licensed pilot. Such great skill was required of a pilot on this river that he might command a salary of $1,000 a month. He had complete charge of all the boat's movements except that he could not give orders on when to start or to stop. He had to know 1,500 miles of one of the most changeable rivers in the world. Obstructions were constantly shifting. High or low water, daylight or darkness—each altered the appearance of the stream. Besides, the very early pilot had no guide except eyesight and memory. Lighthouses and buoys were yet to be constructed, though navigation of the Mississippi would never be easy.

Pilot versus Captain

The boat captain took second place to the pilot, though the captain was often part owner of the vessel and was always its official master. It was a very foolish captain who dared to give orders to the

burned wood. Soon nearly every settler along the banks of the Mississippi River was chopping down trees and keeping a woodpile handy so that he might sell the fuel to the steamboat companies.

Practically all large steamboats had sleeping quarters, a dining room, a men's room and bar, and a ladies' parlor. The last was always at the stern of the vessel as that was the safest place when an explosion occurred. This happened all too often, because steamboat captains had a

GREAT DAY IN UTAH. On May 10, 1869, near Ogden, the last spike, a golden one, was driven in, completing the first transcontinental railroad. East and West were now linked.

pilot concerning navigation. The engineer, then as now, reigned supreme over the machinery.

Rough work on the boats was done by the roustabouts, most of whom were Negroes. They cleaned decks, stoked the furnace and loaded and unloaded the cargo. This group originated many folk songs—made up on the spur of the moment to lighten its labors. Any number of these songs are on record today, and those quoted below were published in the *Christian Science Monitor Magazine* from the collection made by Horace Reynolds.

As a Negro polished the brass in a pilot house, he sang:

> Wake up, Rose, put on your clothes;
> Day done broke, an' de sun done rose.

A roustabout who had hoped but failed to secure work sang this sad ditty:

> Boat all loaded
> And ready to back out,
> And the mate's going to leave
> This old roustebout.

One worker advertised his good nature and willingness to work with this:

> I loves everybody
> No matter how rough I seems,
> I wuk hard for muh livin'
> There's no use leavin' me.

Sometimes the verses consisted of only two lines:

> The prettiest girl I ever saw
> Lived on the banks of the Arkansas.

> Way down there in Arkansas
> The bullfrog kissed his brother-in-law.

Often a Negro would sing to show his pride in the boat on which he worked:

De City of Cairo is a mighty fast one,
But jus' lemme tell yuh what dat Monroe done,
She left Natchez at half-past one,
And landed at Vicksburg at the settin' of de sun.

Though the Negro contributed an important share to American humor, it was white men who brought it to public attention. Jim Crow Rice, the first of these men, roamed the rivers on showboats. He made up an act featuring the Negro stories and songs he had heard, painting his face black for the performance.

However, the first real minstrel shows were led by Dan (Daniel Decatur) Emmett. The appearance of his Virginia Minstrels in Boston in 1843 is regarded as the first genuine full-length minstrel show.

The Far West swung into the national limelight again with the discovery of gold at Sutter's Mill, near the present city of Sacramento, California. The lure of the yellow metal brought fortune hunters not only overland but also by way of the Isthmus of Panama and even all the way

and horse broth. A number of horses had become exhausted and died along the banks. Those who passed through the Mormon community in Utah, however, were able to buy food from the successful farmers there.

The Panama route took very little longer than the overland trail, and the sea voyage to the isthmus was fairly comfortable. But many migrants came down with fever as they passed through the jungles of Panama. (It was yellow fever, and the cause was yet to be discovered.)

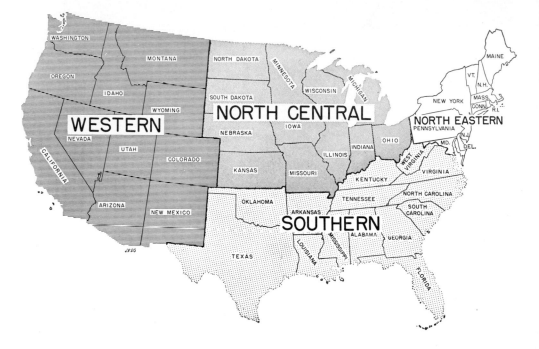

around South America. In the expectation of getting rich quick, they started out in high spirits. On the trail and on the ships, the strains of *Annie Laurie, Arkansas Traveler* and many another familiar song might be heard. Most of the singing of the overland group was done, however, before it reached Fort Hall, in Idaho. From there on, food and water ran short. Some of the weary travelers, wracked by hunger, ate soup made from their boots. Often they went for miles and miles without water. When they reached the Humbolt River (Nevada), its waters had the horrible taste of alkali

Once the gold seekers had reached the Pacific side of the isthmus, they often had to wait a long time for a ship. Vessels sailing north were dangerously overcrowded.

Long as the route around Cape Horn was, there were compensations on the voyage. If a vessel was at sea during the Thanksgiving season, there was a series of Thanksgiving dinners as each person on board insisted on keeping the Thanksgiving Day his state observed. It was not yet a national holiday.

On the heels of the gold rush, so many thousands of people settled in California

THE SERENE INTERIOR of Christ Church, in Boston, belies the Revolutionary drama associated with it. It is supposed to be the North Church in whose belfry the lanterns warned of the approach of the British—"One, if by land, and two, if by sea." Thence came Paul Revere's "midnight ride."

185

Where memories of the past remain strong

AT WILLIAMSBURG the visitor steps into a faithful reconstruction (the Governor's Palace, above) of Virginia's gracious colonial capital. It was a center of political activity on the eve of the Revolution.

MARDI GRAS in New Orleans is one of the gayest festivals in the whole United States. Then high carnival is king, and the revelers vie with each other in the creation of imaginative costumes and decorated floats.

ON LOOKOUT MOUNTAIN, near Chattanooga, Tennessee, was fought the Civil War "Battle of the Clouds," in November 1863, when Union forces were driving deep into the South. Well named, the mountain looks out over the broad valley of the winding Tennessee.

THE ALAMO, in San Antonio, the cradle of Texan liberty. There, in 1836, less than two hundred defenders, including Davy Crockett, died rather than surrender to a Mexican army.

FORT CLATSOP, Oregon, on the Columbia River, is a memorial to the Lewis and Clark Expedition. On its way through the wilderness the party camped on the site.

MARK TWAIN would have been astounded by this modern Mississippi River steamer. Its sleek design and gleaming metal structure are a far cry from the wooden, boiler-bursting side-wheelers that Twain once piloted on his beloved stream.

«

CATTLE roam peacefully today near the site of the Battle of the Little Bighorn, Montana. There, in 1876, General George A. Custer and his men were all slain by Indians in one of the last engagements before the Indians were finally subdued.

MONUMENT TO FLIGHT on Kill Devil Hill, Kitty Hawk, North Carolina. It was here, in 1903, that Wilbur and Orville Wright became the first men to fly an airplane successfully.

FOUR GREAT PRESIDENTS—Washington, Jefferson, Theodore Roosevelt and Lincoln— memorialized for the ages, carved in granite by Borglum on South Dakota's Mount Rushmore.

INDEPENDENCE HALL, above, and the landscaped mall that runs north of it, in Philadelphia. At right, visitors read treasured documents—the original Declaration of Independence and the Bill of Rights—preserved in the National Archives, Washington.

THE JEFFERSON MEMORIAL and the Washington Monument in the national capital. Between the two landmarks ripple the blue waters of the Tidal Basin.

MARINE CORPS' MEMORIAL—the Iwo Jima Monument (at Arlington, Virginia)—commemorates a fierce battle on a Pacific isle in World War II.

Shrines to great men and great events

»

THE DIGNITY and strength of Lincoln are caught in Daniel Chester French's heroic statue in the Lincoln Memorial, in Washington. The war President's Second Inaugural Address and Gettysburg Address are inscribed on nearby walls of the surrounding structure.

191

THE CAPITOL DOME in Washington gleams in the floodlights, as a shower of fireworks bursts nearby. The center of the building is of sandstone, the wings are of white marble.

that transportation became an urgent problem. The West now adopted forms that the East had used at an earlier period. Because distances were much greater, however, the West had more money invested in its transportation system than the East ever had during its stagecoach and freight-wagon days. One of the largest freight companies in the West was the firm of Russell, Major and Waddell. It transported military supplies along the Oregon Trail. Some idea of the scale of the company's operations is indicated by the fact that at the peak of its trail-freighting activity, it used 6,250 wagons, each with a capacity of 6,000 pounds, and 75,000 oxen. In 1859, Horace Greeley estimated that the property of this firm was worth $2,000,000.

Ben Holladay, however, was the greatest of the Far Western freighters and stagecoach operators. Between 1861 and 1866 he ran stagecoaches over a distance of 5,000 miles. He owned 500 coaches and express wagons, 500 freight wagons, 5,000 horses and mules and innumerable oxen. During his first year of business, the cost of equipment and of operating the lines amounted to $2,425,000. Holladay also ran steamship lines between Oregon, Panama, Japan and China.

Silver on Whip and Harness

Nearly every Western stagecoach driver worshiped his whip. He hated to lend it even to his best friend. Many of the whips had stalks ornamented with silver ferrules and silver caps. Harnesses also were adorned with silver, and a horse might have a silver bit worth $25 to $40. This lavish use of silver was considered a good investment because it advertised the mining industry of the West.

With the completion of the Union Pacific Railroad in 1869—joining East and West by track—stage lines began to go out of business.

Besides transportation, faster communication was needed between the West and East. The first mail received in California came by ocean steamer, and a letter from New York City to San Francisco was usually about four weeks in transit. Kit (Christopher) Carson, whose exploits as a trapper, guide and Indian fighter had made him a Western hero, carried the first mail overland from the Pacific coast to the East, in 1848. Ten years later the Butterfield Overland Mail started a more efficient service by stage, but it was still slow.

The upshot of all this was the Pony Express, a relay system that sped the mail through two thousand miles of an almost absolute wilderness, between St. Joseph, Missouri, and San Francisco. The first run started on April 8, 1860.

Pony Express Steeds

The "ponies" were really small, wiry horses. California mustangs were favorite steeds. Along the route, mounts were changed at about fifteen-mile intervals. Such a grueling pace was set that only young men, light in weight, physically strong and with iron nerves, were chosen as riders. Usually a rider was clad in a buckskin hunting shirt, cloth trousers tucked into high boots, and a jockey cap or a slouch hat, and a scarlet handkerchief was tied around his neck. A complete buckskin suit protected a rider in bad weather, for he was expected to keep going regardless of storms. Only two minutes were allowed in which to exchange horses and transfer the mail pouches at the relay stations. Buffalo Bill (William Cody, who organized his Wild West Show later) had the reputation of being one of the most able riders. It is claimed that on one occasion he rode 320 miles in 21 hours and 40 minutes.

One of the greatest enemies of the riders was the prairie dogs. A horse might step into one of their burrows and break a leg, throwing the rider and injuring him as well. Indians caused little trouble. During the nineteen months that the Pony Express was in operation, the Indians interfered seriously with the mail only once.

Each rider carried four small mail bags covered with oilskin silk to keep them dry. The total weight of any one mail could be no more than twenty pounds, and it usually weighed less. At first the

FREDERIC LEWIS

VIRGINIA CITY, Nevada, the most rip-roaring of all Western mining camps around 1880.

now moved westward to the rich timberlands of the Northwest—northern California, Washington and Oregon. Side by side with the lumberjacks paced their mythical hero, Paul Bunyan. If there was ever a real Paul Bunyan, who he was is lost in the mists of time. The giant lumberjack of legend, however, is one of the most amusing figures in American folklore. In the "dead-pan" style of the tall tale, he is credited with having dug about every deep crease in the surface of North America—the St. Lawrence River, the Grand Canyon, Puget Sound. For his Blue Ox, Babe, Paul gouged out the Great Lakes because Babe was always drinking the rivers dry. The Blue Ox was so huge that the width between its eyes measured twenty-four ax handles and a plug of tobacco. The mythical John Henry of Southern folklore was perhaps an adaptation of Paul Bunyan.

To return to the main thread of our story, while all the exciting activity we have discussed was going on in the Far West, back east the "iron horse" was coming to the fore. Though the Baltimore and Ohio, the first passenger railway in the United States, was begun as early as 1828, intense opposition to the railroads

Pony Express charged $5.00 for each ounce of mail or fraction thereof. A little later the rate was $1.00 a half ounce. In addition to the Pony Express charge for a letter, the regular United States Government postage of ten cents had to be paid.

On the average the Pony Express dashed from the Missouri River to San Francisco in 10½ days. The best time it ever made was when it carried the news of the election of Abraham Lincoln to the presidency—exactly 6 days, between the telegraph terminal at Fort Kearney, Nebraska, and Fort Churchill, in western Nevada. The end of the exciting Pony Express came abruptly, when the first telegraph line to California was completed on October 24, 1861.

In the preceding two decades, a "lumbering frontier" had opened in northern Wisconsin and Minnesota. This frontier

BLACK STAR

BOOT HILL GRAVEYARD, in Tombstone, Arizona. Desperadoes died with their boots on!

ON THE SALT FLATS in northwestern Utah, the wagon-wheel tracks of the Donner party are still visible.   The little band passed this way before its grim ordeal in the Sierra Nevada.

WHERE SUTTER'S MILL stood on the American River, near Sacramento, California. Today the stream, once roiled by a host of prospectors in feverish haste, swirls by the site placidly.

A TALE THAT IS TOLD. The discovery set off an extraordinary stampede. Lured by hopes of quick wealth, men rushed overland and by sea, even all the way around Cape Horn.

SAN JOSE MISSION in San Antonio, Texas, is called the Queen of the Missions for its architectural beauty. Founded 1720, it was restored in the 1930's as a national historic site.

lingered for some time. In 1832, at Lancaster, Ohio, for example, an attempt was made to hold a meeting in the school for the promotion of a railroad. The school board replied:

"You are at liberty to use the schoolhouse to hold meetings for all proper purposes. But railroads and telegraphs are impossible and rank infidelity. If God had intended his intelligent creatures should travel at the frightful speed of 16 miles an hour by steam, he would clearly have foretold it in the holy prophets. It is a device of Satan to lead immortal souls down to Hell."

Steam Locomotives Appear

In the face of the railroads' obvious advantages, of course, opposition could not last. Even before locomotives appeared, there were crude trains drawn by horses on a track. Steam locomotives, however, took over in the 1830's. The first American locomotive designed for practical service was the Best Friend engine, built in New York City in 1830. But it was in use for only a short time when it exploded. In fact, train accidents were frequent for a number of years. Nevertheless, as engines were improved and safety measures came into effect, the general public was persuaded that travel by train—certainly much faster than by horse-drawn vehicles—was no longer fraught with peril.

At the same time, a ride on an early train was none too pleasant. The coaches were open, and passengers held spread umbrellas to protect them from the flying sparks from the engine. The cars looked as gay as a child's toy train. Locomotive and coaches were painted in vivid reds, blues and greens, and were lavishly ornamented with brass.

There were no timetables. A prospective passenger simply went to the depot and waited until a train came that was going in the direction he wanted. In places where one could see for a long distance, train officials sometimes erected a "lookout pole." A watcher climbed to the top of it and as soon as he saw any smoke, he dropped a note to the ground.

PHILIP GENDREAU

SACAJAWEA—a statue in Portland, Oregon, of the guide of the Lewis and Clark party.

Both railway and steamboat companies used a unique form of advertising. They pictured their trains and steamboats on Reward of Merit cards for children, evidently in the hope of catching the imagination of the coming generation of passengers.

At first each railroad builder used his own judgment as to the proper width of the track. The result was that there might be tracks of four or five different widths within one state. This meant that at the end of one line, passengers and freight had to be transferred to the next. Naturally the transfer consumed considerable time, and villages sprang up at the ends of lines to catch the trade the long waits brought. Passengers needed food and, often, lodgings. As a standard gauge came into use, making the halts unnecessary, the folk who had come to rely on the trade sometimes tore new tracks up overnight.

The Indians also tore up many railroad tracks because they knew that the railroad would bring white settlement. They had not forgotten that the white man had almost killed off the buffalo, depriving the Indians of clothing, food and shelter. While the Union Pacific Railroad was being constructed, through wild country, the Government had to post soldiers along the roadbed to protect the track.

Today Americans are likely to take railroads and all the other swift means of transportation and communication for granted. They can fly overnight to Europe or South America seated in a warm cabin, or talk with casual ease to a friend halfway around the globe. Yet all this is but the climax to an extraordinary story of development, which paced the whole history of the United States. Tracing the beginnings of the story and what it meant in human effort yields greater understanding of the modern nation.

BY ORA BROOKS PEAKE

THE UNITED STATES: FACTS AND FIGURES

THE COUNTRY

The total area of the states of the Union, including Alaska and Hawaii, is 3,615,194 sq. mi. (land area, 3,552,198 sq. mi.); population, approaching 177,719,000.

GOVERNMENT

Federal republic of 50 states; executive power vested in a president and a cabinet of 10 members; legislative power in a Congress consisting of 2 houses, a Senate composed of 2 members from each state and a House of Representatives of 437 members (each state is given representation according to its population). Each state, except Nebraska, has a legislature of 2 houses, a governor and other executive officials. Both houses of the legislature are elective, but the senators have larger electoral districts.

COMMERCE AND INDUSTRY

The United States ranks first in world production of corn and cotton; other important crops are wheat, hay and forage, vegetables, fruits, oats, rye, barley, buckwheat, rice, tobacco and sugar crops. Swine, sheep and cattle are raised in great numbers; latest figures, 216,700,000 head of livestock. Mineral resources are rich and varied; of the metals, iron ore is first in value, followed by copper, zinc, lead, gold, ferroalloys, silver, tungsten, bauxite, mercury, platinum. The non-metals include coal, petroleum, natural gas and a variety of building materials. Petroleum is the most valuable mineral product. The chief timbers are fir, pine, hemlock, spruce and redwood. Extensive salt- and fresh-water fisheries. Manufacturing has become highly developed; some of the important industries are motor vehicle manufacture, slaughtering and meat-packing, iron and steel, steel works and rolling mills, petroleum refining, printing and publishing, flour mills, textile mills and electric light and power generation. Chief exports are raw cotton, petroleum and its products, industrial and agricultural machinery, automobiles and accessories, grains and grain products, iron and steel products, tobacco, cotton manufactures, lumber products; leading imports are wool, rubber, coffee, sugar-cane, paper and paper manufactures, cocoa, petroleum, hides, skins, furs and copper.

COMMUNICATIONS

Railways, about 390,000 mi.; roads about 3,455,000 mi.; some 60,000,000 telephones; international—4 cable, 6 radiotelegraph and 1 radiotelephone carriers; 1,200,000 radio transmitters and 15,400,000 radio sets; 545 TV stations and 50,000,000 TV sets; 12 major airlines, some operating overseas, and about 7,000 municipal and commercial airports; seagoing merchant fleet of 32,900,000 deadweight tons—more than 3,000 ships, including tankers; about 1,800 newspapers are published daily.

RELIGION AND EDUCATION

No established church; all denominations represented. Protestants about 59 per cent of church membership. Each state has a system of free public primary and secondary schools supported by state and local taxation. There are 122,756 elementary schools; 29,582 secondary schools (both public and private). There are 1,864 colleges and universities. Included in this number are junior colleges and professional schools.

CITIES

Washington, the capital, in District of Columbia. Population, 850,000. For other cities, see sectional facts and figures.

OUTLYING TERRITORIES AND POSSESSIONS

The Commonwealth of Puerto Rico, Guam, American Samoa, Panama Canal Zone and the American Virgin Islands. Total area of these possessions, 10,900 sq. mi.; total population, about 2,500,000.

The Northeastern States ...from Maine to Maryland

AMONG the states running southward from the fragrant green woods of Maine to the sandy flatlands of Delaware and eastern Maryland, the Republic first took shape. Nine of the thirteen original states are in the northeast. Here the industrial revolution, later to sweep the country, took root. New England is still a great shoe and textile center. Today these states remain pacesetters for the nation in industry and culture, though their leadership is being challenged.

The Northeast is the most densely populated part of the country and there also the average income is highest. The demands of this rich market absorb vast quantities not only of the products of its own skilled labor force but also of goods from the other states and from abroad. At the same time a steady stream of manufactured articles flows in the other direction. The eleven northeastern states (Maine, New Hampshire, Vermont, Massachusetts, Rhode Island, Connecticut, New York, New Jersey, Pennsylvania, Delaware and Maryland) regularly produce 40 per cent of the nation's manufactures and account for 40 per cent of its annual personal income. The range of occupations in these states is heavily on the side of business, the professions and entertainment.

The cultural influence of the Northeast is widespread, in part a heritage from the past. The region was settled much earlier than the rest of the country, and schools and colleges were founded almost as fast as homes were erected. The Northeast was turning out educated men to man the professions and run the Government long before the rest of the country had hardly been explored. Saving only Virginia, Massachusetts had more influence on the intellectual life of the nation from the beginning until about 1900 than any other state. Historians like Parkman and Henry Adams, writers like Thoreau and Hawthorne, philosophers like Edwards and Emerson, statesmen like John Adams and his son, John Quincy, Daniel Webster and Edward Everett, educators like Horace Mann and Charles W. Eliot—all helped to mold the American mind.

The Northeast still boasts the greatest single concentration of first-rate colleges in the nation, though excellent state and private universities are rapidly coming to the fore elsewhere. The list includes Harvard, Yale, Dartmouth, Smith, Massachusetts Institute of Technology, Mount Holyoke, Wellesley, Brown, Columbia, Vassar, Cornell, Rochester, Princeton, Rutgers, Pennsylvania, Bryn Mawr, Johns Hopkins and Brandeis.

Thanks to its early lead the Northeast remains the book- and magazine-publishing center of the country. It was in Philadelphia that Benjamin Franklin turned out his *Poor Richard's Almanack*. The famous "Brahmin" literary circle of Boston—among its members, Lowell, Holmes and Longfellow—dominated American literature through much of the nineteenth century. Then, in 1888, William Dean Howells, who, as editor of the *Atlantic Monthly,* in Boston, had become the most influential figure in American letters, moved to New York. In doing so Howells shifted the literary spotlight from Boston to New York, where it has stayed.

Magazine publishing also gave New York an early lead in advertising. Its expansion into the big business we know today, however, came with the development of radio and then television—mass communications. In fact, the volume of national advertising increased from $2,200,000,000 in 1941 to $11,100,000,000 in 1959. It is advertising that pays the direct costs of most programs. They require writers, artists, actors and musicians as well as engineers and technicians.

They absorb many of the gifted young people drawn to New York in the hope of literary or artistic success. "Madison Avenue" has become almost a synonym for advertising because so many of the national advertising agencies as well as market-research organizations have offices on that New York street. The industry has severe critics. They contend that in view of its influence on American life the standards that it introduces into the nation's living rooms are not as high as they should be.

Because of their dense population, the northeastern states have a powerful voice in the national political conventions and in the Electoral College. This body, which some political scientists think

CHANGE OF SHIFT at a New Jersey plant; there are as many cars as workers.

should be discarded, does the actual electing of presidents and vice-presidents. By custom not law, all the electors from a state vote for the candidates of whichever party received the highest popular vote in their state. Each state has the same number of electors as it has members in both houses of Congress. As the number of members a state has in the House of Representatives is decided by the census, population growth is a basic factor in national political life. It is on this ground that the western states, including Alaska and Hawaii, are today nudging the Northeast for political leadership.

Within the northeastern states (and in some other states as well) there is another basic political problem. Dating from the days when the country was far more agricultural than it is today, rural regions frequently have far more representatives in Washington and in the state capitals than large cities do in proportion to population. This gives the vote of someone living in the country much greater weight than the vote of a city dweller. As big-city voters frequently have more liberal views than rural voters, the consequence is that state governments and city governments are often on opposite sides of the political fence and at loggerheads.

Yet as suburbs grow and ever larger areas have such problems as transportation and water supply in common, the most efficient solutions require co-operation between state and city governments.

As the Northeast includes most of the country's oldest cities the problem of urban blight has been especially severe there. The trek to the suburbs has meant that many once fine old residential neighborhoods have deteriorated. Philadelphia has been leading the way in renewal of such neighborhoods. There, for example, between 10,000 and 12,000 new homes are being built in the Eastwick project, in the historic area between Washington Square and the Delaware River. Independence Hall today has a beautiful mall.

Among New York City's most ambitious projects are the Lincoln Center for the Performing Arts as well as a great bridge across the Narrows, the entrance to the inner harbor.

Great manufacturing cities dot the map from Maine to Maryland, and farms of many kinds help feed the millions engaged in commerce and industry. The countryside is extremely varied and each section beautiful in its own way, whether we like best the flat salt marshes of the Jersey shore, the Finger Lakes of western New York or the stony elm-shaded pastures and the rocky coast of New England.

These contrasts in the landscape vividly illustrate the fact that the state boundaries do not follow natural physical lines. Of all the eleven northeastern states, Delaware is most nearly a unit. Except for a small section near its northern boundary, it belongs entirely to the coastal plain which stretches from Texas and Florida to Long Island and includes the low sandy point of Cape Cod. Half of Maryland and much of New Jersey are thus part of the plain. West of it, in Maryland, Pennsylvania and northern New Jersey, are the rolling hills of the Piedmont belt, and then come the Appalachian ranges—the mountain backbone of eastern North America. The rough plateau country west of the Appalachians covers all western Pennsylvania and most of southern New York. The Adirondacks are separated from the mountains of northern New England by the valleys of the Hudson River and Lake Champlain. Vermont is almost entirely mountainous and so is half of New Hampshire, but the coastal region is lower.

New England

Of all the northeast sections, New England was the least inviting when the first colonists from Europe came looking for new homes. Nevertheless, its people early took a leading part in American development. The various colonies at Plymouth, Massachusetts Bay, Providence, New Haven and elsewhere gradually came to be connected by more settlements, and a certain sort of unity was forced upon them by the necessity of fighting off French and Indian attacks.

ROUND TOWER or Old Stone Mill—Newport, Rhode Island, landmark. Whether it is an eleventh-century Norse relic or a seventeenth-century mill remains a mystery to this day.

New York, of course, was settled by the Dutch, and did not come into English hands until 1664, when upper New Jersey also became English. In Delaware the Swedes had been first, but the Dutch governor of New Netherlands, sturdy old Peter Stuyvesant, conquered New Sweden and held it until he himself was expelled by the English. Maryland was the first to insist upon religious freedom. Pennsylvania, also famous for its toleration, was not founded until 1682, but it grew rapidly and attracted colonists from the British Isles and Germany.

Just as New Englanders were forced at an early date to join together for mutual protection, so the whole group of English colonies learned a certain sort of co-operation in the almost continuous fighting against the French and the Indians. Yet such was the self-reliance and independence necessarily developed by each colony that it is a wonder they ever stuck together firmly enough to carry through the Revolutionary War. Boston was from the first a center of resistance, and Philadelphia was the meeting-place of the Continental Congress and the Constitutional Convention. Everywhere throughout the Northeast are reminders of Colonial and Revolutionary days. The number of houses where Washington slept or made his headquarters has become proverbial.

We are less likely to find monuments commemorating important events of the industrial revolution which followed upon the political one. Mechanical and economic changes of far-reaching importance coincided roughly with westward expansion. At the beginning of the nineteenth century the United States was a nation of small farms and hand industries; small cities and many farms were scattered along the seaboard north of Florida, and a few outposts stood in the wilderness between the Appalachians and the Mississippi. By the early twentieth century, the territorial boundaries had reached the Pacific and extended overseas, and the nation was largely urban and in-

STANDARD OIL CO. (N. J.)

THE STATE OF POTATOES

Many hours of backbreaking labor are eliminated by this tractor-drawn machine that is shown digging up potatoes on a farm in Caribou, Maine. In spite of the fact that only 33 per cent of the total acreage of Maine is suitable for agricultural purposes, it exceeds by many thousands of bushels the potato crop of any other state in the Union.

FRESH OYSTERS from the beds planted in Long Island Sound are prepared for market.

dustrial, with manufacturing done in factories on a gigantic scale. Water power, steam power and finally electric power—the development of such resources accompanied and made possible the invention of complicated and delicate machinery which took industries out of the home and required large capital resources.

The Northeast experienced these industrial changes first. In New England, especially, thousands went into the factories as farming grew less and less profitable, while other thousands went west to settle new states. Hardy spirits took to the sea in greater numbers than before, as fishermen, whalers and sealers, and fast clipper ships from Boston or Baltimore did much of the carrying trade of the world until steam-driven ships of iron destroyed their supremacy. Fresh immigration kept adding to the cities, so that the racial make-up of the population had entirely changed, and newcomers from Europe and their descendants outnumbered the descendants of the original colonists. In New York City the results of immigration and industrialization were

most pronounced of all, on account of its commanding location and its fine harbor, but Philadelphia and Baltimore also grew to be great seaports and railway terminals, and Pennsylvania coal and coke made Pittsburgh into a center of the iron and steel industry.

Thus the wilderness of 1620 was transformed in three centuries. Could the Puritan leaders see Boston today—could Peter Stuyvesant see Manhattan Island, or Penn his Philadelphia—they would think themselves in another New World. Yet if we travel from end to end of the Northeast we shall find the transformation not always complete. There are stretches of countryside in New England which still look much as they did in Colonial days; there are old farmhouses and meeting-houses in Pennsylvania and New Jersey which date almost from Penn's time, and boxwood grown from cuttings of English shrubs still grows on old estates of the Maryland Eastern Shore. Such survivals of an earlier day give the East much of its beauty.

Those who have not seen New England

THE QUIET LIFE of a small New England town is pictured in Farmington, Connecticut.

THE CAPE COD CANAL is bridged at Sagamore, a resort village on the Buzzards Bay end of the waterway. About eight miles long, it connects Buzzards Bay and Cape Cod Bay.

CRAIGIE HOUSE illustrates the charm of Cambridge, Massachusetts. The stately colonial mansion served as headquarters for Washington and, later, was Longfellow's home.

LONGWOOD GARDENS, in Pennsylvania just across the border from Delaware, is an estate of the Du Pont family of Delaware. Gardens and conservatories are open to the public.

A STATUE OF NATHAN HALE, Revolutionary patriot, overlooks a corner of the old garden court of the Deacon Richard Hale House in Coventry, Connecticut, Nathan's birthplace.

cannot realize its charm. Compared with western North America or South America its scenery is not at all spectacular; here are no stupendous peaks fifteen or twenty thousand feet high, no snow-covered volcanic cones, no enormous glaciers. The low wooded mountains, the rocky fields, the pockets of good soil, the many lakes large and small tell the geological story of an old land, with hills eroded and scarred by glacial action. Valuable granite and marble quarries are concealed in those hills, and the beautiful lakes to-day provide ideal locations for many a summer camp, in Maine, New Hampshire and Vermont. Spruce and pine, hickory and hemlock still cover large areas, fringe the tortuous coast of Maine, and seem to summer visitors like the forest primeval, but most of it is second and third if not fourth growth. Lumbering is less and less profitable in the Northeast and much reforestation is necessary. The tourist business has become, in some parts of New England, even more important than lumbering or farming. Farmers take summer boarders or rent summer camps; old inns become famous, new hotels are built and the resort trade of three months supports many a community for the balance of the year. Along the cool Maine coast, Mt. Desert, Bar Harbor, Penobscot Bay and Boothbay Harbor are names known alike to tourists, week-enders, tired vacationists and fashionable summer colonists. The combination of surf and rock and forest has a strong appeal for many people while others prefer the deeper woods of the interior, where long and exciting canoe trips lead from stream to stream and lake to lake.

Hills and Mountains

For those who like the hills better than the sea, Vermont has its Green Mountains and New Hampshire its White Mountains. Both ranges are green in summer and white in winter, and the call of winter sports in this section is now almost as insistent as the summer lure of mountain villages, forest trails and blue lakes hidden away in the green hills. Massachusetts in turn has the lovely Berkshire Hills,

and in addition a coastline of superb variety. The North Shore—that is, the shore above Boston—boasts a succession of beautiful headlands and wholly delightful old towns: Marblehead, fascinating Salem, Beverly, and Gloucester in the lee of Cape Ann. This is the region of fishing-schooner and clipper-ship fame; sails are still mended on Gloucester docks and codfish spread out in the drying yards. Gloucester and Boston ship cod, herring and mackerel even to distant points, but those who have never eaten fresh Gloucester mackerel or swordfish new-caught off Martha's Vineyard do not realize how delicious fish can be.

Plymouth and Cape Cod

Then there is the South Shore, past Quincy and Hingham to Plymouth and Cape Cod. "The Cape" is known to thousands who love its sandy roads and high dunes, its beaches and its tough, wind-bent pine and juniper trees, its weathered old frame houses with door-yards of asters, and its white picket fences lined with tall dahlias. Nantucket and Martha's Vineyard, those two low islands across Nantucket Sound from Chatham and Falmouth, are akin to the Cape geologically; they were settled by the same kind of sea-faring folk, who went on fishing and whaling voyages and built the same kind of low charming houses.

Little Rhode Island

The greatest whaling port of all was New Bedford, as readers of Moby Dick well remember. Then it became one of the great cotton textile towns, like Fall River just to the west and Pawtucket and Providence across the line in Rhode Island. The smallest state in the Union has almost more water than land, for Narrangansett Bay divides it in two, cutting deeply inland. The low hills of Rhode Island and Connecticut are much alike in character, and are beautiful with many swift-moving streams whose waterfalls—as in the rest of New England—have determined the locations of factories. A full description of New England's manufacturing towns is here impossible.

ATLANTIC CITY, POPULAR PLAYGROUND OF THE NEW JERSEY COAST

The boardwalk and the wide, sandy beach make Atlantic City a Mecca for vacationers. The boardwalk is lined with luxury hotels, shops, restaurants, a convention hall and movie theaters.

FRITZ HENLE, PHOTO RESEARCHERS

KIM MASSIE

AN EXPRESSWAY, edging a crowded cemetery, links Manhattan and Long Island, New York.

DOWNTOWN—the financial district of New York. Thousands work there but almost no one lives there.

Megalopolis—the continuous strip of

IN BOSTON, auto traffic stops at a corner to let rush-hour workers cross at will.

COMMUTERS in a hurry create blurred images in Grand Central Station, N. Y.

A BIG-CITY TOT accepts endless duplications of Santa Claus with aplomb.

DAVID LAWLOR. SHOSTAL

KIM MASSIE

JANE LATTA

MIGRATION of so many families to the suburbs has resulted in huge housing developments—here Plainview, Long Island—on what was once farmland or open country. Some business firms have also moved in the hope of escaping congestion. The building in the center houses offices and the technical center of a camera and instrument company.

CITY SUMMERS bring open-air concerts. The Boston Pops plays to enthusiastic music lovers, in a shell on the Esplanade, overlooking the placid Charles River.

DAVID LAWLOR, SHOSTAL

PETER ROLL, PHOTO RESEARCHERS

cities and suburbs

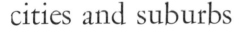

STRING BANDS and fanciful costumes—Philadelphia's Mummers' Parade, January 1.

HIGH-STEPPERS—Maryland Majorettes go through their paces at a bowl game.

A. JACK DI TORO

ROBERT LEAHEY, SHOSTAL

211

There are the huge paper mills of Millinocket in the heart of the Maine woods, the woolen and cotton mills in the cities of Lowell and Lawrence, the shoe factories of Haverhill, Lynn and Brockton; watches come from Waltham and clocks from Waterbury, jewelry from Attleboro and typewriters from Hartford. It is surprising how many articles of every-day use are made in this small area.

The Effect of the Lakes

New York in turn presents a fascinating combination of scenery and industry. The Adirondacks are more varied than the Green Mountains, from a geographical point of view. Lake Ontario and Lake Erie influence the climate and the products of western New York favorably, so that it is a country of orchards and vineyards, and in good years fruit has been so plentiful as to go unpicked. Throughout the Northeast, farming must be intensive and specialized or it is profitless, and abandoned farms, whether in Vermont, New York or Pennsylvania, tell the same story of non-adaptation to economic and local conditions.

The Route to the West

It is the Barge Canal and the railroads following its route which link east to west in New York. Add cheap transportation to hydro-electric power, and the result is a string of manufacturing cities from Buffalo to Albany, each well known in its line: optical and photographic goods from Rochester, collars and cuffs from Troy, electrical machinery from Schenectady. Down the Hudson Valley from Albany pours the volume of commerce which determines New York City's leadership in trade. On each bank is a railroad, and the river itself is a highway. It is one of the country's most beautiful streams, cutting its way down from the heart of the Adirondacks, joined by the Mohawk and flowing on past the Catskills through the highlands until it spreads out at Tappan Zee into a bay four miles across; then suddenly just below Nyack the Palisades begin, and those magnificent cliffs line the

west side of the river until we are opposite the Manhattan skyscrapers. The counties along the Hudson were settled by the Dutch, and place-names from Staten Island to Rensselaer are echoes of the days when New York was New Netherland, and stocky, vigorous settlers built white frame houses with gambrel roofs in the style which we call Dutch Colonial.

No description of the state, however brief, could leave out Long Island, with its beautiful estates and towns, and fertile truck gardens growing produce for city markets. There is a pleasant and comfortable atmosphere which often gathers about fields well cultivated and clusters of communities, and these Long Island has in good measure. The long sand beaches and dunes proclaim the island's relationship with the Jersey coast to the south.

The Surface of New Jersey

One-third of New Jersey is hilly country with parallel mountain ridges walling pleasant valleys and well-kept dairy farms. Factory towns like Paterson and Passaic, with their silk mills, half encircle New York City. But from the Raritan south the land is relatively flat, and literally so on the beaches which barricade the coast. Southern Jersey is all sand, as though it had been raised from under the sea only yesterday, and such, geologically speaking, is the case. How can anything grow in that sandy soil? Many things, such as grass and grain crops, will not, but melons, potatoes, fruits and truck crops will. So will stubborn pines and scrub oaks. Thus the central Jersey landscape is one of flat fields carefully fertilized, cultivated and watered. A few country towns, farms and fine old homes still stand as reminders of the colonial past. But the countryside is steadily giving way to industrial communities and hundreds of acres of housing development. Farther south are wide stretches of pine woodland where white sandy trails show up distinctly against the dark green foliage. The Jersey which most people know is the shoreline itself, that series of beaches each isolated by its bay or inlet and by wide, desolate salt marshes. On the beaches the Atlantic breakers pound steadily, and there is good surf bathing by the mile. Consequently this coast is practically one long summer resort. Asbury Park, Seagirt, Barnegat, Beach Haven, Atlantic City, Ocean City, Wildwood, Cape May— every city dweller in the near-by metropolitan districts knows one or all of them. In fact so many people run away from the suffocating heat of Philadelphia and New York that the barrier islands are almost entirely built up with cottages, hotels and board-walks and there are few of the big sand-dunes left.

Away from the sea breezes and the fishy salt smell of inlets, once across the flat truck lands and, finally, the Delaware River, the different character of Pennsylvania landscape is immediately evident. Southeastern Pennsylvania is rolling, hilly, Piedmont country of good soil and many streams. It has been well cultivated for two hundred years, and more than one family still holds land by deeds from William Penn. The Quaker settlers built houses and barnes of local sandstone, and developed an architecture known as the Pennsylvania farmhouse type, different from the New England and Dutch Colonial homes, but quite as satisfying to look at. North and west is the belt of country settled by Germans who are often called "Pennsylvania Dutch." These people long kept their racial identity, their customs and their German dialect almost intact. Big stone houses and great red barns painted with white circles and stars are characteristic of the region, which stretches around in a wide quarter-circle from the Maryland line through the to-

BLACK STAR

WEST POINT cadets march past the ivy-covered gray walls of the Military Academy on their way to the parade ground.

bacco fields of Lancaster County to Reading, Bethlehem and the Delaware.

River transportation has helped to concentrate a ring of industrial cities around Philadelphia, and is especially responsible for the shipyards of Camden and Chester, while blast furnaces smoke up the valley of the Schuylkill which leads down from the hard coal fields. One of the country's greatest steel plants is located at South Bethlehem, on the edge of the Appalachian ridge country, where Lehigh Valley coal is easily obtained. Much cement is manufactured in this limestone country, while the biggest slate quarry in the world is near Bangor, above Easton.

Almost all the anthracite coal in the United States is in one relatively small

STEEL MILLS of a large company in Pittsburgh dominate a web of railroad tracks, roads and river. The city's position between sources of iron ore and coal has been further strengthened by multiple transportation facilities to make it a prime steel producer.

BUSINESS BAROMETER— stock-price listings in a Wall Street broker's office.

LARGE CORPORATIONS must keep accurate and often complicated records. The job requires thousands of business-machine operators.

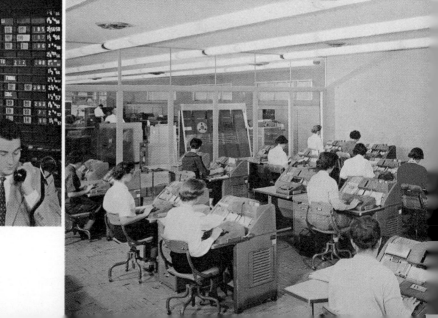

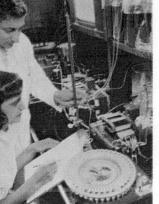

ROTOR HEADS are assembled in a Connecticut helicopter plant. Other firms supply most of the parts.

LABORATORY of a drug company in New Brunswick, New Jersey, a center of drug manufacture.

AT DUSK, Manchester, New Hampshire, textile mills are dark—symbol of New England's decline in textiles.

National hub of business, finance and manufacturing

PRODUCTION of costume jewelry braces a town's economic health—Plainville, Massachusetts.

WHEELED RACKS of new-fashion dresses thread traffic in New York's garment district, wholesale center of ready-made women's clothes.

MIRROR LAKE (LAKE PLACID), SUMMER VACATIONERS' PARADISE

Upper New York State has a strong lure for vacationers and sports' lovers the whole year round. Mirror Lake (above) is one of the most picturesque spots in the Adirondack Mountains.

BOTH PHOTOS, CHARLES PHELPS CUSHING

WINTER SNOWS FIND SKI ENTHUSIASTS FLOCKING TO LAKE PLACID

The long winter season makes Lake Placid a popular spot with skiers and skaters. It is also the answer to a photographer's prayer, for no season of the year is without its rare beauty.

MILKING TIME and the cows wend their way through a stony pasture in New Hampshire. Cattle can forage on such boulder-strewn soil but it is poor for the raising of any crops.

THE BEAR AND THE SEALS, amusing sculpture in ice. Such displays are a feature of the merry winter carnival held at Dartmouth College, in Hanover, New Hampshire, every year.

A RACING SLOOP scuds before the wind in Long Island Sound. Sailing, for profit or for pleasure, has been a natural element of life on the northeast coast from the earliest days. There the great clipper ships were built and set forth for China.

The old lure of the sea: for pleasure,

AT MYSTIC, Connecticut, a last haven for many famous sailing vessels, the oldest existing wood whaling ship is berthed.

FREIGHTERS tie up at piers jutting out into the East River from Brooklyn. Manhattan skyscrapers loom across the water. Miles of waterfront help to make New York the nation's leading port.

H. ARMSTRONG ROBERTS

THE BOARDWALK (Steel Pier in background), Atlantic City, New Jersey, draws Easter holiday throngs.

BIRTHPLACE of the textile industry—Slater Mill, Pawtucket, Rhode Island; its spindles started to turn in 1793. For many years, New England held the lead in manufacturing while the South supplied raw materials such as cotton. Easy sea transport facilitated the arrangement.

ERIC M. SANFORD

M. L. WARREN, SHOSTAL

beauty and work

ROCKBOUND COASTS, the New England settlers' first sight of America, may still be glimpsed at Acadia National Park, Maine.

CADETS on parade at the United States Naval Academy, Annapolis, Maryland—where naval officers have trained since 1845.

RUSS KINNE, PHOTO RESEARCHERS

FINE MARBLE is cut and lifted in huge blocks from Vermont's world-famous quarries.

region of northeastern Pennsylvania. Riding up from Philadelphia into the Blue Ridge one comes suddenly to the coal country, with no warning except that the water in the tumbling mountain streams has become black. Green mountains give place to hills of dull black coal dirt, refuse from the "breakers" where the coal is sorted and graded after being hauled from the deep mine shafts. Railroad tracks cover every valley-floor and hug the banks of streams, and loaded freight cars by the mile stand on the sidings, waiting to be made up into trains. Where mining towns were once very dirty and unattractive, much progress has been made toward better living conditions.

Scranton, Pennsylvania's third largest city, and Wilkes-Barre have grown up in the heart of the anthracite mining area. But there is a great deal of industry other than coal in this region. Allentown, Bethlehem and Easton join Scranton and Wilkes-Barre as centers of machinery, truck, textiles, clothing and tobacco manufacture and railroad operations. Noted for its steel industry, Bethlehem is also remarkable for its many cultural interests as a Moravian community.

As abruptly as it begins, the region of coal veins ends, and the hills are beautiful once more. The Susquehanna winds its shallow way down through the mountainous centre of Pennsylvania, and is joined not far above Harrisburg by the lovely Juniata. The Great Valley of the Appalachians is well marked in Pennsylvania, and here as in other states to the south it is remarkable for its fertility and beauty. West of the mountains begins another great industrial section, and soft coal, oil and natural gas have all contributed to the growth of Pittsburgh, Johnstown, Altoona, Connellsville, Erie and other places where manufacturing is supreme, be the product glass, steel, pig-iron, coke or silk.

The westernmost tip of Maryland belongs in the soft coal country, and it is connected with the eastern part of the state by a narrow strip of land where the Great Valley swings south from Pennsylvania. Eastern Maryland and Delaware belong together geographically, for they are in a very real sense the product of two rivers, the Susquehanna and the Delaware. The peninsula between Chesapeake Bay on the one side and Delaware Bay and the Atlantic on the other includes all of the state of Delaware and that part of Maryland called the Eastern Shore. The western shore of the Chesapeake is also lowland built up by river silt. This level land is like New Jersey in its fertility for truck crops. The shores of Chesapeake Bay are so indented with small streams that boats can quickly and easily bring the fresh fruits and vegetables across from almost any part of the peninsula. The bay itself, stocked with fish, oysters and other shellfish, is also a prime source of revenue.

The factories and shipyards around Wilmington make upper Delaware look very different from lower Delaware and Maryland, where the atmosphere of the South begins to make itself felt. The Mason and Dixon line between Pennsylvania and Maryland was long the boundary between free and slave states, and south of it the Negro population is noticeable outside the cities, which is not the case in the North. Down on the Eastern Shore one can still see fine old Southern houses that once belonged to the owners of large plantations. Thus these two states are an area of transition between the North and South, although today there is much less difference in customs and economic organization between the two regions.

THE NORTHEASTERN STATES: FACTS AND FIGURES

POPULATION (States and Important Cities)

The areas of the states, in square miles, are in parentheses after the name; state capitals are in italic letters.

CONNECTICUT (5,009), 2,517,000; *Hartford,* 161,000; Bridgeport, 156,000; New Haven, 149,000; Stamford, 92,000; Waterbury, 107,000.

DELAWARE (2,057), 443,000; *Dover,* 7,000; Wilmington, 94,000.

MAINE (33,215), 962,000; *Augusta,* 22,000.

MARYLAND (10,577), 3,072,000; *Annapolis,* 10,000; Baltimore, 921,000.

MASSACHUSETTS (8,257), 5,115,000; *Boston,* 682,000; Cambridge, 107,000; Fall River, 100,000; Lowell, 92,000; Lynn, 94,000; New Bedford, 101,000; Quincy, 87,000; Somerville, 94,000; Springfield, 174,000; Worcester, 186,000.

NEW HAMPSHIRE (9,304), 601,000, *Concord,* 29,000; Manchester, 87,000.

NEW JERSEY (7,836), 6,019,000; *Trenton,* 114,000; Camden, 125,000; Elizabeth, 113,000; Jersey City, 270,000; Newark, 396,000; Paterson, 141,400.

NEW YORK (49,576), 16,655,000; *Albany,* 126,000; Buffalo, 528,000; New York, 7,660,000; Niagara Falls, 91,000; Rochester, 316,000; Schenectady, 81,000; Syracuse, 215,000; Utica, 99,000; Yonkers, 153,000.

PENNSYLVANIA (45,333), 11,219,000; *Harrisburg,* 79,000; Allentown, 109,000; Erie, 135,100; Philadelphia, 1,960,000; Pittsburgh, 601,000; Reading, 98,000; Scranton, 110,000.

RHODE ISLAND (1,214), 845,000; *Providence,* 207,000.

VERMONT (9,609), 387,000; *Montpelier,* 9,000.

PRODUCTION (Agriculture and Industry)

Much of the area's land is not suited to agriculture, but good farming has made it highly productive. Truck farming and fruit growing are important in New York, New Jersey, Pennsylvania, Delaware and Maryland; New York and Maine are among the leaders in the production of potatoes. Pennsylvania and New York have large interests in stock farming and dairying. About one fourth of the fish products in the United States (by value) comes from the northeastern states. All the hard coal and about one fifth of the soft coal of the nation are mined in Pennsylvania, which was second in the value of its mineral products until California surpassed it in 1949. The value of building stones, including granite, marble, sandstone and limestone, quarried in the northeastern states is more than two fifths of the nation's total. The value of manufactures in the northeast is two fifths of the national total. Leading manufactured products are clothing, electrical and non-electrical machinery, textiles, food, iron and steel, chemicals, fabricated metals and transportation equipment. Printing and publishing are carried on. Principal ports: New York, Philadelphia, Boston, Baltimore, Providence. Shore and mountain vacation resorts are important.

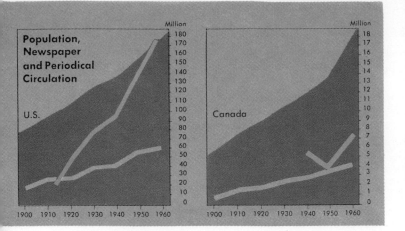

Population, Newspaper and Periodical Circulation

U.S.

Million — 180, 170, 160, 150, 140, 130, 120, 110, 100, 90, 80, 70, 60, 50, 40, 30, 20, 10, 0

1900 1910 1920 1930 1940 1950 1960

Canada

Million — 18, 17, 16, 15, 14, 13, 12, 11, 10, 9, 8, 7, 6, 5, 4, 3, 2, 1, 0

1900 1910 1920 1930 1940 1950 1960

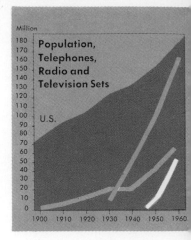

Population, Telephones, Radio and Television Sets

U.S.

Million — 180, 170, 160, 150, 140, 130, 120, 110, 100, 90, 80, 70, 60, 50, 40, 30, 20, 10, 0

1900 1910 1920 1930 1940 1950 1960

POPULATION GROWTH 1900–60 is shown by top lines of dark areas; newspaper circulations by orange lines; and periodical circulations by green. Figures at left are for both populations and circulations in millions. Magazine exceeds newspaper circulation in both nations.

TELEPHONES are represented by orange lines; radio sets by green; and TV sets by yellow. Soon after radio's invention, set ownership quickly

Communications in Canada and the United States

IN CANADA and the United States the major lines of communication have experienced radical changes since the turn of the century. Around 1900, newspapers and the postal service were dominant. Most large cities had several competing newspapers and even the small town usually had its own daily or weekly. What magazines there were had comparatively small circulations. Telephones were just beginning to come into use. Today, although suburban and rural papers seem to have a new lease on life, most big cities have only one paper or none. (Of cities of over 50,000 population, 1 in Canada and 46 in the United States had none in 1960.) In such cities, as far as newspapers go, readers have no way of comparing news coverage—a requirement for well-informed opinion. This helps to explain the growth of news magazines in particular. The arrival of radio in the 1920's and of TV after World War II speeded up communications to a degree undreamed-of in 1900. Yet it is doubtful that they will ever fully supplant the printed word because the time limitations of broadcasting prevent the presentation of current news in any great detail. Radio and TV do mean, however, that news of a crisis in foreign relations, of a disaster, spreads almost at once. The average citizen is thus made aware of public affairs as never before.

Location of Newspapers and Television Coverage

- Cities over 50,000 with newspapers owned by a single company
- Cities over 50,000 with newspapers owned by two or more companies

Television-station coverage (the diameter of each circle is 100 miles)

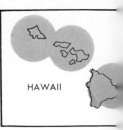

HAWAII

222

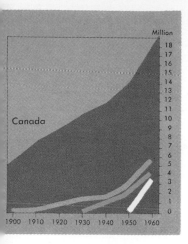

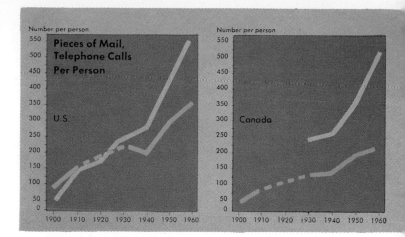

overtook telephone installations in the United States. In Canada, in 1960, telephones still exceeded ownership of both radio and TV sets.

PIECES OF MAIL handled (green lines) as compared with telephone calls (orange lines) per person—figures at left. Use of the telephone began to

pass that of mail in the 1920's even though "mail" includes a vast amount of advertisements and the like besides first-class letters.

WHILE NEWSPAPER circulation has increased, competition among papers has been declining. In 1960 among the 23 Canadian cities of over 50,000 population only 8 had 2 or more competing papers; among the 314 United States cities of over 50,000 only 43 has competing papers. Many newspapers have failed and others have merged. Two main reasons cited are high produc-

tion costs and TV competition. Green and yellow-green circles on map show that southeastern Canada and the eastern United States are almost blanketed by TV. Only the Appalachian Mountains (dark streak) interfere —as do the higher ranges in the far west. In any case, TV stations are set up to reach the greatest number of people, and the west still has comparatively empty spaces.

223

The Southern States

THE South is variously defined. Here we are including the states of Virginia, West Virginia, North Carolina, South Carolina, Georgia, Florida, Kentucky, Tennessee, Alabama, Mississippi, Arkansas, Louisiana, Oklahoma and Texas. But regardless of limits the South is a unique region, with an experience of tragedy and defeat unknown in any other part of the country.

Today the South is the focus of the United States' most serious internal problem, discrimination against Negro citizens, one tenth of the total population. In part this is because about two thirds of the Negroes live in the southern states.

(Thousands have moved north though discrimination is not limited to the South.) It also springs from the unhappy relations between Negroes and whites that developed in the South during the bitter, poverty-stricken years following on the Civil War. Feeling against the Negro was especially strong among the poorer white Southerners. They had never owned slaves but now the Negro was in economic competition with them. The idea took hold of having separate (segregated) public services, including schools, for the Negroes. Several Supreme Court decisions in the late 1800's gave sanction to this idea though the

... *from Virginia to Texas*

phrase used was "separate but equal." But the services were not equal.

Part of the trouble, as we have indicated, was that for a long time after the Civil War the South lagged behind the rest of the nation economically. Most of the battles had raged on southern soil; and at war's end the South was in ruins, its prewar agricultural economy wrecked. Recovery was slow and painful. While the North surged ahead industrially and the West was opened up the South remained largely a rural backwater.

Then, beginning in the 1930's, the South began to catch up with the rest of the country. The Tennessee Valley Authority transformed a vast area. In providing power it opened the South to big industry. The demands of World War II further hastened industrial growth.

Meanwhile, more and more Negroes were becoming educated, many in northern colleges. Dissatisfaction with their limited opportunities, growing out of discrimination, came to a focus on the school issue. The Supreme Court decision of 1954, declaring racial segregation in public schools unconstitutional, resulted. In view of the drastic adjustment it would require in deeply entrenched southern attitudes, complete desegregation was not ordered at once but "with all deliberate speed." The issue today is not the Supreme Court decision but the rate at which desegregation is being accomplished. By 1960, 6 per cent of all Negro pupils in the southern states were attending classes with whites. The border states had made the greatest advances and there was steady if slow progress elsewhere. It lagged most in the core of the Deep South—South Carolina, Georgia, Alabama, Mississippi and Louisiana —where there is a high percentage of Negroes in the population.

No group of Americans has greater respect for the law than Southerners. The fear of many white southern parents that their children's education may suffer because of desegregation is understandable, however. Through no fault of their own the Negro children have had poorer schooling. Until they caught up in desegregated schools they could hold the other children back.

The battle over the rate of school desegregation is on legal grounds. However, Negro college students in the South began taking matters into their own hands in 1960 by insisting on sit-in service at lunch counters along with whites. In doing so they were breaking local laws. Nevertheless they showed remarkable re-

GLITTERING MAZE—night view of part of an oil refinery at Baton Rouge, Louisiana. Among the states, Louisiana is second only to Texas in the production of petroleum.

225

The spread of cultural activities in the United States

THE FOUNDATION of any culture is education, which includes not only schools and colleges but also home and religious training. These set the pattern for an individual's way of life and how he makes use of his time apart from earning a living. Together with education a people's leisure-time activities—whether watching television, reading a book, going to church or visiting a foreign country —make up a nation's cultural life. Americans spend millions of dollars today on what is loosely labeled "entertainment," but it includes many fields—books, music, theater, ballet—that bring satisfactions beyond the passing moment. Moreover, as the map below shows, interest in the most rewarding forms of culture has been spreading out from the Northeast, which had the earliest start.

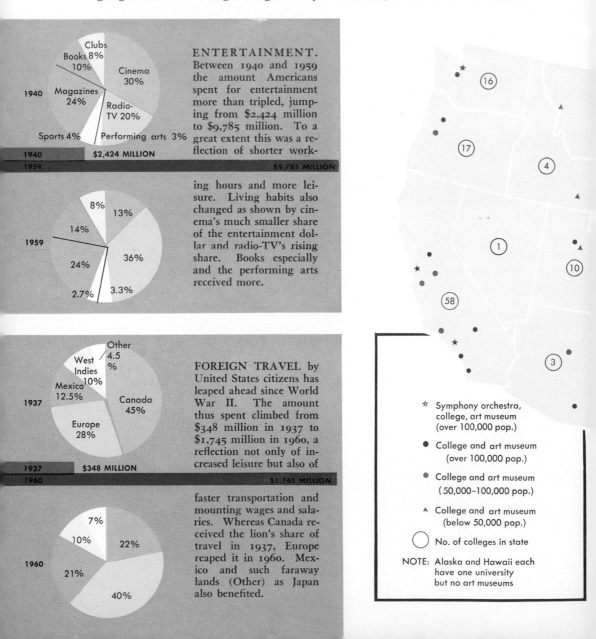

ENTERTAINMENT. Between 1940 and 1959 the amount Americans spent for entertainment more than tripled, jumping from $2,424 million to $9,785 million. To a great extent this was a reflection of shorter working hours and more leisure. Living habits also changed as shown by cinema's much smaller share of the entertainment dollar and radio-TV's rising share. Books especially and the performing arts received more.

1940 pie chart:
Clubs
Books 8%
10%
Cinema 30%
Magazines 24%
Radio-TV 20%
Sports 4%
Performing arts 3%

1940 $2,424 MILLION
1959 $9,785 MILLION

1959 pie chart:
8%
13%
14%
36%
24%
2.7%
3.3%

FOREIGN TRAVEL by United States citizens has leaped ahead since World War II. The amount thus spent climbed from $348 million in 1937 to $1,745 million in 1960, a reflection not only of increased leisure but also of faster transportation and mounting wages and salaries. Whereas Canada received the lion's share of travel in 1937, Europe reaped it in 1960. Mexico and such faraway lands (Other) as Japan also benefited.

1937 pie chart:
Other 4.5%
West Indies 10%
Mexico 12.5%
Canada 45%
Europe 28%

1937 $348 MILLION
1960 $1,745 MILLION

1960 pie chart:
7%
10%
22%
21%
40%

Map legend:
★ Symphony orchestra, college, art museum (over 100,000 pop.)

● College and art museum (over 100,000 pop.)

● College and art museum (50,000-100,000 pop.)

▲ College and art museum (below 50,000 pop.)

◯ No. of colleges in state

NOTE: Alaska and Hawaii each have one university but no art museums

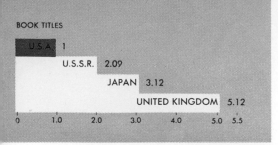

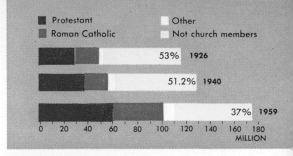

BOOK PUBLICATION in the United States as compared with other nations of confirmed readers. For every 12,220 persons in the United States, 1 book (separate title) is published a year. For an equal number of persons in the U.S.S.R., 2.09 books are published; in Japan, 3.12; in the United Kingdom, 5.12. Figures below show exact number of titles per 12,220.

CHURCH MEMBERSHIP grew between 1926 and 1959 not only among Protestants and Roman Catholics but also among other religious groups such as the Jews. This was not merely the result of an increasing population. Rather, church membership increased faster and nonaffiliation, as the percentages show, declined. Population figures are given below, in millions.

ART MUSEUMS, symphony orchestras and colleges and universities are the measure of cultural advancement. The communities that have any or all of these institutions are, by and large, intellectual leaders, supporting as they do the nation's creative life in the arts and sciences. The orchestras, museums and colleges are clustered in the most densely populated and longest settled areas.

straint, taking their cue from the civil-disobedience, nonviolent methods of Mohandas K. Gandhi, the great Indian leader. Even from among die-hard white Southerners they won reluctant admiration. Moreover, some white college students joined in the demonstrations.

Another side to the over-all problem is the civil-rights issue. In many rural areas of the South the Negro is kept from registering, and hence voting, by various devices. How to enforce and protect the Negro citizen's civil rights is a matter that Congress has still to resolve satisfactorily. In the process the long domination of the Democratic Party in the South may well be broken. The Republicans are already making inroads in such states as Florida.

Regardless of the resistance to equality for the Negro, most thoughtful observers, southern included, believe that full integration is inevitable. A growing body of white Southerners is, in fact, in sympathy with the Negro's aspirations. The question also bears on foreign policy. In relations with the colored peoples of Africa and Asia the United States cannot afford discrimination at home. Economic factors are likewise at work. Industrial plants, branches of northern corporations, have been sprouting all over the South, to the South's benefit. (In many of these factories, Negroes and whites work side by side amicably.) On the other hand, any corporation would think twice before investing further millions of dollars in an area likely to erupt into violence. Also, as the country's prosperity has been seeping down to the average Negro, his buying power has increased. This is a lever that businessmen can hardly ignore.

The South can take pride in its cultural contribution to the nation. It has a number of colleges and universities of first rank, including Vanderbilt University and the University of North Carolina. Above all is the literary flowering of the South in this century, producing such novelists as William Faulkner (Nobel Prize winner), Thomas Wolfe and Katherine Anne Porter, poets Robert Penn Warren and John Crowe Ransom, playwrights Lillian Hellman and Tennessee Williams, newspaper editors Hodding Carter and Harry Scott Ashmore. Though they reflect the travail of the South these are not strictly regional writers. Rather, their best works have the stature of universal meaning. One of the South's most distinguished scientists was a Negro, the chemist George Washington Carver.

However, the greatest cultural contribution of southern Negroes has been in music. The haunting spirituals developed during slavery. Jazz, considered the distinctive American musical idiom, began late in the 1800's among Negro musicians in New Orleans.

The South is a vast area with many differences in elevation, soil and climate. Texas alone is much larger than all the states classed as northeastern. It is farther from Richmond to Memphis, in an adjoining state, than from Richmond to Portland, Maine. The distance from Richmond to El Paso is longer than to the farthest point in North Dakota. The total area of these fourteen states is 887,-048 square miles; in them live 45,000,000 people—white, black and Indian.

Most of the physiographic divisions mentioned in an earlier chapter are represented in these states. The Atlantic-Gulf Coastal Plain extends the whole length of this area, from the Potomac to the Rio Grande, and along the Mississippi stretches northward to the southern tip of Illinois. Florida, Mississippi and Louisiana are altogether within this division. Parts of Virginia, North Carolina, South Carolina, Georgia and Alabama are included in the Piedmont Belt or Plateau. The Appalachian Mountains are west of the Piedmont in all these states and occur also in West Virginia, Kentucky and Tennessee. West Virginia, however, is almost entirely in the Appalachian Plateau, which also covers parts of Kentucky, Tennessee and Alabama. East of the Mississippi the Central Plains dip down through Kentucky and Tennessee into the northern part of Alabama, and to the west of that river extend through Oklahoma into

TOBACCO LEAVES FLAP IN THE WIND ON A VIRGINIA FARM

When the tobacco leaves change from deep green to yellow, they are ready for harvesting. Usually each leaf is cut from the plant by hand, and then strung with others to be dried.

SELECTING SPECIAL LEAVES FOR VARIOUS BLENDS OF TOBACCO

After the tobacco has been cured it is taken to the factory. Here dried leaves of various kinds are sorted together in specific blends. Later they will be shredded for cigarettes.

From cotton fields to ranches

RICE FIELDS in Arkansas, their contours sharp as viewed from the air. The crop is grown on irrigated land in the state.

STRAWBERRIES in commercial quantities will come from this well-tended plot, protected by pines, near Mobile, Alabama.

CORN SILAGE, fodder for livestock, is kept in a trench for winter feeding, in the state of Georgia.

ELLIOTT ERWITT, MAGNUM

ROBERT L. GODWIN, SHOSTAL

C. LEROY LITTLE, SHOSTAL

MILLING HORSES raise the dust of a corral as the hands on a large Texas ranch select their mounts. The favorite breed on the western ranges is the quarter horse; it is very fast for short distances—about a quarter of a mile, hence the name.

JOHN LEWIS STAGE, PHOTO RESEARCHERS

AN EVAPORATOR for the processing of oranges into frozen juice, a major source of income for Florida. In the huge machine, water is extracted from the natural juice. The resulting product is then canned and frozen, for nationwide shipment.

FLORIDA CITRUS COMMISSION

»

JOE CLARK, SHOSTAL

TOM HOLLYMAN, PHOTO RESEARCHERS

SORGHUM is gathered in the mountains of Tennessee. A sirup similar to molasses—and often called that—is pressed from the stalks.

GRADING APPLES from the orchards of the Shenandoah Valley, Virginia. The state produces some ten million bushels of apples a year.

PICKING COTTON, the crop that is still a mainstay of Southern economy, in eastern North Carolina. Although cotton-picking machines have been in use here and there in the South for some years, on many farms the bolls are still gathered by hand, a tedious task.

ANDY BERNHAUT, PHOTO RESEARCHERS

»

A TOBACCO AUCTION in Winston-Salem, North Carolina. Before sale the leaf has already been cured to a gold color. The man with hand upraised is the auctioneer; men holding tobacco are trained buyers. Beyond them the growers follow the bidding, hoping to sell at a high price.

R. J. REYNOLDS TOBACCO CO.

»

A DOG and a gun, cherished possessions of an elderly mountaineer in the Great Smokies.

On the other hand, in the higher Appalachians the vegetation is Alpine, and the climate is delightful. As a matter of fact, summer temperatures in most of the South are seldom so high as they are in Central United States, but the summers are longer, and there is little escape from the heat except along the seacoast and in the Appalachian Highlands.

Many metals and other minerals are found in the section, but only a few can be worked profitably. These few are so profitable, however, that three Southern states are found among the first seven in mineral production. During the seventeenth and eighteenth centuries, iron was smelted in the older states, but the discovery of richer deposits elsewhere closed the rude furnaces. Until the discovery of gold in California, North Carolina and Georgia were a source of gold, but today few of these mines are worked. There is some iron and much coal through the Appalachian region, and Alabama has be-

Texas. The Great Plains also extend southward into the two states last named. The Ozark-Ouachita Uplands include parts of Arkansas and Oklahoma, while in the extreme west of Texas, the Big Bend country, are the Trans-Pecos Highlands, a semi-arid region of mountains and filled valleys. Other divisions might be made. Texas, for example, is a sort of transition region. Some would separate the Edwards Plateau from the Great Plains, and the Central Basin from the Central Plains, and also call attention to the Central Mineral region, the oldest part of the state, a region of worn-down mountains, rich in minerals.

The section has the highest mountains east of the Rockies, and much low alluvial land little raised above the sea; high plateaus and fertile plains; land where much rain falls, and also land where there is too little for agriculture without irrigation. Southern Florida reaches almost to the tropics, and southern Texas nearly as far.

SHIP ISLAND light is a friendly beacon to sailors along the Gulf Coast of Mississippi.

THE SHRIMP FLEET has produced a major industry along the Gulf Coast. Vast quantities of the delicious shellfish are netted by the trawlers and shipped fresh or canned.

Heritage—
the natural landscape
and the human story

WASHBOARD BAND in Brunswick, Georgia. Jazz grew out of such prosaic beginnings—church music, field hollers, funeral parades, and dances like the quadrille adopted from Europe.

TOM HOLLYMAN, PHOTO RESEARCHERS

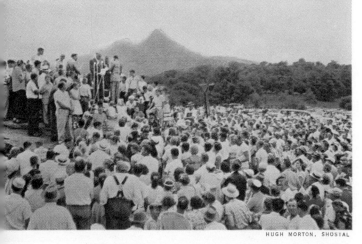

LOUISIANA BAYOUS are a maze of swampy woods and innumerable sluggish creeks. Early in the 1800's they

KENTUCKY DERBY. The country's most thrilling horse race is run at Churchill Downs, Louisville.

JERRY COOKE, PHOTO RESEARCHERS

HUGH MORTON, SHOSTAL

SINGING on the Mountain, a nondenominational convention, gathers on Sundays in June near Boone, North Carolina. Attracting as many as 25,000 persons, it reflects the region's religious interest.

gave shelter to pirates. Today, besides shrimps and muskrat pelts, they are yielding oil and natural gas.

POLING through Okefenokee Swamp. Most of the tract (in Georgia), teeming with mammals and birds, is a national wildlife refuge.

MAGNET for tourists— Mount Vernon, Washington's Virginia home.

PLAYLAND for the nation—Miami Beach, Florida. Catering to visitors seeking the sun, the resorts account for about a third of the state's income.

come an important coal, iron and steel state. West Virginia and Kentucky also rank high in mineral production because of coal, natural gas and petroleum, and Arkansas has a respectable position due to the same products. Virginia and Tennessee produce coal, Texas and Louisiana furnish much of the world's supply of sulphur, zinc is mined in Oklahoma, and Tennessee and North Carolina produce some copper.

Petroleum and Natural Gas

It is petroleum and natural gas, however, which give the section its high place in mineral values. Texas and Oklahoma lead all other states in the combined values of these two products, and Louisiana also has a considerable production, in addition to the states named in the preceding paragraph. This has been almost entirely a development during the present century.

Many of the states have building stones of good quality. Tennessee and Georgia produce much marble, and North Carolina ranks third in the production of granite. There is much stone suitable for making cement, and Florida is first in phosphate rock. The clay deposits are widely spread, and are considerably worked. Dozens of other minerals are found, and some are worked on a small scale, but these are the most important.

The South and Agriculture

There are millions of acres of land, level enough for agriculture, and the long growing season is favorable to crops. Somewhere or other in the section nearly every crop will grow. The region is the world's great source of cotton, which is the nation's largest single export. Winter wheat, corn, oats, sorghum, tobacco, clover, alfalfa, all the legumes; all the vegetables; nut trees of several sorts; fruits of the temperate zone as apples, peaches, pears and plums and cherries; sub-tropical fruits as oranges, lemons, grapefruit and figs; the small fruits as strawberries and blackberries—all of these are grown somewhere in the South.

Not all of them are grown in sections where they can easily be grown. In the cotton belt, and in the regions where tobacco flourishes, many of the farmers devote all their attention to one or both of these crops and buy most of their food, just as many of the wheat farmers of the Northwest raise wheat exclusively. If their "money crops" bring a good price they can pay their debts and are satisfied; if the crop is poor or the price is low, they sometimes go hungry. Many farmers in regions where the pasture is fair, or even good, keep few or no cows.

Better methods have been introduced into many parts of the South, however. Through the Extension Service of the Department of Agriculture, the farmers are taught how to make the best use of their soil. The Tennessee Valley Authority has also brought prosperity to the farmers of the region it serves.

Early Fruits and Vegetables

The climate gives the section great advantages with certain crops. Early vegetables from the lower Rio Grande or from Florida appear in the markets of northern cities before the snow has gone from the streets. Additional supplies from Georgia, the Carolinas and Virginia follow when seeds in suburban gardens in New England have hardly sprouted. Peaches from Georgia come to market early, to be followed a little later by others from North Carolina or Virginia. Local passenger trains must take the sidings in order that solid trains of refrigerator cars may pass on their way to the northern cities.

The South can raise more cotton than the world is able to buy, in spite of the ravages of the boll weevil. Texas is always first, Mississippi second, with Georgia, Alabama and Arkansas contending for the third place. Some cotton is grown in all Southern states except one; North Carolina, Kentucky and Tennessee grow two-thirds of the tobacco of the United States. Nearly all the sweet potatoes are grown in the South with North Carolina and Georgia leading, and peanuts are a southern crop almost exclusively.

At one time, a century or more ago, the older states of the South manufactured in small shops or little factories most of the

FORT SUMTER guarded the harbor of Charleston, South Carolina, at the time of the Secession. A Confederate attack on Union troops in the fort marked the beginning of the Civil War.

PEACEFUL AND PRIMITIVE is life in the bayou country along the Gulf Coast. The marshes and sluggish streams teem with birds and small mammals as well as water plants.

Industry—raw and finished products

ART D'ARAZIEN, SHOSTAL

COOKING FAT from vegetable oil is packaged at a plant in Memphis, Tennessee. The processing of food—as well as the growing of it—is important to the Southern economy today.

«

TOM HOLLYMAN, PHOTO RESEARCHERS
THURSTON HATCHER, SHOSTAL

BOBBINS of nylon thread are tested in a knitting machine in a mill at Chattanooga, Tennessee. Such industries have grown as result of power provided by the Tennessee Valley Authority.

«

JOHN LEWIS STAGE, PHOTO RESEARCHER

«
STEEL MILL at Birmingham, Alabama. Situated in the midst of a coal, iron-ore and limestone region, the city expanded side by side with the iron and steel industry. Many other products are turned out as well—textiles, clothing, chemicals, construction materials.

238

CUTTING PULPWOOD in South Carolina. Manufacture of such forest products as pulpwood (for paper), boxes, cellulose (for cellophane) is a prime source of income for the Palmetto State.

»

OIL RIGS are etched against the sky on the edge of a wheatfield in the Texas Panhandle. The state leads the country in oil production.

«

HILLSIDE DWELLINGS in the coal-mining region of West Virginia. Mechanization, unemployment made it a "depressed area" in the early 1960's.

LOADING SULFUR on a freighter at Galveston, Texas. The value of the state's annual mineral production is over four billion dollars.

AROUND THE FIRST TURN AT CHURCHILL DOWNS ON DERBY DAY

On the outskirts of Louisville, Kentucky, is Churchill Downs, the site, since 1875, of the most famous, most colorful spectacle in American horse racing—the Kentucky Derby.

OUTSIDE LEXINGTON IN THE BLUEGRASS OF CENTRAL KENTUCKY

Like their great father, Man o' War, Thoroughbred colts of Faraway Farm near Lexington, Kentucky, nibble the rich bluegrass that builds the sinews and stamina of champion runners.

PHILIP GENDREAU

COTTON FIBERS GLIDE into cloth on a loom in a textile mill in Georgia. The state is a leader in the production of sea-island cotton, which has an exceptionally long, silky fiber. Other southern states exceed Georgia in the production of short-staple cotton.

articles the people needed. As the world's demand for cotton and tobacco increased, more and more attention was given to agriculture, and manufacturing declined, though it was never entirely given up. There were numerous little cotton factories in 1860, many sugar mills, and some factories of other sorts. During the last quarter of the nineteenth century manufactures began to grow. Now there are five states, Texas, North Carolina, Maryland, Georgia and Virginia, each of which reports annually products valued at more than a billion dollars, and the production of several other states is worth noting.

The Growing Cotton Industry

The first important industry to develop was the manufacture of cotton. In 1890 New England mills used three times as much cotton as the Southern, but by 1905 the Southern mills had forged ahead, and now they use almost four times as much. Though Massachusetts still has many spindles, three states, South Carolina, North Carolina and Georgia, sometimes run more spindle hours in a year. This term means that the number of spindles is multiplied by the number of hours they run. Southern mills usually run more hours in a week and most of them have run steadily, while, for several years, many New England mills did not run full time. New England still manufactures a large part of the finer goods, but Southern mills are doing more and more of this class of work, and their total product is worth much more. North Carolina leads in the number of spindles, with South Carolina not far behind. Georgia follows with Alabama in fourth place. Tennessee and Virginia also manufacture considerable cotton. There are many knitting mills, especially in North Carolina and Tennessee. The cotton industry has not taken root in any other Southern state.

New Social Problems Appear

The growth of the textile industry introduced many new problems. The workers, nearly all white, were drawn from the rural districts, where they were tenant farmers or small landowners. Their change to factory life brought about real difficulties in adjustment. There was at first little industrial friction, as the workers appeared to be fairly contented with their wages and working conditions. Discontent eventually raised its head, however. By the year 1951, all-out campaigns had been undertaken for the purpose of organizing the textile workers of the South. It was estimated that between 15 and 20 per cent of the men and women in the textile industry had been unionized.

The manufacture of cotton is not the only industrial activity. North Carolina now manufactures more tobacco and snuff than any other state, and makes nearly half of all the cigarettes. Virginia makes another third. Florida and Virginia also make cigars. Largely as a result of the tobacco industry North Carolina pays more taxes to the Federal Government in some years than any other except New York. In the memory of many men yet living cottonseeds were thrown away. Now the products are worth over $400,000,000 a year. The oil is used for food, and in making soap and candles. Formerly some of it was exported to Europe, there mixed with olive oil, and then crossed the ocean again to be sold as pure olive oil. The meal and hulls are valuable for feeding cattle, and some of the meal is also used in making fertilizer. The refining of petroleum has become an enormous industry in the oil-producing states.

The Production of Lumber

There is considerable timber left in the South. Mississippi, Louisiana, Alabama, Texas, Arkansas, Georgia and North Carolina each produces more lumber than any states except Washington, Oregon and California. Some is hardwood, but more is pine and cypress. Though most of the lumber is exported, a considerable quantity is taken a step or two farther. High Point is the southern center of the furniture industry, and there are many other factories scattered through the South. There are several large pulp mills which are increasing their production, but the industry is not yet important. Turpentine and resin, obtained from the pine, have always been Southern products. Georgia and Florida lead.

There are hundreds of other factories producing scores of articles in the South. One advantage is the recent extensive development of hydroelectric power. The South Atlantic states generate more horse power than any other group, except the three Pacific states, and Alabama and Tennessee have extensive developments. Tennessee, Alabama and North Carolina, ranking fourth, fifth and sixth, top the other Eastern states except New York. The ease with which electric power may be transmitted puts the village on an equality with the city as a site for manufacturing, and is causing the development of many towns rather than a few great cities. It will be noted that these states which have developed large amounts of power are those a considerable portion of whose surface is mountain or plateau. The Tennessee Valley Authority (TVA), a government agency, has developed hydroelectric power, better farming methods and control of floods.

Atomic Energy Plants

World War II and its subsequent tensions left their mark on the South. When the atom bomb became a possibility in 1942, one of the first three atomic plants, known as the Clinton Engineer Works, was constructed at Oak Ridge, Tennessee. The 60,000-acre government reservation on which it is built became an "atomic town," its population composed of plant workers and their families. Houses and stores are rented from the Government, and the area has its own schools, hospitals, recreational and welfare facilities. During the war, the population reached a high of 70,000 but that had dropped at the latest census to half that number.

Early in 1952 the great Savannah River hydrogen-bomb project in South Carolina began to take shape. Ellenton, a small town on the 202,000-acre tract, was moved, lock, stock and barrel, along the highway and relocated at Jackson. This was to make way for the plant installation of the Atomic Energy Commission.

In spite of the many factories and the great atomic developments, the South is still rural. No state is "industrial-minded," though a few are becoming so. The largest city in the section ranked fourteenth in 1950.

Rural Population in the South

This rural population is interesting from many standpoints. Before the Civil War—in the states east of the Mississippi and in Louisiana—the English ideal of life on a country estate was dominant, though as in England the wealthy owner of a plantation might have a city house. Even the professional man who was forced to live in a city often had a plantation to which he hoped to retire. While, of course, there were cultured and wealthy individuals in the cities, in general it may be said that the city was considered a convenience only, if not, in fact, an evil. Most of the famous Southern mansions were on the plantations rather than in the cities. Certainly there was more culture in the rural districts.

This condition no longer exists. The destruction wrought by Civil War and Reconstruction destroyed the old plantation system, and the families have generally moved to town or city.

Problems of the Rural South

The rural situation is complicated by the presence of the Negro, who must always be considered. After Reconstruction, the people who had not money enough to maintain one efficient public school system felt themselves obliged to maintain two, with the result that neither was even moderately satisfactory. Only slowly has improvement been manifest, and even now the rural and small town schools, as a whole, are less efficient than those in other sections. While more progress has been made in some states than in others, there has been real progress in all, and the amount of illiteracy both black and white has been greatly lessened. Between 1920 and 1930 white illiteracy was reduced about one-third, and Negro illit-

P. & A. Photos

THE SINGING TOWER

This superb tower, with its carillon of 71 bells, was built by the famous editor, Edward W. Bok, who is buried here. It is at Iron Mountain, the highest point in Florida.

eracy almost one-fourth. By October 1947, illiteracy had reached an all-time low throughout the country.

Twelve of these fourteen states had slavery in 1860, and there is a considerable proportion of Negroes in all of them, though that proportion is decreasing. Mississippi and South Carolina had a small majority of Negroes in 1920, though before 1930 the latter state had a majority of whites. In West Virginia and Oklahoma, the proportion is small, but in several other states it is over 35 per cent. In the section as a whole the proportion is a little less than one-fourth.

When the Negroes were freed, in 1865, few could read or write. It is a measure of their advance that almost 90 per cent can do so today. There are a number of Negro colleges and technical schools; and Negro race is no bar to admission in many of the country's leading universities. By law Negroes are supposed to have educational opportunities equal to those provided for whites. This is still not true in some parts of the South, but the picture is changing by slow degrees.

Even before slavery was abolished, a few Negroes achieved fame, among them Joshua Johnston, Benjamin Banneker and Frederick Douglass. Today there are hundreds of Negroes who are outstanding, in almost every field—music, art, science, literature, sports—and many of these men and women were born and brought up in the South. Relations between the colored and white people are still not easy, but a hopeful note in the situation is that both sides today are providing responsible leadership.

Reference has been made to the tenant system, which has handicapped Southern agriculture. While, perhaps, the best system possible when it was put into effect after the Civil War, its continuance has resulted in unsatisfactory farm conditions. Though a number of tenants, both white and Negro, do manage to purchase land, many of the farms are still operated by tenant farmers and sharecroppers. Because they are often short-time occupants, they do not have the same interest as a farmer-owner in improving the land

A POWER SHOVEL loads railroad dump cars with tons of bauxite ore, near Bauxite, Arkansas. The region is the United States' chief home source of the ore, which yields aluminum.

AN OIL PUMP in the middle of the street reminds visitors to the town of Barnsdall, in northern Oklahoma, that it is in the midst of a fabulously rich petroleum-producing area.

A BEAUTIFUL SPECIMEN OF FISHERMAN'S LUCK

From the southern tip of Florida a long succession of coral islands (called keys) extends in a southwesterly direction. From Key West, at the tip of the island chain, sportsmen go out in boats large and small, lured by tarpon and other large fish that abound in the deep waters. The tarpon pictured here is a summer fish, though occasionally one may be caught in winter.

or preserving the equipment, and so this tenancy is unsatisfactory to both the owner and the tenant and has an adverse effect on the community as a whole. Recently there has been some reconversion of plantations from sharecropper to hired labor and the general standard of farming is rising, although slowly.

One cause of the backwardness of the rural population in some states was the isolation caused by roads that were almost impassable in winter. Recent years have marked a tremendous improvement, and all the Southern states now boast highway systems that include from one to thirteen thousand miles of high-type surfaced roads, with more constantly being constructed. The hordes of motorists who head south each winter give ample proof of this change.

The schools in the towns and cities are generally good, and some invite comparison with those of any other section, in buildings, standards of instruction, and qualifications of the teachers. There is

more property to tax in the towns and cities, and in some cities the citizens have voted heavy rates for school purposes.

Some of the oldest colleges and universities in the country are in the South. The College of William and Mary at Williamsburg, Virginia, was founded (1693) next after Harvard, and the University of North Carolina was the first state university to begin operation, graduating the first class in 1795. Thomas Jefferson wore with pride the title "Father of the University of Virginia." Every state has a state university, and while not all are real universities, some are recognized as first-class institutions in every respect. Private philanthropy has established other universities, some under the auspices of a church and others independent. Duke University at Durham, North Carolina, through the will of the tobacco and power magnate, James B. Duke, is one of the best endowed institutions in America with imposing buildings, admirably equipped. Rice Institute in Houston, Texas, is another institution amply endowed by a millionaire which has high standards.

There are scores of denominational colleges, too many perhaps. In some cases a denomination has established several colleges in the same state. Many do excellent work. But others, handicapped by the lack of sufficient funds, have voluntarily become junior colleges.

The cities of the South have grown rapidly, becoming busy centers of manufacturing and trade. Oil in the southwest, shipping from ports along the Atlantic and Gulf coasts, the tourist trade in Florida and a general industrial advance throughout the region have contributed to the great increase in the number of cities with more than a hundred thousand people. In 1940 there were twenty; the 1960 census showed thirty-nine; Texas had ten; Florida, Tennessee and Virginia, four each; Alabama, Georgia, Louisiana and North Carolina, three each; Arkansas,

Kentucky and Mississippi, one each. Only West Virginia and South Carolina had no cities of more than a hundred thousand.

The tourist industry is becoming important in the South. All through the Appalachian country there are excellent hotels, which attract visitors from the South in summer, and from the North in winter. Asheville and the "sandhill country" of North and South Carolina attract many visitors, and Georgia also gets its share. Florida attracts increasing numbers of winter residents and many have established permanent homes. In the decade 1950 to 1960 Florida's population almost doubled, real estate boomed and new communities mushroomed. New towns on the Gulf of Mexico, older towns on the Atlantic, like Miami and Palm Beach, and historic New Orleans lure people from the North to spend, to play and to settle in the South.

THE SOUTHERN STATES: FACTS AND FIGURES

POPULATION (States and Important Cities)

The areas of the states, in square miles, are in parentheses after the name; state capitals are in italic letters.

ALABAMA (51,609), 3,244,000; *Montgomery,* 134,000; Birmingham, 339,000; Mobile, 192,000.

ARKANSAS (53,102), 1,771,000; *Little Rock,* 106,000.

FLORIDA (58,560), 4,886,000; *Tallahassee,* 48,000; Jacksonville, 198,000; Miami, 285,000; St. Petersburg, 178,000; Tampa, 271,000.

GEORGIA (58,876), 3,911,000; *Atlanta,* 485,000; Columbus, 116,000; Savannah, 147,000.

KENTUCKY (40,395), 3,016,000; *Frankfort,* 18,000; Louisville, 383,000.

LOUISIANA (48,523), 3,234,000; *Baton Rouge,* 151,000; New Orleans, 621,000; Shreveport, 164,000.

MISSISSIPPI (47,716), 2,163,000; *Jackson,* 144,000.

NORTH CAROLINA (52,712), 4,532,000; *Raleigh,* 93,000; Charlotte, 201,000; Greensboro, 119,000; Winston-Salem, 111,000.

OKLAHOMA (69,919), 2,304,000; *Oklahoma City,* 322,000; Tulsa, 259,000.

SOUTH CAROLINA (31,055), 2,358,000; *Columbia,* 99,000.

TENNESSEE (42,244), 3,532,000; *Nashville,* 166,000; Chattanooga, 128,000; Knoxville, 110,000; Memphis, 492,000.

TEXAS (267,339), 9,488,000; *Austin,* 186,000; Amarillo, 137,000; Beaumont, 119,000; Corpus Christie, 166,000; Dallas, 672,000; El Paso, 272,000; Fort Worth, 347,000; Houston, 933,-

000; Lubbock, 126,000; San Antonio, 584,000; Waco, 97,000; Wichita Falls, 100,000.

VIRGINIA (40,815), 3,899,000; *Richmond,* 218,000; Newport News, 113,000; Norfolk, 273,000; Portsmouth, 107,000; Roanoke, 96,000.

WEST VIRGINIA (24,181), 1,847,000; *Charleston,* 85,000.

PRODUCTION (Agriculture and Industry)

Agriculture is the most important occupation in the southern states, though today they are setting a rapid pace in industry as well. The soil, climate and rainfall all make it possible to grow many temperate and semitropical crops. The most important crops are cotton (these states furnish over 70% of the world's supply), tobacco (North Carolina, Kentucky, Virginia, South Carolina and Tennessee furnish over 80% of U. S. supply) and sugar-cane (Louisiana). The South Atlantic and Gulf Coast states produce quantities of early vegetables. Virginia raises large quantities of apples, North Carolina and Georgia, peaches, Florida and Texas, citrus fruits. Dairying has become important in these states; one fourth of dairy cattle of the United States are now found here; Texas raises many beef cattle and sheep. Rich forest and mineral resources. Among the mineral products are petroleum (a large percentage of world's supply comes from Texas, Oklahoma and Louisiana), iron ore and coking coal, sulfur (Louisiana and Texas), bituminous coal (West Virginia), bauxite and a variety of building materials.

North-Central States

...the Middle West

THE north-central states—the Middle West—include Ohio, Indiana, Illinois, Michigan, Wisconsin, Minnesota, Iowa, Missouri, Kansas, Nebraska, South Dakota and North Dakota. Settlement of the area did not begin until the dawn of the nineteenth century, some years after the eastern coastal states were well established. Once the barrier of the Appalachian Mountains was breached the pioneers found beautiful, fertile country. The Ohio and Mississippi valleys filled up rapidly. West of the Mississippi River lay the treeless Great Plains—to early frontiersmen the Great American Desert. But when transcontinental railroads were built after the Civil War the plains too were settled, especially by immigrants from continental Europe. Old Americans and new, they made the Middle West.

On the plains, always under threat of drought, life was hard. Well into our own century the Midwest as a whole lagged behind the East culturally. This is no longer true. No other region in the country is more devoted to education and the arts. The massive state university is virtually an invention of the Midwest. Backed by enormous state funds, these institutions open their doors to thousands upon thousands of students. The Big Ten alone (Illinois, Michigan, Northwestern, Ohio State, Wisconsin, Michigan State, Iowa, Indiana, Minnesota and Purdue) have 200,000 students a year. Critics claim that these mammoth universities resemble assembly-line factories Their defenders claim that they are the backbone of democracy—that they provide quality education for numbers of future citizens who might never have received it otherwise.

In and around these institutions flourish a multitude of painters, writers and musicians, most of them faculty members. Nowhere else do universities support the creative arts so enthusiastically. The

248

CORNELL CAPA, MAGNUM

and educated in Iowa. Nor that Robert M. La Follette of Wisconsin was the most daring governor in the country during the early 1900's. It was under La Follette that Wisconsin became the first state to offer workmen's compensation and social security. In these years there was also an upsurge of literature in the Midwest, which included such names as Carl Sandburg, Vachel Lindsay, Theodore Dreiser and Sherwood Anderson.

The University of Chicago has rivaled the boldness of Wright and La Follette in another field—education. While at Chicago in the early 1900's, John Dewey established an experimental school to try out what we now call progressive education. Dewey's theories revolutionized American teaching methods. Robert Hutchins, president of the university from 1929 to 1945, was also eager to experiment. His "Chicago Plan," adopted in 1930, allowed bright undergraduate students to bypass the four-year residence requirement and take a degree as soon as they were qualified. Modifications of his plan have been put in use elsewhere.

The basis of economic life in the north-central states, of course, is the phenomenally productive farms and steel mills. When crops are poor or farm prices down, however, states like North Dakota, South Dakota, Nebraska, Kansas, Indiana, Iowa and Ohio (usually referred to as the "farm states") suffer severely. Manufacturing states like Michigan and Minnesota are in much the same situation when a strike or recession hits the steel industry, the nation's economic barometer.

The farm problem is especially serious. It first reared its head in the 1920's, when farm output, thanks to new methods and machines, began to pull ahead of the population increase. Demand did not again meet supply until World War II, when the Government established a series of price supports to encourage even

Creative Writing Workshop at Iowa, the Hopewood prizes at Michigan—these are just two examples of the way young writers are encouraged there. The drama departments staff and run a number of remarkable university theaters. Visiting orchestras, dance troupes and lecturers are invited to use the theaters when the students aren't. Nobel Prize-winning poet T. S. Eliot once delivered a lecture on poetry to an audience of 13,743 at the University of Minnesota. "Never before," said one American poet, referring to such phenomena, "over so wide an area and reaching so many people, have so many paintings been shown, pieces of music played, plays performed, or so many examples of the arts created."

A bold zest characterizes everything these states put their hands to. It is no accident that the controversial Frank Lloyd Wright, whose imaginative designs dominated American architecture during the first half of this century, was born greater production. The Government guaranteed to buy great quantities of food at fixed prices for its allies and armed forces abroad if the farmers would grow them. Though farm population was decreasing year by year, twentieth-century technology—machines, fertilizers—produced ever greater yields. Food prices inevitably dropped. Once again, the Government had to step in and buy up the surpluses during the postwar period—this time to keep the small farmers from going bankrupt. Despite government aid, however, the large farms continued to grow richer and the small ones poorer. Everyone agrees that the huge subsidies paid out each year are an unfortunate drain on the Treasury, but few can agree on how to remove both price supports and keep farm income high. Meanwhile the Government has continued to pile up food surpluses, though a great part of the world's population goes hungry.

The farm states have traditionally been the stronghold of the Republican Party. As elsewhere in the nation, though, traditional party loyalties are breaking up. South Dakota, Nebraska, Kansas, Iowa and Ohio have all elected Democratic governors in recent years, while Democratic congressional and mayoralty candidates have been successful in the other farm states. Michigan, Illinois and Missouri exchange allegiances between the Republicans and the Democrats fairly regularly. Minnesota and Wisconsin have a strong "reform" tradition. La Follette's record in Wisconsin has already been mentioned. Minnesota has been home to a number of "third parties," among them the Farmer-Labor Party, which made a formidable alliance with the Democratic Party in 1940.

Almost two thirds of the population lives in cities and towns with 2,500 or more inhabitants. Approximately one sixth of the people live on farms, and the remainder in small towns and villages.

The central plains cover most of the region. There is, however, a border of Superior highlands in upper Wisconsin and Minnesota, a lovely region of woods and lakes. A bit of the Appalachian plateau extends into eastern Ohio; and the Ozark plateau covers a large part of southern Missouri. Down the center of this group of states flows the mighty Mississippi, "Father of Waters." Its great tributaries are the busy Ohio and the muddy Missouri—which is almost as long as the main stream. Between the Missouri and the Mississippi lies Iowa, the champion corn state, in the heart of the Corn Belt—Ohio to western Nebraska.

North of the Corn Belt around the Great Lakes is a strip of country that depends heavily on hay and dairying. There are two huge wheat-growing areas, the northern devoted to spring wheat, the southern to winter wheat which is planted in the fall. Of course, the farms of these several outstanding regions are not confined entirely to the produce named. A certain amount of general farming is the rule and portions of Michigan, tempered by the lakes, specialize in fruits.

There is, finally, a region rich in minerals which, for this reason—coupled with the ease of transportation by water and by the straight-laid rails of the prairie country—has become a great manufacturing region. The lower Great Lakes region, with an accessible supply of metals, coal and wood, has become the heart of the nation's automobile industry and a center for manufacture of farm machinery.

Before the Revolution had ended hardy pioneers had made their way into this region. The migration from the east and the southeast grew during the early years of the Republic until it became a flood. In 1803 the region was extended when most of the territory now in the west north central states was included in the Louisiana Purchase. Later other thousands of Southerners sought opportunities in the West. Some loaded all their household goods into wagons and made the long trek. Other pioneers came by way of the Erie Canal after it was opened; still others reached the Ohio and floated down until they came to their destination. Later the foreign-born came—chiefly Germans and Scandinavians at first—until now these states form a cross section of the United States of today.

THE AMPHITHEATER of the Toledo, Ohio,
Zoo provides a lovely setting for a concert.

THE WOOD YARD of a paper mill in Munising, Michigan, is piled high with the raw material
needed for pulp and paper. Munising is on Lake Superior, in a lumbering and farming region.

THE KEOKUK DAM AT THE FOOT OF THE CANAL AROUND THE DES MOINES RAPIDS, IOWA

The Federal Government built the first lock of the Mississippi River, Gulf water. This dam, a mile and a half long, was constructed primarily with a lift of forty-one feet, at Keokuk, Iowa, which is 1,461 miles from as part of a great hydroelectric power project.

With characteristic energy the settlers of these Midlands converted them into what is today a region of fertile farms and progressive cities. Highways criss-cross the countryside; today's farmhouse is equipped with such modern comforts and conveniences as telephones, radios, television, automobiles and many labor-saving devices. Some farmers even own airplanes, which they use in connection with their work as well as for pleasure. The region has its own charm of sparkling white winters, summers of goldenrod, wild roses and black-eyed Susans, autumns—in the hardwood regions—of gorgeous red and yellow foliage, of ripening grapes, and, later, hazelnuts, hickory-nuts and black walnuts. There are still deer near the Canadian border, and the early settlers used to be able to shoot prairie chickens on the plains.

The twelve states under consideration are all important agriculturally, those with extensive mines and manufactures less so than the others, however. The state with the greatest percentage of land in farms is Nebraska, and of over 47,000,-000 acres in farmland, about 19,000,000 are sown to cultivated crops, chiefly corn and oats. The state with the next greatest percentage of land in farms is Iowa. This state has almost twice as many swine as any other state, and more cattle than any state except Texas.

Half a century ago the typical farm, nearly self-sufficient with its mixed crops and home manufacture of butter, bacon, clothing and other necessities, was laboriously cultivated by human labor, chiefly that of the immediate family. Today the larger corn-grower, with his tractor and four-row planter, has been known to cover as much as forty-six acres a day, and with a four-row cultivator he can often cultivate sixty-five acres in a ten-hour working day. In the old days he could harvest only one or two acres of corn a day. Now that he has a corn-picker and husker operated by tractor, he can gather eight to ten acres a day. This complicated machinery not only appreciably reduces the need of human labor on the farms, releasing large num-

SHIPS THAT PASS IN THE LOCKS OF THE SOO

A passenger ship and a freighter move in opposite directions through the Sault Sainte Marie Canals. They avoid rapids in the St. Mary's River and connect Lake Huron and Lake Superior.

PRODUCTION LINE OF STRATOJETS IN A WICHITA, KANSAS, PLANT

The Midwestern city of Wichita has for years been a leader in the manufacture of airplanes and plane parts. Thousands are employed in its aircraft factories. Situated on the Arkansas River in the southeastern part of Kansas and reached by highways and major railroads, its manufactured items are easily shipped throughout the United States and to other countries.

bers of young people—who tend to go to the cities—but it very greatly reduces the cost of harvesting the mammoth crops after the initial investment in such machinery has been met. The figures that will shortly follow show the extraordinary quantities of grain produced.

One even hears of an occasional woman farmer, as, for instance, a large wheat farmer of western Kansas who harvests her 4,500 acres by hiring employees in three eight-hour shifts. These men operate seven combines, each of which cuts a twenty-four-foot swath, while at night they hitch the tractors to plows and turn the stubble under. Meals are served from a commissary car that follows the tractors. Of course there are many smaller farms which employ simpler machinery. The typical farm is said to be that operated by one farmer, his sons and a hired man. However, in rush seasons, plowing is often done at night.

The North Central states, taken as a whole, produce two-thirds of the corn crop, more than half of the wheat crop, over three-quarters of the oats and over three-fifths of the barley.

Where corn and wheat do not grow so well, hay and dairy animals thrive. The North Central states produce over two-thirds of the butter made in factories in the United States and about the same proportion of the butter made on farms. Wisconsin leads the country in cheese production, making more than half of all produced.

Kansas City (neighbor to Independence, Missouri, which was once the terminal of the Santa Fe cattle trail) has an important meat-packing industry. The livestock raised in Kansas includes nearly three times as many cattle as swine and a rather small number of sheep. Its stockyards and packing plants are the second largest in the world. But the products of the meat-packing firms in Illinois (chiefly in Chicago) are worth much more. Chicago's packing plants have, in fact, played an appreciable part in making that city the commercial capital of the North Central states.

Chicago is the world's largest food-distributing center. The refrigerator car made it possible for Chicago to slaughter and pack meat for the world. It has an entire section known as Packing Town with a square mile of stockyards. Milwaukee has been likened to a miniature Chicago. When Michigan lumber was plentiful, Grand Rapids and Saginaw started as sawmill towns and later became centers for the manufacture of furniture. Certain firms of the region introduced the now widely used knock-down furniture, which may be shipped flat, and knock-down garages and houses made in sections which may readily be put together. These, like the clothing and other products of the big Midwestern mail-order houses, may be sent to remote regions by rail or water. It is part of the reason why the words "standardization" and "efficiency" have come to be applied to things American.

It has been said that the lower lake region started as "a Yankee outpost of New England." This region, with its cheap water transportation, its wool and metal, has become the heart of the automobile industry. Since the turn of the century this has been perhaps the chief element in multiplying the population of Detroit by six, as well as greatly stimulating the growth of Flint, Lansing, Toledo, Cleveland and Akron. The last three are tire centers. Cleveland and other cities along the south shore of Lake Erie, where coal and iron ore meet, manufacture machinery on a large scale.

Ease of transportation, whether by water or by rail, has been an important factor in the growth of St. Louis. The nearness of the wheat to be milled or stored for shipment has helped make Minneapolis, Milwaukee, Indianapolis and Kansas City, and has formed one of many factors in the growth of Chicago—

UNION PACIFIC RAILROAD

THE SPACIOUS BUILDINGS and grounds of Boys Town, just west of Omaha, Nebraska. The famous "town" was founded by Father Flanagan to give neglected boys a better start in life.

second in size only to New York City. Chicago is a huge transportation center and has many miles of belt-line rails for shifting freight from road to road. The city is also a distribution center, famous for its mail-order houses, from which one may buy almost every possible product. Chicago is convenient to the grain regions, and its constant need for manufactured goods often keeps the freight carriers two abreast—loaded on their return trips. Thanks to the canals, the Great Lakes form one navigation unit. Six-hundred-feet freighters are so constructed that they can negotiate canals, locks and artificial channels; and besides the freighters, there are fine passenger steamers. Chutes and gigantic scoops make loading and unloading possible with incredible rapidity. Iron ore thunders, steel clangs, lumber echoes, cattle bellow, soft-coal billows; and the mingled odors of all these activities combine to give an impression as different as possible from the papery rustle of cornfields and the sunny peace of waving wheat or the lovely lake resorts that are all within the region that the metropolis serves.

The upper lake region was once high mountains but has been worn down by streams and weather almost to a plain, with hills of harder rock which contain lodes of iron and copper. Lakes are abundant in the ice-formed basins. Minnesota has 11,000 such lakes, Michigan 4,000 and Wisconsin 2,000. Unfortunately there is considerable territory covered by muskeg, swamp and rock. The forests, chiefly pine and spruce, maple and hemlock, once attracted Eastern lumbermen, and upper Michigan, Wisconsin and Minnesota successively led in lumber production, the work of which the deep snows facilitated. But so thoroughly was the timber crop reaped without replanting that tremendous problems in forest conservation were left. In many places nothing but jack pine grows. Wisconsin, however, still supplies an important paper industry.

BY STERN WHEELER THROUGH THE DELLS OF THE WISCONSIN

In south-central Wisconsin, the Wisconsin River has carved an eight-mile gorge—the scenic waterway called the Dells. The deepest part has sandstone walls, sculptured by the water.

EWING GALLOWAY

GIANT SENTINELS! GRAIN ELEVATORS AT A GREAT LAKES HARBOR

The huge, concrete cylinders at the harbor of Duluth are a familiar sight in the wheat-growing states. Often grain is cleaned, blended and dried in the elevators, as well as stored.

257

Midwest farms—from family holdings to field factories

SOYBEANS, thriving under the summer sun, are cultivated on a farm in Iowa. In recent years, soybeans have become a lucrative commercial crop.

HILLS AND WOODS give pleasing variety to a farm landscape in Ohio. In this part of the Midwest the farms are usually close together. It has been thickly settled almost since the Revolution.

«

SEED CORN, which is used for planting, is processed at an Iowa plant. Piled corn is loosened so that it will slide into conveyer, covered by planks, at bottom.

PROSPEROUS FARMS in the vicinity of Libertyville, Illinois. The terrain is flattening out and the farms are farther apart. Good roads are a necessity. Although this region usually receives enough rainfall, planting windbreaks—the rows of trees—helps to protect the land from the vagaries of the weather.

"

A LINE OF BUTTES, carved by wind and weather, forms a backdrop for a wheat field in Nebraska. Only one farmhouse is visible, hinting at the vast distances that still separate human habitations on the prairies.

COMBINES KEEP PACE with each other as they harvest and thresh a Kansas wheat field in one operation. The machines are symbols of the technological revolution in farming by which more and more food and fiber are being produced by fewer and fewer workers. On the horizon are concrete elevators for grain storage.

MACHINERY does the work of many men in picking and husking corn on a farm near Nodaway, Iowa. Good food crops in this region mean a great deal to people all over the world.

Along the south shore of Lake Superior, where Indians were once able to secure copper at the surface, mines must now be driven very deep to get at the large deposits of the metal. In the hills around the western end of the lake, iron ore is easily mined. The great quantities of ore that this area has yielded have helped build the great steel-making centers in Ohio, Indiana, Illinois, Michigan and Minnesota, as well as those in the East. By far most of the iron ore of the United States comes from the land at the head of Lake Superior.

Kansas is one of the leading oil-producing states of the nation. Illinois is also a source of considerable petroleum in addition to being a major coal-mining state. It is worth noting that the Black Hills district makes South Dakota, instead of one of the far western states, the nation's largest producer of gold. Missouri leads the United States in mining lead, Ohio as a source of lime, and Michigan as a producer of salt and gypsum. The belt running through Ohio, Michigan, Indiana and Illinois yields much of the nation's stone, gravel, sand and clay.

Of the five principal manufacturing states, three—Ohio, Illinois and Michigan—are in the North Central region. Indiana, Wisconsin and Missouri also rank very high in this respect. Leading manufacturers include automobiles, farm machinery, household appliances and products of iron and steel, rubber and clay.

The North Central states have excellent educational facilities, including sixty thousand public elementary and secondary schools and more than five thousand private schools. This region has approximately six hundred universities, colleges, junior colleges and professional schools, a third of which are public-supported. Each state has one or more state universities. Among the largest of these are Ohio State University, the universities of Illinois, Minnesota, Michigan, Wisconsin and Indiana, and Michigan State College. Ranking with the above in the number of students are Wayne University of Detroit, operated by the city, and the University of Cincinnati. One feature of many of these institutions is that they offer extension courses.

The state universities have grown up on lands that were granted long ago by the Federal Government or were purchased with Federal funds. These schools have come to play an important part in the democratic life of the region. They not only provide a liberal college education at a low cost to thousands of deserving students but through the years they have assumed tasks not generally a part of a university's program. They carry on extension classes in all parts of their states, correspondence courses and technical research centers that often develop important new products and techniques. Staffs of experts from these centers help to keep farmers and businessmen abreast of modern advances. Apart from their university programs, the states look after many other phases of public education. Indeed, we

FUEL AND FOOD. Oil wells stand erect against the Kansas sky, altering the agricultural look in the heart of the winter wheat belt. Kansas ranks high among petroleum states.

FOOD PROCESSING provides a living for thousands of Midwesterners. Left, a Chicago meat-packing employee coats jackets on sides of beef for shipping.

Center, a Missourian inspects his prize hickory-smoked hams. Right, skilled cheese makers check ripe wheels of the delicious Wisconsin product.

THE LAND, the climate and man combine to make the region the national breadbasket. Today, with laborsaving devices, most chores are light: (from left) inspecting grain, feeding chickens, selling produce.

THE CITIES call on talents for newspaper reporting (left) and civic leadership (right).

The human variety—in look,

MANUFACTURING ABSORBS a large segment of the labor force. Many of the factory jobs call for a high degree of skill. Left, an experienced glassblower shapes an

X-ray-tube unit. Center, an operator controls the tempering of cold-rolled sheet steel. Right, a pressman adjusts the plates for printing a dress pattern.

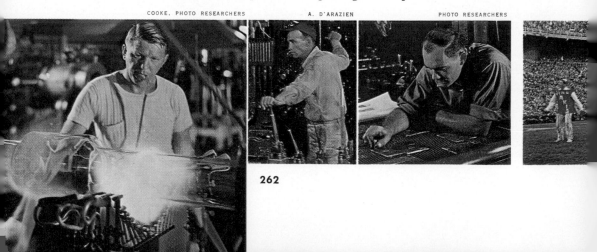

WAYNE MILLER, MAGNUM

<< RAPT ATTENTION is given the sermon during church service in an Illinois town. The typical Midwesterner is concerned with religion. Summertime attire may be informal but the deep seriousness of the congregation cannot be in doubt.

occupations, interests—of the Midwest

STATE UNIVERSITIES are lively centers. Big Ten athletics mold young bodies—Ohio cheerleaders (far left). Young minds are stimulated by gifted teachers—a painter at Iowa (left), an Ohio psychologist (far right). Grateful alumni often help with handsome endowments: the white-haired man (right) donated a new campus library to North Dakota.

MAGNUM   MAGNUM   UNIVERSITY OF NORTH DAKOTA   MAGNUM

CHEESE-MAKING, ONE OF THE MAJOR INDUSTRIES OF WISCONSIN

At a Swiss cheese factory in Madison, Wisconsin, the curd is lifted from the whey to drain. The curd is the basis of cheese, and the watery, vitamin-rich whey is used for other foods.

cannot begin to name all of the opportunities for practical education in this part of the country.

Some great scholars are in the universities of the Middle West and some of the most popular poets and novelists were born in one or another of these states. The writers include George Ade, Theodore Dreiser, Mark Twain, Sinclair Lewis, Edgar Lee Masters, Booth Tarkington and James Whitcomb Riley.

The section has also produced many women of historical importance. One was Jane Addams, the celebrated humanitarian, who founded—and directed for forty-six years—Hull House in Chicago, the first and most famous settlement house in the United States. Another noted woman was Carrie Chapman Catt, the reformer. Largely through her efforts, the country adopted the Nineteenth Amendment, in 1920, giving women the vote.

Moreover, the people of these twelve states have played a great part in the national political scene. Among such activities have been the presidential nominating conventions. Between 1868 and 1952 inclusive, 18 of the 22 Republican and 18 of the 22 Democratic conventions have been held in large cities in this region.

In addition, from these states have come nine of the seventeen presidents since the Civil War—Ulysses S. Grant, Rutherford B. Hayes, James A. Garfield, Benjamin Harrison, William McKinley, William Howard Taft, Warren G. Harding, Herbert C. Hoover and Harry S. Truman.

The people are fond of calling their region by such names as the "Heart of America" or the "Valley of Democracy." They have some justification for their boasts. They are, on the whole, democratic; the level of intelligence is certainly up to, if not above the average, and the same may be said for the standard of morals. The average of material comfort is rather high, and the prospects for future development are bright.

THE NORTH-CENTRAL STATES: FACTS AND FIGURES

POPULATION (States and Important Cities)

The areas of the states, in square miles, are in parentheses after the names; state capitals are in italic letters.

ILLINOIS (56,400), 10,006,000; *Springfield,* 83,000; Chicago, 3,512,000; Peoria, 103,000; Rockford, 126,000.

INDIANA (36,291), 4,633,000; *Indianapolis,* 469,000; Evansville, 140,500; Fort Wayne, 161,-000; Gary, 178,000; Hammond, 112,000; South Bend, 132,000.

IOWA (56,290), 2,743,000; *Des Moines,* 207,-000.

KANSAS (82,276), 2,177,000; *Topeka,* 119,-000; Kansas City, 121,000; Wichita, 254,000.

MICHIGAN (58,216), 7,778,000; *Lansing,* 108,-000; Dearborn, 111,000; Detroit, 1,656,000; Flint, 195,000; Grand Rapids, 175,000.

MINNESOTA (84,068), 3,393,000; *St. Paul,* 313,000; Duluth, 105,000; Minneapolis, 481,000.

MISSOURI (69,674), 4,293,000; *Jefferson City,* 28,000; Kansas City, 473,000; St. Louis, 747,-000; Springfield, 96,000.

NEBRASKA (77,227), 1,405,000; *Lincoln,* 127,-000; Omaha, 300,000.

NORTH DAKOTA (70,665), 627,000; *Bismarck,* 27,000.

OHIO (41,222), 9,637,000; *Columbus,* 465,000; Akron, 288,000; Canton, 113,000; Cincinnati, 488,000; Cleveland, 870,000; Dayton, 258,000; Toledo, 316,000; Youngstown, 166,000.

SOUTH DAKOTA (77,047), 677,000; *Pierre,* 10,000.

WISCONSIN (56,154), 3,930,000; *Madison,* 126,000; Milwaukee, 733,000.

PRODUCTION (Agriculture and Industry)

The north-central states produce nearly one half of all the farm crops in the United States, over half of the wheat crop, three fourths of the corn crop, four fifths of the oat crop and more than two fifths of the barley crop. Enormous quantities of hay, potatoes, rye, buckwheat, sugar beets, tobacco and fruits are grown each year. Throughout these states there are active livestock industries; dairying is highly developed; hogs, cattle and sheep are raised for the market. More than four fifths of the iron ore of the United States comes from the Lake Superior ore lands in Minnesota, Michigan and Wisconsin. Illinois ranks high among the states in the production of coal; it is also mined in Ohio, Indiana, Kansas and Missouri. Michigan leads in the production of salt and is important for its copper. Missouri mines large quantities of lead, and the quarries throughout the north-central states yield sandstone, limestone and gypsum; there is an enormous output of Portland cement, bricks and tiles and other clay products. Silver and gold are mined in South Dakota. These states produce, by value, one third of the manufactured products of the United States; three fourths of the farming implements and over one half of the world's output of automobiles are manufactured in Michigan. Furniture and paper products are important around the Great Lakes. The cereal crops and livestock industries have given rise to flour production (Kansas, Minnesota, Missouri) and meat-packing (Illinois, Wisconsin).

EWING GALLOWAY

STEEL PLANT IN YOUNGSTOWN, OHIO, DURING THE NIGHT SHIFT

Ohio is the geographical center of steelmaking in the United States. Its leading industry is iron and steel, and most of its other industries, in general, are based on these materials.

MINING ORE, Mesabi Range, Minnesota. High-grade ores are depleted but new methods are making low grades profitable today.

»

CLEVELAND—the industrial area on the Cuyahoga River. The maze of factories includes gigantic steel mills. They help make the city a major supplier of steel wire, wire nails, bolts and nuts.

GROOVES are cut in a steel gear (for an oil tanker) 14 feet 2 inches in diameter. Rough cutting takes 105 hours; the watch-like finishing, 110 hours.

Iron and steel

STACKS of cold-rolled steel are measured at a plant in Ohio. From such rolls an infinite variety of parts for finished articles is stamped out.

266

THE GLOW of open-hearth furnaces frequently lights the nighttime sky over Gary, Indiana, a leader in the production of crude steel.

»

PLANNING an automobile production line. The entire sequence is mapped out, to the tiniest detail, on a table model. Detroit is the world symbol for this kind of industrial know-how.

PARTS for farm tractors are carried by an overhead conveyer belt along the assembly line of a factory in Milwaukee, Wisconsin.

—economic barometer

STEEL PLATES are cut by an ingenious oxygen-torch device that yields several copies at once—and needs only one operator. Plants like this are basic to the whole United States economy because almost every other kind of heavy industry is to some degree dependent on supplies of steel.

PRAIRIE SENTINELS—grain elevators at Hatton, North Dakota. Wheat from the valley of the Red River of the North is stored here, awaiting shipment to markets at home and abroad.

THE CONSOLIDATED SCHOOL at Sterling, North Dakota, takes the place of many little schoolhouses once scattered over the countryside. Busses bring children from a distance.

268

THE EERIE LANDSCAPE of the Badlands of South Dakota. Wind and weather have carved the dry plateau into strange pinnacles and rifts, where scarcely a blade of grass can grow.

PHOTOS, STANDARD OIL CO. (N. J.)

TRIBUTE TO KING CORN—the Corn Palace in Mitchell, South Dakota. All of the decorations, including the murals, on the fantastic building are made of corn, both kernels and cobs.

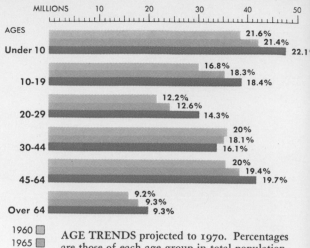

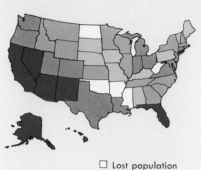

MILLIONS 10 20 30 40 50

AGES

Under 10 — 21.6% / 21.4% / 22.1%

10-19 — 16.8% / 18.3% / 18.4%

20-29 — 12.2% / 12.6% / 14.3%

30-44 — 20% / 18.1% / 16.1%

45-64 — 20% / 19.4% / 19.7%

Over 64 — 9.2% / 9.3% / 9.3%

☐ Lost population
☐ Below 18%   ■ 37-72%
☐ 18-36%   ■ Over 72%

MOST STATE POPULATIONS increased between 1940 and 1960. States in red hues increased above the national average of 36%.

1960 ☐
1965 ☐
1970 ■

AGE TRENDS projected to 1970. Percentages are those of each age group in total population. Population figures are given above.

Population and economic trends in the

NOTABLE SHIFTS are taking place in the population and in the economy. Three major changes in population are illustrated above: movement to the western states—and to Florida —adding to their political as well as economic strength; a decline in the age group 30-44 (the most productive group) while the over-64 group (largely retired) increases; movement to cities and suburbs, making the United States a predominantly urban nation. Economically (see charts below), labor-saving machines, including automation, are helping to bring about increased production of many kinds with fewer employees. This is especially true in agriculture and in such automated industries as petroleum refining. At the same time the city-based service industries have been expanding; today they employ more than half of the work force. Manufacturing continues to hold the lead in dollar value. It is also the base of the coun-

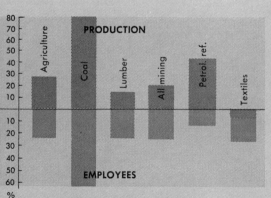

PRODUCTION

Agriculture Coal Lumber All mining Petrol. ref. Textiles

80 70 60 50 40 30 20 10 / 10 20 30 40 50 60 %

EMPLOYEES

RESULTS OF AUTOMATION and the like in major industries. Bars above base line show increase; below, decline—by per cents, at left. Production declined only in textiles but employment declined in all.

NATIONAL INCOME as drawn from six major industrial fields. In each case, figures are given for 1930, 1945 and 1960. Dollar amounts each contributed are shown beside colored bars, with per cent of national income each represents given just below. Manufacturing, for example, yielded $18.2 billions (24%) in 1930; $52 billions (28.5%) in 1945; and $125 billions (30%) in 1960. Agriculture-forestry-fisheries lagged.

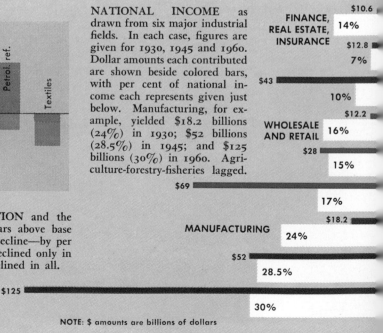

FINANCE, REAL ESTATE, INSURANCE
$10.6 — 14%
$12.8 — 7%
$43 — 10%

WHOLESALE AND RETAIL
$12.2 — 16%
$28 — 15%
$69 — 17%

MANUFACTURING
$18.2 — 24%
$52 — 28.5%
$125 — 30%

NOTE: $ amounts are billions of dollars

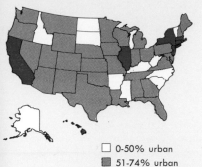

CITIES and suburbs have bulk of population. Figures indicate general percentage of urban dwellers per state.

United States

try's foreign trade, as graphs at right show. Exports are mainly factory products, where imports are raw materials. But as more machinery is exported, fostering manufacture in underdeveloped lands, the old export-import pattern may well be challenged, certainly not immediately but sometime in the future.

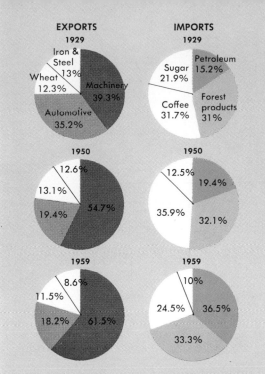

EXPORTS
1929
Iron & Steel 13%
Wheat 12.3%
Machinery 39.3%
Automotive 35.2%

IMPORTS
1929
Petroleum 15.2%
Sugar 21.9%
Coffee 31.7%
Forest products 31%

EXPORTS 1950
12.6%
13.1%
19.4%
54.7%

IMPORTS 1950
12.5%
19.4%
35.9%
32.1%

EXPORTS 1959
8.6%
11.5%
18.2%
61.5%

IMPORTS 1959
10%
24.5%
36.5%
33.3%

FOREIGN TRADE. Pie-graph colors indicate same leading exports and imports as labeled on top two. Percentages stand for the share of each in the total value (in dollars) of exports or imports in the given years.

RELATION of exports and imports to Gross National Product (value of all goods and services produced per year) and world trade. Above base line, whole bar length indicates per cent of total world trade; colored section, per cent of GNP. Below line, length shows dollar value. Figures are at left.

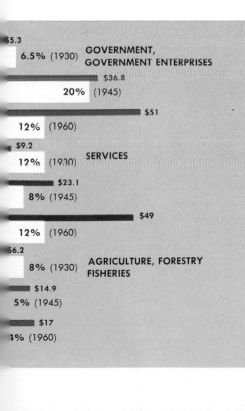

$5.3
6.5% (1930)
GOVERNMENT, GOVERNMENT ENTERPRISES

$36.8
20% (1945)

$51
12% (1960)

$9.2
12% (1930)
SERVICES

$23.1
8% (1945)

$49
12% (1960)

$6.2
8% (1930)
AGRICULTURE, FORESTRY FISHERIES

$14.9
5% (1945)

$17
4% (1960)

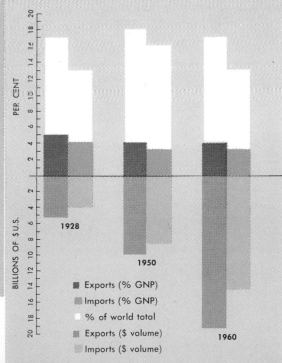

PER CENT
BILLIONS OF $U.S.
20 18 16 14 12 10 8 6 4 2
2 4 6 8 10 12 14 16 18 20

1928
1950
1960

■ Exports (% GNP)
▨ Imports (% GNP)
□ % of world total
▨ Exports ($ volume)
▨ Imports ($ volume)

Mountain and Pacific States

...the far West

THE area usually referred to as the "West" includes eleven states with a total area of 1,187,753 square miles. The mountain states are Montana, Idaho, Wyoming, Colorado, New Mexico, Arizona, Utah and Nevada; the Pacific states are California, Oregon and Washington.

Today these states loom large in the United States' political and economic life. If the rest of the country is growing fast the West is growing faster. It is estimated that by 1970 the East's population will have risen 11 per cent, the Midwest's 10 per cent, but the West's will have shot up 22 per cent. By 1970 the West is also expected to more than match the East in political influence. The West will not only send as many Congressmen to the House and Senate as the East; it may well top the East in electoral votes, by which the president and vice-president are formally elected.

Industrial growth is part of the picture. Until recent years the West had an inadequate labor supply, but today the movement of the American population as a whole is westward. The influx cannot fail to stimulate the economy of the region further. Already the West is turning out about half the steel it consumes.

Because of the mild climate, yielding favorable testing conditions, the West is producing most of the country's aircraft. In addition, with the speed of modern transportation the West has access to the rising Pacific market.

However, it is in light, not heavy, industry that most experts expect the West to expand. More than a quarter of the nation's total electronic equipment is now made along the west coast and in Phoenix, Arizona. The growth of the western market itself is a stimulant to light industry. More people mean a greater demand for construction, consumer goods, and trade and service activities. Statehood for Hawaii and Alaska will no doubt accelerate the trend. It is bringing a welcome touch of economic diversity to the mountain and northwestern states. The economies of Oregon and Washington in particular have been strengthened by a host of new petroleum refineries using imported crude oil, and an upsurge in the chemical industry.

Expansion is not limitless. Development in the West has always been handicapped by the relative scarcity of rainfall east of the rampart of mountains in California, Oregon, Washington and throughout the mountain states. The need for irrigation and power, both served by giant hydroelectric projects, is of prime concern in the West. In this century its wild rivers have been tamed in many places: by the Hoover, Parker and Davis dams on the Colorado River; Fort Peck on the Missouri in northeastern Montana; Grand Coulee, Bonneville and the Dalles on the Columbia; and Shasta on the Sacramento. These have turned thousands of once dry acres into fertile farmland. Water from the Colorado has made the Imperial Valley in southeastern California perhaps the lushest farmland in the world. Without that irrigation the valley would be desert.

Hardly less important to the economy of the West is the power these dams generate. Politics in the West is deeply concerned with development and control of water resources. Should it be in the hands of government or of private concerns?

Vast tracts of magnificent wilderness are held by the Federal Government in the form of national parks, such as Yellowstone. They are set aside to preserve natural beauty and provide recreational and vacation facilities. The United States Government owns 47.7 per cent of the land in the eleven western states, including 87.4 per cent of Nevada and 71 per cent of Arizona.

The ever increasing importance of the West in national affairs is not limited to the purely economic. The universities in this area are carving out an imposing record in science. California Institute of Technology, for example, is second to none in atomic science. Located at Pasadena, its presence, together with the nearby astronomical observatories on Mounts Wilson and Palomar, make southern California a center of scientific research. Its fine public schools should also be mentioned. Some of these states support their primary and secondary schools to an extent unmatched elsewhere. California spends about $35 more per pupil than the national average and pays its teachers more than any other state. The

URANIUM MINE in Utah. The openings lead to the rich layers of ore-bearing rock hidden for eons beneath the dry tableland.

BEDS of desert plants set off the gleaming whiteness of the Mormon Temple, Mesa, Arizona.

ARIZONA CATTLE in feeding pens. The animals are a mixture of Brahman and Hereford stocks.

CRISP CARROTS ready for market, in the fertile, irrigated San Jose Valley, New Mexico.

CRUMBLING ADOBE is all that remains of a pueblo church in New Mexico.

Inheritors of Spanish and Indian traditions —Arizona and New Mexico

"APARTMENT" HOUSES and storage platforms—a Taos, New Mexico, Indian village.

PHOTOS, CAMERA CLIX

states of Oregon and Washington are also among the leaders in both respects.

The West is understandably proud of its present and growing political importance. San Francisco and Los Angeles have each been host to national conventions during recent years. Earl Warren, former Republican governor of California, was appointed chief justice of the Supreme Court in 1953 and has presided over several controversial, far-reaching decisions. Many of the most vocal leaders in both parties today come from this region. An important field of debate between the two parties in this area concerns how far the Federal Government should intervene to spur economic progress. The Democrats usually support government power projects for example while the Republicans prefer the backing of private enterprise. Neither party, however, can claim unbroken allegiance from any of these states. The West is by no means a one-party area, though recent years have seen a steady growth of Democratic strength, particularly on the Congressional level.

The Land

Most of this region was once beneath a great inland sea. Marine fossils have been found eleven thousand feet high in the various ranges of the Rockies, and California has what are called raised beaches which are as much as fifteen hundred feet above the present sea level. For the most part the mountains have undergone a slow elevation through the ages. In the arid southwest there are vast tracts where the sandstone has been eroded into buttes and canyons. Along the Pacific, a line of volcanoes once flamed red where now rise the mountain ramparts. The mountains have innumerable small lakes of great scenic beauty, of which Lake Chelan in Washington is one of the largest; but there are no vast lakes save Great Salt Lake in Utah.

The Pacific states are broken into narrow valleys that lie between the ranges paralleling the ocean. On the west, in Washington, Oregon and California, are the Coast Ranges; on the eastern side of California and extending into central Washington, a generally north-south ridge of higher mountains composed of the Cascade Range in Washington and Oregon and the Sierra Nevada in California. The latter has occasionally been likened to a long granite block with spurs running westward like the teeth of a giant comb. There is an abrupt drop on the eastern face. Now come three vast high plateaus; that to the north is called the Columbia lava plateau, the next, the Great Basin, and that to the south, the Colorado Plateau. As the Cascades and the Sierras rob the winds from the Pacific of their moisture, these plateaus require irrigation where agriculture is practiced. Now come the scattered ranges of the Rocky Mountain system, rising from the Great Plains and the deserts, a part of the rocky backbone of the continent. There the Continental Divide separates the rivers that flow west from those that flow east.

The Pacific coast is uncommonly regular as compared with the Atlantic seaboard, except for the two huge indentations of Puget Sound—a trough once occupied by glaciers—and San Francisco Bay and also the smaller one at San Diego. So narrow is the continental shelf that there are comparatively few islands save in these bays and sounds; the United States Coast Guard is therefore obliged to maintain far fewer lifesaving stations than on the Atlantic seaboard. A warm ocean current that sweeps northward from Japan, then westward and southward keeps the Pacific coast winters mild, though a narrow belt of cold near-shore water causes fog on the coast. West of the Sierra Cascade mountains wall, rains occur in winter. In the higher altitudes of these mountains, however, almost daily thundershowers are common. While the seaward slopes of the Cascades receive exceptional rainfall, from 60 to 120 inches a year, much of the West is semiarid, and in the extreme south arid. People who live around Puget Sound wear rain togs all winter as a matter of course, for when it is not pouring it is likely to be drizzling; but the tourist with an umbrella in southern California may be laughed at. Parts of Arizona are usually entirely

WHITE-FACED HEREFORD CATTLE pause to drink from a cold stream in Wyoming. The backdrop of snow-clad ranges gives some idea of the splendor and spaciousness of the West.

MONUMENT to Buffalo Bill (William F. Cody) at Cody, Wyoming, the town named for him. He had a home there. Every year Cody has a Frontier Ball on his birthday.

BRANDING calves on a Wyoming ranch. Their mothers look on anxiously from a corral at left.

MARBLE SLABS from a quarry in Colorado, which is a leading western producer of the handsome stone.

Beauty and industry
in Colorado and Wyoming

THE GUNNISON RIVER, a branch of the Colorado, lies entirely within the state of Colorado. Part of the Gunnison's winding course is through the spectacular Black Canyon.

279

ATOMIC ENERGY PLANT AT HANFORD, WASHINGTON

Now a vital spot in world affairs, this area on the Columbia River was desert until it was chosen in 1942 as the location of the world's first atomic energy plant. Hanford had fewer than five hundred inhabitants, but it mushroomed during World War II, until its population reached sixty thousand. Today its buildings cover thousands of acres.

rainless. As for temperature, that varies from the Montana blizzard far below zero along the Canadian border and the eternal snows of the high peaks to the 120 degrees above zero in a city of southeastern California where the writer's heels dented the melting asphalt. The vegetation varies likewise, from the gigantic cedars, spruces and Douglas firs of the moist Pacific northwest, the fog-laved coast redwoods of California and the Big Trees of the Sierra to the prickly plants of the desert and their sage-brush and greasewood.

The Southwest has many palms and other sub-tropic plants, while Washington gardens often look not unlike those of Maine. As for wild life, it still abounds in the remoter regions, although the buffalo that once roamed the plains can now be found only within the boundaries of one or two of the National Parks, and wolves are infrequent save for the little yellow coyotes. A few grizzly bears in the Rockies and a few mountain lions (cougars) in various mountain fastnesses are the only formidable creatures left. There are rattlesnakes in the sunny arid places. Elk and deer are still abundant where there are woods; a few mountain sheep and goats are seen by huntsmen in the northern Rockies and wildcats, rabbits, chipmunks and other small animals may be found in abundance. Western birds migrate up and down the rim of the Pacific and the inland waters are usually alive with trout, besides which salmon by the millions swim up the Columbia at spawning time, actually leaping the falls.

The Spanish explorers early wandered into the interior; and while they made no settlements, the later Spanish influence survives to-day—in the southern half of the region, at least—in many words common in western vocabularies, in place-names and in the modified Spanish architecture, with its patios and loggias of native adobe or tinted stucco or Portland cement. The Indian aborigines varied from the Apaches of desert and plain, who once fiercely combatted the white intruder, to the peace-loving Klatsops, at the mouth of the Columbia, who, in an earlier era dwelt in wooden long-houses with totem-poles before their doors and fished in carved high-prowed canoes, and the peace-loving Pueblos of Arizona who for centuries had practiced a crude system of irrigation.

What we know as New Mexico was visited by the Spanish conquistadores over three centuries ago, and the region has had a continuous Spanish civilization, with few changes, since that date; for not until after the war between the United States and Mexico was American influence felt in that region. The Mission Fathers followed in the wake of the adventurers, and old Spanish Missions are still standing here and there throughout the Southwest. At Mission San Carlos

near Monterey lies California's first great missionary, Father Junipero Serra, a Franciscan monk who traveled half the length of the state to bring Christianity to the Indians.

In 1792 Captain Robert Gray, of Boston, sailed in his good ship Columbia into a great river which flowed through what was known as the Oregon Country. This region President Jefferson sent Meriwether Lewis and William Clark to explore. Led by traders of the American Fur Company, which had penetrated as far westward as the Rockies, and by Indian guides, they started in 1804, making their way up the Missouri and across the mountains into the Columbia and keeping such a careful record that it served to guide those who came after them. Now the British George Vancouver, who had served under Captain James Cook, commanded an expedition in 1792 which ex-

EWING GALLOWAY

SHEETS OF PLYWOOD, fresh from the sanding machine, are inspected in a mill at Longview, Washington. The town is one of the most important lumbering centers in the country. It has an excellent site, at the junction of the Cowlitz and Columbia rivers.

SALT FLATS near Great Salt Lake, Utah. Far off, covered with snow, is the Wasatch Range of the Rockies.

A UTAH RANCH snugly sheltered by folded hills. Such ranches are usually given over to the raising of sheep.

CASTLE PEAK, an oddly shaped rock formation near Moab, Utah. Uranium and vanadium are mined not far away.

282

AT BROWNING, Montana—the Museum of the Plains Indians. Inside are costumes, headdresses, utensils.

Under the "big sky" in Utah and Montana

PHOTOS, ERNST PETERSON

BLAZING MOLTEN COPPER pours into casts at a smelter in Anaconda, Montana, a world copper-smelting center.

GIANT SPRINGS are near the Great Falls of the Missouri River, in Montana. The springs help to feed the Missouri.

FROM THREE FORKS in southwestern Montana, where the Jefferson, Madison and Gallatin rivers unite, the mighty Missouri begins its 2,547-mile course to join the Mississippi.

plored Puget Sound on both sides of the island of Vancouver (discovered in 1778 by Cook himself). Both the Northwest Fur Company and the Hudson's Bay Company were active in that region.

Thus the Oregon Country came to be claimed by Great Britain, Spain, Russia and the United States. Spain had laid claim to territory on the west coast, but finally by her treaty selling Florida to the United States, agreed to relinquish claim to anything north of what has become the northern boundary of California. Russia, then occupying Alaska, agreed to remain north of 54° 40′, the present southern boundary of that territory. Great Britain desired the Columbia River as the dividing line, while the United States claimed what has become British Columbia, clear to 54° 40′. The two English-speaking nations compromised on the 49th parallel, which gave Washington to the United States. The Oregon Country was gained by right of exploration and settlement, while the Mexican territory was acquired in the war of 1846–47 fought as the result of conflicting territorial claims. A small part was added by purchase.

As early as 1842 John C. Fremont and his guides began a series of explorations of the Rockies, discovering South Pass, one of the three points at which the Rockies can best be crossed (the oldest is that of the Santa Fé Trail). In 1843 a party of settlers, banded together for protection against hostile Indians, made

FILM EDITORS of a motion-picture studio in Los Angeles check prints of a day's "takes." The movie industry has played a leading role in the rapid growth of Southern California.

their way to Oregon in ox-drawn covered wagons, a journey of five months via Fort Laramie and South Pass; and in 1847 the Mormons followed Brigham Young through South Pass to the Great Salt Lake, which had been discovered by Captain Bonneville in 1832. These Latter-day Saints, who even now constitute three-quarters of the church membership of Utah, brought water from the mountains to irrigate their crops and practically made the state. Later those who branched off the Oregon Trail on the way to California left at Fort Hall for what became known as the Salt Lake Trail. To name but one more of the leading steps in the westward course of empire, Captain J. A. Sutter had built a fort in 1839 on a Mexican land grant on the Sacramento River and at his mill, in 1848, gold was discovered in such large nuggets in the gravel of the river bed as led the great migration known as the gold rush of the

Forty-Niners. People in all walks of life in other parts of the United States and elsewhere went to California, whether by ship around the Horn, over the Isthmus of Panama or across the plains. It was a race in which the winners were the hardiest or the most acute.

A Spanish post and mission had been established on a hilly peninsula on a land-locked inlet of the Pacific, and in 1835 a town was laid out named Yerba Buena for a small flower that abounded. In 1846 a U. S. man-of-war took possession, the name was changed to San Francisco, and three years later it was a gateway to the gold-mines which drew nearly one hundred thousand people to the state in one year. (The Mission Dolores still stands.)

The harbor filled with the sails of all nations, canvas hotels sprang up like mushrooms, a path over the tide-flats was hastily laid of bales of surplus tea, sand-

Playlands in Montana and Idaho

GROTESQUE SHAPES hewed by time in Makoshika Badlands State Park in eastern Montana. Only scrub can grow on such land. The region has severe winters, with howling winds.

A WARM-WATER POOL steams mid the snow at the fabulous resort of Sun Valley, Idaho. The buses take skiers to the slopes. After a day of skimming down snowy trails, one can soothe aching muscles in the steam-heated pool.

CHATCOLET LAKE, in Heyburn State Park, is just south of the much larger Coeur d'Alene Lake, in the beautiful panhandle of Idaho. Through Chatcolet Lake's placid waters the St. Joe River flows, making a distinct channel.

lots were auctioned off, the Spanish dons from the ranches were quickly outnumbered by miners in red flannel shirts and knee boots and all was high enthusiasm.

The Santa Fé Trail, primarily a trade route, led from Independence, Missouri, eventually to Los Angeles, and the ponderous freight-wagons had worn a way both wide and deep in the sun-baked sands. There followed the horse-stages and for two romantic years preceding the first telegraph line, the pony express. In time bands of steel rails were flung across the continent, and while they were ex-

tremely costly, they laid the way to more rapid settlement. Where herds of buffalo had sometimes stopped the trains, the cattle country in time gave way to fields of waving wheat, and later to oil derricks or mine mouths with debris like giant ant-hills; and today the luxurious transcontinental trains offer one radio music while the scenery whizzes by. The Moffat Tube under James Peak penetrates the Continental Divide fifty miles west of Denver, rising to an elevation of nine thousand feet; and there is an electrified tunnel through the Cascade Range a hundred

GIANT HOOVER DAM KEEPS THE COLORADO RIVER UNDER CONTROL

The tremendous power plants below Hoover Dam look like toys when seen from the top of the dam. But if you go down to the plants through one of the towers, you will find the roaring machines that provide electric power for much of California, Arizona and Nevada. Blocked by Hoover Dam, the Colorado River forms Lake Mead, the world's largest artificial lake.

PATIO AND SWIMMING POOL of a luxury hotel on the "strip," in Las Vegas, Nevada. The "strip" is a road leading out of the city, lined with beautiful homes and palatial hotels.

miles east of Seattle. Now great national highways parallel the railroads across deserts and mountains and from Vancouver down the coast to San Diego. The considerable distance of San Francisco and Los Angeles to other population centers made California an important state in the dramatic history of the airplane.

And what of the people who make up the West? While in 1950 the three Pacific states averaged 45 persons to a square mile, the eight Mountain states averaged just about six, that is, 5.9, including Indians; Wyoming has but 2.9 persons to a mile and Nevada averages 1, as compared with 300 of the Middle Atlantic states and the average of 50.6 for the entire United States. Yet the area of the Mountain states is 863,887 or between a third and fourth of the continental United States. Including the Pacific states, the West totals 1,187,753 square miles.

Even today there are mountain and desert regions where one may ride for days without seeing a human habitation, although in other places one finds thronged motor highways, vertical architecture in the downtown districts and shop windows which display the latest styles from the fashion centers.

The stricter laws put through in the 1920's cut off immigration from abroad to a thin trickle. Earlier, however, many newcomers came from northwestern Europe, Canada and Italy and there were a few from China and Japan. People from the Scandinavian countries were particularly attracted to the big lumbering operations of the Northwest. Italians were drawn to the vineyard slopes—reminding them of their sunny homeland—

of California. Seasonal workers flooded across the border from Mexico—some of them illegally. This situation became a serious problem after World War II. For every worker who came in officially there were perhaps five "wetbacks"—as the workers who enter illegally are called. Some of them swim or wade the Rio Grande, hence the name. In an effort to control matters, Mexico and the United States agreed in 1955 to provide more effective border patrols and better living conditions for legal entries.

We can see that in a region of such varied geography, there must be a number of ways for people to earn their livings. Agriculture is possible in certain areas, only by irrigation; but stock-raising may be practiced over large expanses, and where range-cattle cannot find a living, there may be enough forage for sheep, which are able to go for longer periods without water. In the forested regions, lumbering is the leading industry; along the coast and the Columbia, fishing is important, and in the region around Los Angeles, the sinking of oil wells and refining of petroleum take high rank, for California is one of the most important oil states of the Union. The milling of the lumber, the canning of salmon, fruit and vegetables and the milling of wheat flour are to be expected, and California refines Hawaiian sugar. The sunshine of southern California also makes possible a gigantic moving-picture industry, and airplane factories cluster around Los Angeles. In the slopes of the Rockies, mining for copper, silver and lead is of tremendous importance.

Where People Own Their Farms

In this division of the country, farms are, in the majority of cases, worked by owners though tenancy is increasing rapidly. The proportion of tenancy in some of the Mountain states is somewhat less than in the Pacific states. The farms of the Mountain states are on the average somewhat larger than those of the Pacific states, though there are many great tracts under one management in California particularly. Many years ago tall stories were told of the "bonanza farms" so large that a man could plow only a furrow or two in a day. There are now some enormous farms worked almost entirely by machinery where tractors pull many ploughs and wheat is reaped and threshed in one operation by combines. On the other hand, there are many small farms and orchards upon which the farmer's family does all, or nearly all, of the regular work.

On many of the farms of these Western states, wheat and hay are the principal staple crops, aside from the fruits and vegetables of certain limited regions. Washington recently has run second to Montana in its wheat crops with Idaho and Oregon next. These two groups of states usually produce something less than a fourth of the total wheat crop. The proportion of hay produced in the section is about the same as of wheat, that is between a fourth and a fifth.

A Famous Fruit Region

One is likely to think first of California fruit, but some years California's leading single crop is hay. In that mild, dry climate successive crops of alfalfa may be raised and the hay of the state all put together amounts to very nearly five million tons a year. But California produces millions of boxes of oranges, to say nothing of apples, peaches, pears, lemons, prunes, apricots, figs and grapes—wine, table and raisin. California truck-farms produce millions of dollars worth of lettuce alone. The Inland Empire east of the high ranges in Washington and the Hood River Valley of Oregon are two regions which raise quantities of fine apples. Oregon is also famous for its berries, especially loganberries, which spring up quickly when planted on cutover or burned lands and have been known to send out runners fifty feet in length the first season. California's long interior valley between the Sierras and the Coast Range is one of the richest in the world and the Imperial Valley in the extreme south is fertile. But in much of the West irrigation is necessary and Colorado, for one, has an extensive system of canals which have long been the property of the

A CABLE CAR takes sight-seers up Mount Manitou Incline, which is near Pikes Peak. From the top of the mountain, there is a sweeping view of the eastern ranges of Colorado's Rockies.

state. Since 1902 a Federal Reclamation Service has established irrigation projects where, by intensive cultivation, even deserts have been made to yield food for men or cattle, although sometimes the costs exceed the productive capacity of the land.

Cattle-ranching Important

On the vast ranges of these states are millions and millions of cattle. Colorado has the largest number among the Mountain states with Montana next while California leads among the Pacific states. There are some great ranches though most such establishments as we read about in stories of the Old West have been broken up. Much of the public lands on which the cattle ranged has passed into private hands, and cattle are no longer allowed to roam at will in the national forests.

At one time the wild horses appeared to be on the point of disappearing, but their numbers seem to have increased. In some regions they have become a pest, as they eat the grass needed for cattle and themselves have little value. There are half-wild horses upon ranches which are broken with difficulty. This was the origin of the rodeos which are now held as a spectacle to which tourists and others pay admission. Some of the horses are trained to buck and rear to excite the wonder of the tenderfoot. Montana and Colorado have the greatest numbers of ranch horses but motor cars, motor trucks and tractors are being substituted for horse power both in town and country. Strange to say, many people still believe that the wild horses are native to America. As a matter of fact, they are descendants of the Spanish horses which escaped from the early explorers, and also from many strays which have run away from their owners and joined their free kindred.

Where the forage is too scanty for cattle, sheep can find a living. Almost half of the sheep in the United States are in these two groups of states. Montana is usually first with California next but all these states have many sheep and are extensive producers of wool. Wyoming leads in wool production with Montana second and California third.

Wealth of Mines and Timber

There is more lumber produced in the Pacific states than anywhere else in the continental United States—in fact, 44.9 per cent of the whole amount (besides wood pulp, shingles, turpentine and rosin). The Pacific states are producing more than fourteen billion board feet per year. Unfortunately, the dry summers see many destructive forest fires.

While the fisheries produce much wealth, the mines of the Western states are the largest producers of wealth. The figures of mineral production are stupendous, though gold and silver no longer hold their proud positions. Some of the commoner metals now have a greater annual value than that of gold and silver. Copper, for example, has a much greater value than gold. Arizona is the great copper state, followed by Utah and Montana though all of these states produce more or less of this useful metal. In fact, Michigan is the only important producer of copper outside of these two groups of states. The humble lead is worth more than the gold. Idaho leads the West, with Utah, Arizona and Montana following.

Petroleum and natural gas are the most valuable mineral products of the Western states as of the country as a whole. California is the chief producer though Wyoming and New Mexico furnish appreciable quantities and several other states produce less. California, in fact, is one of the chief oil producing states in the nation.

Mineral Production in the West

The Western states produce about three-fourths of the gold and nearly all the silver mined in the United States proper. California is first in gold with Utah next, in the section (South Dakota in another group is actually first). Idaho is easily first in silver with Montana generally second though in some years Utah is ahead. Arizona, Colorado and Nevada are also large producers of silver. Much of the silver secured is a by-product from mines worked for copper, lead or zinc.

Western educational facilities are good. Every state has a state university. Men from all of the Mountain states attend the University of California, with its main headquarters at Berkeley and a branch at Los Angeles. The university is by far the largest in the West and in point of numbers ranks as one of the three largest in the United States. Its southern branch includes Scripps Institution of Oceanography at La Jolla and Lick Astronomical Department at Mount Hamilton, where the dry, clear air is wonderful for observing the stars. Other well-known astronomical observatories in California are at Mount Wilson, near Pasadena, and at Palomar, near San Diego. Palomar's 200-inch telescope is the world's largest. Stanford University, near Palo Alto, has been provided with a remarkably large endowment, over $39,000,000, much of it given in memory of the boy whose name it bears. The University of Southern California has more than 17,000 students enrolled. There are many denominational and independent colleges. The Mormon Church in Utah maintains the Brigham Young University and the Latter Day Saints University, which has a business college and night school. But there is not space for mention of all the educational facilities of the West. There is a general desire for education, and every state has compulsory education. There is a good showing of every kind of school from primary to normal, state university and private institution, especially in proportion to the population.

Hardy, self-reliant, brave to the point of daring were those first pioneers into the unknown West. The virtues of the times—which the survivors handed in large degree to their progeny—were courage and enterprise, generosity to those in need and summary justice for the fugitives from eastern justice and other "bad men" who showed no respect for life and the means to life, notably, horses. Toward the few women of the early days there was a gallantry which made them safe to a degree seldom met in the world's history. Initiative and creative energy still stamp the western mind, as does an intellectual independence and readiness to

Courtesy Reno Chamber of Commerce

PYRAMID LAKE SPIRES, SET IN THE RUGGED TABLELAND OF NEVADA

Most of Nevada, a huge state of but little more than 160,000 population (including Indians), lies in the Great Basin from four to five thousand feet above the level of the sea. Broken by buttes and high ranges, its valleys contain a few lakes like those above, and more mud lakes up to fifty miles in length but only a few inches deep, which evaporate in summer.

experiment on a large scale. As one outcome, certain of the western states were the first to grant equal suffrage. A fondness for exploration and a readiness to rough it has led to an unusual degree of camping and mountaineering. Local patriotism runs high. There are historical pageants like one once held at Eugene, Oregon, which displayed covered wagons and the Indian dugout canoes. There are flower festivals—tulips in Washington, roses in Oregon, and on every New Year's Day in Pasadena a Rose Tournament is held in which thousands of flowers of every kind are wound about floats from nearly every town in southern California, before something very like a Spanish fiesta. California celebrates not only Admission Day, the anniversary of the date when the state was admitted to the Union, but every New Year's Eve holds a "Mardi Gras." There is cheerful rivalry among the smaller cities, and the standard joke

of cosmopolitan San Francisco is to ask anyone from Los Angeles, "What part of Iowa did *you* come from?"

Parts of the West still contain a few isolated communities reached only by horse-drawn mountain stages, which up to the turn of the century were common almost everywhere in the country districts. Travelers wore linen dusters—for good reason—and so few were the places on the winding mountain roads where two vehicles might pass that the driver watched for the approaching spiral of dust that betokened an oncoming team. In remote valleys people exchanged their surplus produce and lent mutual aid at house raisings, and entire families drove long distances to parties, where the grandmothers put the babies all to bed in some one room. It was a friendly West—and still is. Even the cities are not like those of the East. The people in them are less formal than the Easterners.

THE MOUNTAIN AND PACIFIC STATES: FACTS AND FIGURES

POPULATION (States and Important Cities)

The areas of states, in square miles, are in parentheses after the names; state capitals are in italic letters.

ARIZONA (113,909), 1,282,000; *Phoenix,* 431,-000; Tucson, 210,000.

CALIFORNIA (158,693), 15,507,000; *Sacramento,* 191,000; Anaheim; 103,000; Berkeley, 108,000; Fresno, 132,000; Glendale, 118,000; Long Beach, 329,000; Los Angeles, 2,450,000; Oakland, 361,000; Pasadena, 115,000; San Diego, 545,000; San Francisco, 716,000; San Jose, 203,000; Torrance, 101,000.

COLORADO (104,247), 1,735,000; *Denver,* 489,-000.

IDAHO (83,557), 663,000; *Boise,* 34,000.

MONTANA (147,138), 670,000; *Helena,* 20,000.

NEVADA (110,540), 282,000; *Carson City,* 5,000; Las Vegas, 64,000.

NEW MEXICO (121,666), 944,000; *Santa Fe,* 34,000; Albuquerque, 199,000.

OREGON (96,981), 1,758,000; *Salem,* 46,000; Portland, 370,000.

UTAH (84,916), 887,000; *Salt Lake City,* 189,-000.

WASHINGTON (68,192), 2,824,000; *Olympia,* 18,000; Seattle, 551,000; Spokane, 180,000; Tacoma, 147,000.

WYOMING (97,914), 328,000; *Cheyenne,* 43,-000.

PRODUCTION (Agriculture and Industry)

Agricultural products of Pacific coast states: apples, peaches, prunes, pears, citrus fruits, apricots, cherries, berries of all kinds, nuts and vegetables, which are either dried, preserved or shipped fresh.

Agricultural products of western states and Pacific coast states: wheat (Montana and Washington); hay (California, Montana and Oregon); sugar beets (Colorado and Utah); cotton (California and Arizona). Cattle and sheep ranching is important in all these states. The area supplies much of the country's fruit and vegetables, most of its wool, some fish and a considerable amount of its timber (Washington and Oregon).

Mineral products: silver (Utah, Montana, Idaho, Arizona and Colorado), copper (Arizona, Utah, Montana and New Mexico), petroleum (California), asbestos, lead, zinc and wolfram (tungsten). The western states account for 98% of the country's silver, 75% of the gold and over 95% of the copper.

Manufacturing (mainly in coastal metropolitan areas): lumber, aircraft, machinery, electronic goods, motion pictures, petroleum products and preserved foods. Though the West has long depended on agriculture and mining, manufacturing industries are expanding rapidly. By 1959 the West was producing about half the steel it needed.

SUN AND SNOW and the Swiss-chalet look of the buildings make a winter wonderland of Sun Valley, Idaho.   Skiing is a popular sport of many mountain sections of the West.

VAST FIELDS OF CROPS, as well as grazing lands, spread across the broad valleys and Plains of Montana. Hay, fodder for livestock, is cut and stacked with modern machinery.

RODEO DAY is the big event of the year in many a mountain-state town. Horse races, trick riding, broncobusting and steer roping are among the most popular cowboy contests.

ASAHEL CURTIS

AWE-INSPIRING MOUNT RAINIER VIEWS ITSELF IN MIRROR LAKE

The ice-clad volcanic peak rises more than fourteen thousand feet above sea level in the Cascade Range in the state of Washington. The Indians named it Tacoma, "the mountain that was God." Mount Rainier National Park, with its deep conifer forests and glaciers, attracts motorists and campers; and the towering peak challenges daring mountain climbers.

The Old West and the New in Nevada and California

LOG FORT at Genoa, Nevada. Here the Mormons founded the first permanent white settlement in the state, 1851.

GHOST TOWN—Virginia City, Nevada. The tremendous Comstock Lode (silver) was discovered on the site in 1857.

MILE-HIGH LAKE TAHOE lies between the Sierra Nevada and the Carson Range, on the California-Nevada line.

GOLDEN WEALTH in California—oil derricks, pumping "liquid gold," framed in a grove of luscious ripe oranges.

FISHERMAN'S WHARF, San Francisco. Here the fleet comes in, heaped high with the sea's bounty. The restaurants on the wharf are world-famous.

THE AMAZING EFFECT of sweeping curves and mountain terraces results from open-pit copper mining at Bingham, Utah. Trains chug along the various levels, carrying out the ore.

INDIANS of the Northwest, like generations of their forefathers, net and spear the big salmon that fight their way over rapids and falls of the frothy Columbia River to spawn.

WILD RHODODENDRON in flower at the base of Mount Hood, the highest point in Oregon. One can climb the peak on an aerial tramway.

SEA LIONS sun themselves on a slippery ledge above the swirling Pacific. Such sights are among the pleasures of touring the Oregon Coast Highway.

302

Resources and eye-catching vistas in the Northwest

GENERATORS in a power house at Grand Coulee Dam, Washington. The generators transform the force of the Columbia River into vast amounts of electric current.

FISH TRAP on the Wind River (southern Washington), a branch of the Columbia. Eggs taken from the salmon caught are raised in nearby hatcheries. These help to keep the Columbia stocked.

APPLE-PICKING TIME near Wenatchee, Washington. The city, in the center of a marvelous fruit-growing region, is called the "apple capital of the world."

TRIAL BY ORDEAL—in Nome, Alaska, style—all in a spirit of fun. Any occasion—a holiday, a birthday, a new baby—serves to toss someone in a blanket. Not even the victim minds although he had better be agile.

Alaska and Hawaii

...the forty-ninth and fiftieth states

ON July 4, 1959, forty-nine stars blazed forth in the blue field of the Stars and Stripes; and since July 4, 1960, the field has had an array of fifty stars. Thus the design of the flag, which had forty-eight stars from 1912, has been altered to give place to the states of Alaska and Hawaii. By long custom the star representing a new state is always added on Independence Day. Alaska officially entered the Union on January 3, 1959; and Hawaii, on August 21, 1959.

Despite extreme contrasts in such features as size, climate and topography, Alaska and Hawaii have several things in common. Both were territories for a long period. The United States bought Alaska from Russia, for $7,200,000, not long after the Civil War, in 1867. The Hawaiian Islands were annexed, at the request of the numbers of Americans and Europeans already living there, in 1898. (Hawaii's last monarch, Queen Liliuokalani, had been forced to abdicate in 1893.) In part, however, because of the Klondike gold rush at the turn of the century, which spilled over from the Yukon into Alaska, the efforts to win statehood began in these same years in both territories. They entered the Union in less than a year of each other.

Neither Alaska nor Hawaii has any

304

TUNA FISHING in Hawaiian waters, which swarm with a variety of delicious food fish and crustaceans.

land continuation with the other states. Alaska is separated by Canada; and Hawaii lies more than two thousand miles out in the Pacific. Noncontiguity, in fact, was one of the major arguments against statehood.

On the other hand, because of their location, both states have unique value in the defense of the country. There are sixteen major military installations in Hawaii today, including the base at Pearl Harbor. Alaska, with northern Canada, guards the polar and most direct approaches to the whole of North America from the heart of Eurasia. Thus the DEW Line, the chain of radar stations

extending westward from Baffin Island, is joined at Cape Lisburne (north of Bering Strait) by the West Wall. This is another chain of electronic signal stations. From headlands and peaks they watch over Bering Strait and Sea. Six radar stations in the Aleutians continue the line of sentinels out to Umnak Island. Since 1958, clear reception even during the magnetic storms that sweep Alaska has been insured by the "White Alice" system. White Alice is a code name for the network of sixty-foot radio screens perched high in the mountains.

Defense expenditures are therefore extremely important to the economy of both

THE HARBOR at Honolulu where large oceangoing ships dock. In the foreground, just behind the vessel, is the Aloha Tower. At picture's top is another landmark, Diamond Head. Waikiki Beach, a narrow strip, is on this side of Diamond Head.

PINEAPPLE FIELDS on Kauai. Intensive cultivation requires an investment of several thousand dollars an acre.

POTTING ORCHIDS. Some 700 species, wild and cultivated, thrive.

H. ARMSTRONG ROBERTS

IRVING ROSEN, SHOSTAL

DOWNTOWN in Honolulu. Besides banks and offices there are many smart shops with the latest styles.

THE CREW winning an outrigger race is welcomed by an Aloha Week "king." During Aloha Week, in the autumn, the islands' story is celebrated in colorful pageants.

Hawaii, the Pacific-island state

WEEDING TARO in a flooded field. Taro has a starchy rootstock. This is cooked, pounded into a paste and allowed to ferment. The Hawaiian food poi results.

VOLCANO in eruption on Hawaii island. The crater is part of the Kilauea field, itself on the flank of Mauna Loa.

JOHN LEWIS STAGE, PHOTO RESEARCHERS

JOHN LEWIS STAGE, PHOTO RESEARCHERS

307

states. They amount to $327,000,000 a year in Hawaii, almost two fifths of the state's total income. In Alaska during 1958, contracts for military construction alone came to $75,000,000.

Tourism thrives in both states. Alaska offers majestic mountain scenery; and Hawaii the delights of tropical islands with natural air conditioning, the balmy trade winds. Air travel has made both states easily accessible, and both hope that statehood will heighten interest in their vacation possibilities.

With the admission of Alaska and Hawaii to the Union the westward trend of the American population has been strengthened. Western representation in Congress has thereby been increased, in turn weakening the Southern bloc.

In the mind of the average person Hawaii is typified by pineapple, sugar cane and girls swaying to the strum of ukuleles. Alaska calls up vivid images of Eskimo families in fur parkas, of bushy sled dogs, of salmon canneries and of great brown bears weighing more than half a ton. Neither picture is quite true today.

Hawaii

The Hawaiian Islands are one of the few places under the American flag where the same clothes can be worn Christmas Day as on the Fourth of July. In Honolulu, capital city of this picturesque state, the average temperature for the month of December is 73 degrees. During mid-summer, in July, it is barely 5 degrees warmer, 77.9.

These steadfast temperatures give to life in "the Islands" a languid, restful quality. Bathing in the tepid ocean is the most frequent recreation. Newcomers are surprised to find hard coral beaches rather than soft sand underfoot. At any time of the year a hostess can pile her guests' plates high with luscious fruit from her own garden—pineapples, avocados, bananas.

The big ships from the mainland move slowly into Honolulu harbor. Brown-skinned girls weave gently in their famous hula dance, which is done more with the hands than with the hips and which has a

symbolic meaning deep in Hawaiian tradition. The "grass skirt" worn by the dancers is not made of grass at all but from fresh ti leaves. The ti plant sprouts a long, dark green leaf that resembles the leaf of the banana tree.

This is the romantic side of Hawaii, more often than not simply for show, though island hospitality is genuine. Actually the fiftieth state is bustling.

Island Economy

In spite of the languorous climate the 600,000 people of the islands have created a prosperous economy. Indeed, the Federal Government at Washington, D. C., collects more money in taxes annually from the residents of the Hawaiian Islands than from the taxpayers of any of eleven of the other states of the Union with small populations. Hawaiians are civic-minded. About 95 per cent of Hawaii's registered voters participated in the 1959 elections.

Sugar cane is the basic industry. Production of sugar in a recent year totaled 1,085,000 tons, an immense crop valued at $144,000,000. One out of every eight working Hawaiians is on a sugar payroll. Pineapple, a symbol of Hawaii to all the world, ranks next among the industries of these verdant islands. The first seafaring men on the broad Pacific reveled in the taste of Hawaiian pineapple. In one year Hawaii shipped to the mainland 30,000,000 cases of pineapple products. This sweet fruit with its distinctive flavor was worth $113,000,000 that year. Most of the companies now processing the zestful fruit have existed in one form or another since Americans first came to Hawaii. Mechanization, however, has reduced employment in the fields.

Sugar plantations and waving fields of pineapple are expected in Hawaii. The islands' cattle ranches are not so well known. Yet Hawaii produces $30,000,000 worth of livestock products a year. White-faced cattle graze on lush uplands which look down dizzily on the blue sea. These ranches are patrolled by hard-riding cowboys, as handy and accomplished on horseback as any in Arizona or Texas.

SURF, SUN AND CORAL SAND AT WAIKIKI BEACH

Tropical vacation paradise of the Pacific is Hawaii with its fabulous beaches and clear waters so popular with surf-board enthusiasts. Diamond Head on Oahu Island rises in the background.

An extraordinarily large proportion of the fertile land of the islands is devoted to agriculture. The farms of Hawaii yield $2,700,000 worth of coffee beans annually, in addition to diversified dairy products for the ever increasing population.

The term "Hawaii" is all inclusive. It refers to the eight islands that form the Hawaiian group; yet the name actually comes from the single island of Hawaii, largest in size of the chain. The Hawaiian Islands together have a total area of 6,454 square miles. This is comparatively small as states of the Union run, yet it exceeds the respective areas of Rhode Island, Delaware and Connecticut.

Strangely enough, it is not the dominant island of Hawaii that is the best-known in the Hawaiian group. This honor is reserved for the third largest island in area—Oahu. Honolulu, with half the people of all the islands inside its municipal boundaries, lies on Oahu. And Oahu is the site of the great American naval base of Pearl Harbor. It was here, on December 7, 1941, that occurred the act which the late President Franklin D. Roosevelt said would "live in infamy." When Pearl Harbor was bombed without warning by Japanese planes, the United States was brought into World War II as an active belligerent.

Many Japanese-Americans live in the Hawaiian Islands. They formed the heroic 442nd Battalion, which fought through the Italian campaign and made a brilliant record in battles and campaigns. In spite of the presence of numerous residents of brown skin and Oriental extraction, Hawaii never has been seriously plagued with racial troubles. Democracy has attained a high level in the islands and there is little discrimination. In 1950, people of many ancestries took part in a

PHOTOS, HAWAII VISITORS BUREAU

A WARRIOR KING

Before Honolulu's Judiciary Building stands a statue of King Kamehameha I, the Great.

309

JUNEAU, the capital, has a superb setting—between Mounts Juneau and Robert and the Gastineau Channel.

«

FAIRBANKS from the air. The lively city, which serves as the commercial center for east-central Alaska, is developing rapidly. New structures include several skyscrapers.

IN SUMMER, short but warm, the beach near Anchorage becomes a gay playground. The Chugach Mountains tower in the background. New port facilities opened Anchorage to ocean trade in 1961.

ST. LAWRENCE ISLAND, barren tundra, lies in the Bering Sea near the entrance to Norton Sound. The vapor trails in the sky are of Russian jets flying over Siberia, which here is only about fifty miles away.

Alaska—state of the far northwest

PHOTO RESEARCHERS   PHOTO RESEARCHERS

A HOMESTEADER rests for a moment from digging potatoes on his Kenai farm. He fishes for salmon in season.

WHALING CAMP near Point Barrow, the northernmost tip of Alaska. Arctic whaling is a small home Eskimo industry; commercial whalers today go to the Antarctic.

HERDS OF CARIBOU wander over the tundra of northern Alaska, in July, searching out their favorite food, lichens. Only such tiny plants can survive in this bleak area. When winter comes the herds will migrate south. Many Eskimos depend on the caribou.

CHARLES OTT, SHOSTAL

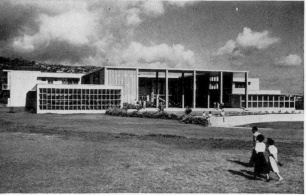

SCHOOL DAYS IN THE TROPICS

The modern style of the administration building
of the University of Hawaii suits the climate.

convention to draft a constitution for the
prospective state of Hawaii. The docu-
ment was modeled after the constitutions
of the United States and of the state of
California.

Visitors to these islands always are
amazed by the great variety in geography.
These "lily pads" in the Pacific do not
conform to the notion of tropical islands
as flat places. The island of Kauai, for
example, is split by awesome Waimea
Canyon, a deep chasm that rivals any
abyss on the mainland except the Grand
Canyon of the Colorado. Mauna Loa, a
mountain battlement on the island of Hawaii, soars to 13,784 feet. Mauna Loa is
actually more massive in circumference
than either Mount Whitney in California
or Mount Rainier in Washington.

Sun visors, shorts, bathing suits, toeless
sandals, beach umbrellas—these are the
standard garb and equipment. Few days
pass without sunshine. A savage rain
squall may drench Honolulu fiercely for
half an hour, but then the sun will pierce
through the overcast and soak up the water
that has fallen to earth. Annual rainfall
in the capital city is rarely more than
thirty-two inches—less than in New York
or Seattle or Portland, Oregon.

In the islands people of Japanese an-
cestry outnumber the Caucasians. Yet
the boys and girls of these families are
educated together in a modern public-

school system, and the relation between
races is one of comradeship. In Hawaii
130,000 children are enrolled in public
schools and 28,000 in private schools.
Teachers are well paid, and there is always a long waiting list of men and women
from the mainland who hope to voyage to
Hawaii to teach. The University of Hawaii offers degrees in scientific and liberal
arts subjects, and its athletic teams compete frequently with colleges from "the
States." Spectators at football games in-
variably marvel at Hawaiian punters who
can kick a ball fifty yards with their bare
toes. They forget that these young men
have run across the firm coral beaches
without footgear almost since they could
toddle. The University of Hawaii is a
land-grant college like many of the schools
in states west of the Mississippi River.

Under territorial status, Hawaii's government was largely a patchwork. The
governor was appointed by the president of the United States. Any law
passed by the Hawaiian legislature could
be set aside by Congress. Yet even before statehood, Hawaiian citizens were
paying more than $81,000,000 a year in

HAWAIIAN COUTURIERES

No souvenir of Hawaii is more popular than the
"grass" skirt these girls are making of ti leaves.

federal taxes. As a state, Hawaii elects its own governor as well as the two senators and one representative who are sent to Congress. In short, it has a government like the other states.

Hawaii lays a claim on the heart of its visitors. As a great liner puts out to sea from Honolulu harbor, the people on shore sing ALOHA to their friends. The plaintive strains of Hawaiian music come across the smooth water. *Aloha* means "good-by" in the lilting language of the native people of the islands. The hard, stern realities of life must be faced again. The pleasant and placid routine of Hawaii

Nenana during the long summer days, bare-chested men frequently load river-boats in sweltering temperatures that touch 100 degrees above zero. Few places on earth record such startling contrasts.

Alaska's forests contain seventy-eight *billion* board-feet of timber. These trees, harvested on a basis of perpetual yield, could supply at least 25 per cent of the newsprint needed on the continent. Early in the 1950's, construction began on the first pulp mill in the North, near Ketchikan, Alaska's principal salmon-packing center. Other mills are eventually planned for Sitka, Juneau, Wrangell

ALASKA DEVELOPMENT BOARD

THE BUSH PILOT DOES HIS PART
The busy Alaskan bush pilot carries both mail and passengers long distances. Here a pilot has landed his plane, equipped with pontoons, on the Taku River, in southeastern Alaska

fades on the horizon. Jack London once wrote that anyone who spent a month in these sunny islands was sure to return before he died.

Alaska

Alaska, land of contrasts, ascends to the 20,300-foot summit of Mount McKinley, loftiest spot in North America, and it has a longer coastline than the rest of the Union. Alaska includes lonely valleys that have never been mapped and bustling cities where a vacant room is rarely available. Winter temperatures often drop to 75 degrees below zero, with anti-freeze solution hardening in automobile radiators. Yet despite its latitude, only 3 per cent of Alaska is permanently blanketed with ice and snow. At Fort Yukon or

and Petersburg. The names of some of these communities indicate the Russian influence in the settlement of Alaska.

From 1940 to 1957 the population of Alaska shot from 72,000 people to very nearly 165,000. This is a 130 per cent increase, largest anywhere under American sovereignty. Most of the recent newcomers have migrated northward to Anchorage and Fairbanks to work on defense projects. A few years ago Anchorage was a tiny outpost. Now it has housing developments, two newspapers, bus routes, department stores, wide avenues and many hotels. These burgeoning Alaskan communities are inhabited by two or three men to every woman. A pretty nurse or school teacher arriving from the states is barraged with early proposals of marriage.

However, local authorities advise women not to migrate to Alaska until they are sure of a place to live. Residential quarters often cannot be obtained for any price.

As Alaska has become a state, Texas has lost its claim to first in size. Alaska measures 586,400 square miles, approximately twice the size of Texas. In addition, Alaska extends so far from west to east that it lies within three different time zones, which are spoken of in the north as "Yukon time," "Alaska time" and "Aleutian time." At its longest and widest points, if we include the great Aleutian archipelago, Alaska is longer and wider than all the other states together. During World War II the Aleutian Islands became the first North American soil (north of the Rio Grande) to feel an invader's tread in nearly a century and a half. Imperial Japanese troops landed on Kiska and Attu but later were expelled by American soldiers fighting in damp cold and chilling fogs.

At the time of the Aleutian invasion, a

CANADIAN NATIONAL RAILWAYS

TRIPLETS ON A TOTEM POLE

These curiously carved figures decorate the totem pole of a chief, on Wrangell Island.

1,523-mile highway was pushed through the spruce solitudes, as an emergency route to Alaska, by seven regiments of the United States Army Engineer Corps. Later the road was widened and steel bridges were built by civilian workers. Until the completion of this highway, Alaska was to all intents and purposes an island—as cut off by the Canadian wilderness as an island is by the sea. But in 1951, for the first time in history, more people migrated to Alaska by land than by boat. These newcomers arrived over the Alaska Highway. Out of the total of 22,-507 men, women and children who drove to Alaska on the gravel road, more than 5,880 stayed on to make their homes.

The airplane also has had a profound influence on modern-day Alaska. Once a wilderness family was cut off completely after the first "big snows" had fallen. A serious illness might mean death because no doctor could get through drifts as high as a lodgepole pine. Now a plane on skis can land almost anywhere that there is open country. The "bush pilot" is to the Alaska of the 1950's what the dog-musher was to the Alaska of 1898, when gold was

ALASKA DEVELOPMENT BOARD

OLD RUSSIAN CHURCH AT KODIAK

This church, with its Russian-style cupola, is a reminder that Alaska once belonged to Russia.

found in the Klondike and in other murmuring creeks of the north.

Alaskan cities now get home delivery of mail. This, too, is directly attributable to the airplane. The old mail schedule of one or two boats a week never justified the maintenance of a force of letter carriers. As a result, all Alaskans were compelled to pick up their mail at the post office. Anchorage had more central-station post-office boxes than even New York City. Now the plane comes with mail every day and so the mailman in his familiar gray uniform is justified at last.

Fisheries are still the principal industry. Alaska produces 88 per cent of the canned salmon sold in American stores. The annual salmon pack is worth about $60,000,-000. Many Alaskans, both Indian and white, troll for salmon offshore in small boats. The large king salmon, or *tyee*, is caught in the southeast and the smaller red salmon in Bristol Bay, near the Bering Sea. Many salmon are snared in fish traps, huge timbered chambers fitted with nets and placed near the mouths of rivers where salmon spawn. Most Alaskans believe these devices threaten the future of the fisheries and they have petitioned Congress to outlaw the traps.

It costs a great deal to live in the new state, even by present-day inflationary standards. A dozen eggs may sell for $1.50, a quart of milk for 35 cents. Haircuts are $2.00 in Fairbanks. Soldiers at Alaskan bases during the war were accustomed to paying 75 cents for a milkshake. Wages are correspondingly high and a carpenter helping to erect a barracks may earn $750 a month. It is often easy come, easy go. Thousands of dollars are wagered on the exact day, hour, minute and second when the ice pack will drift out of the great Tanana River. Perhaps this attitude toward money is due to the preponderance of men and the absence of a hearth and home life.

Tuberculosis has been a particularly grim problem. Some Indian and Eskimo tribes are wracked by the world's highest death rate from tuberculosis, higher even than in famine areas of India and China. For many years nothing was done about this. However, not long ago a governor of Alaska, Ernest Gruening, himself a medical doctor, established Alaska's first

JUNEAU, THE CAPITAL OF ALASKA

Juneau, in southeastern Alaska, on the Gastineau Channel, is the main port of the state. It nestles between the water and the slopes of Mount Juneau and Mount Robert, rising behind.

full-time Department of Health. Hospitals and clinics are being built. A converted Navy vessel, now called S. S. Hygiene, cruises into fiords taking chest X rays of native families. Infected adults and children are immediately isolated from healthy tribespeople so the plague will not spread farther.

Alaska is a lively, tingling realm. Its people are typical frontiersmen. They face danger bravely and seldom quail from hardships, even in sports. Alaskans compete in dog-team races with scarlet-coated Canadian Mounties from Whitehorse across the border. A high-school basket ball team may fly eight hundred miles to oppose the team in the next town. This is equivalent to the distance between New York and Chicago. Alaskan children trudging through the woods to school have been taught to freeze into silence if they hear an ominous growl. It may come from a Kodiak brown bear, the largest meat-eating creature that stalks the earth. Many youngsters catch a fifty-pound salmon before they weigh much more than that themselves.

Indians and Eskimos comprise 20 per cent of Alaska's total population. At one time these people were the victims of discrimination and could not share equally in the use of hotels, theaters and other public places. But in 1945 the territorial legislature at Juneau enacted a civil-rights bill ending such abuses. Six natives have sat as members of the legislature, and a full-blooded Tlingit Indian has served as president of the Alaskan Senate.

Juneau, the capital, is the farthest north seat of government in the Western Hemisphere. It lies on a narrow lava shelf between the salt waters of Gastineau Channel and the great sheer rock precipices of Mount Robert and Mount Juneau. Old Greek Orthodox churches, relics of the Russian occupation of almost a century ago, contrast vividly with the marble pillars of the Federal Building, where the American flag flies. In summer, when the hours of darkness are short, Juneau's people play tennis, hike up the towering mountain and swim in the icy waters fed by near-by glaciers. As statehood has come, with its exciting elections and self-government, gossip about politics has been added to the pastimes of this capital in the glow of the midnight sun.

By RICHARD L. NEUBERGER

ALASKA AND HAWAII: FACTS AND FIGURES

Alaska includes extreme northwestern part of North America and the Aleutian Islands. Bounded on the north by Arctic Ocean, south and southwest by Gulf of Alaska and Pacific Ocean, west by Bering Sea and Strait and east by Yukon Territory and British Columbia. Total area, 586,400 square miles; population 224,100 (1960). Became the 49th state of the Union in 1958, with 2 senators and 1 representative in the national Congress. State government is under an elected governor and a legislature of two houses. The raising of fur animals, fishing, forestry and mining are the principal industries. Exports are salmon, herring, copper, furs, shellfish and gold; imports are iron and steel, tin cans, machinery, mineral oil, meats, provisions and explosives. Road mileage, 4,200; railway mileage, 509. Chief means of transport is by air lines. Telephone, telegraph and radio link Alaska and Canada and the other states. Education compulsory through age 16; schools under Department of Education; also schools for natives under Alaska Native Service. Populations of chief towns: Juneau (capital), 6,350; Anchorage, 43,750.

Hawaii consists of a group of islands, 8 inhabited, in the North Pacific Ocean, about 2,090 miles southwest of San Francisco. Total area, 6,407 square miles; population, 620,350 (1960). As a state, it has a government similar to the other states. It elects its own governor, other officers, and legislature as well as the 2 senators and 1 representative who represent it in Congress. Agriculture, chief industry, especially of sugar and pineapples; coffee, animal products, bananas also important. Chief exports: sugar, pineapples, coffee, bananas, hides and honey. Tourist trade is of considerable volume. Imports: manufactured goods, foodstuffs, oils, rice, lumber and fertilizers. Monetary unit (also Alaska), the American dollar. Shipping important; some 141,000 passenger motorcars; passenger travel mainly by air. Telephone, radio, TV, wireless and cable systems. Education under territorial Department of Public Instruction; compulsory from 6 to 16; public and private schools from kindergarten through 12th year; 1 university. Honolulu (capital), pop., 290,000; Hilo, on the island of Hawaii, 25,600.

MIST WREATHES the skyscrapers of New York so that they seem to float like towers in a fabulous dream.

United States Cities... *centers of*
culture and industry

WHEN George Washington became president of the United States in 1789, the population of the nation was almost entirely rural. Of the few cities then existing, New York, the largest, had but 33,000 inhabitants. During the next century, however, cities grew and multiplied to an amazing extent, spurred by immigration and industrialization. By 1960, if one includes the suburbs, America's population was largely urban, not rural —decidedly so in the northeastern states. There the stretch between Boston and Washington was becoming so thickly built up as to form one gigantic megalopolis.

In the beginning, American cities were light and spacious, in contrast to the overcrowded cities of the Old World with their dark, narrow lanes and alleys. The citizens of the New World laid out broad, sweeping thoroughfares that later accommodated the first influx of automobile traffic easily. When demand for business space increased, American builders simply shot skyscrapers upward on steel frames. Today America's phenomenal growth is beginning to catch up with her cities. The need for space has outgrown ingenuity, and most business districts are a crazy-quilt pattern of contrasting architectural styles, the buildings crammed together. Factories, meanwhile, have ex-

NEW YORK CENTRAL SYSTEM

THE BIRTHPLACE OF PAUL REVERE

The well-preserved house, with a steep, shingled roof, was built in Boston around 1660.

panded into many residential neighborhoods, blanketing once lovely streets with soot and smoke. The 1950's and 1960's, therefore, saw many city residents abandon these areas for the suburbs, with a consequent weakening of the urban economy.

This in turn has led to increased emphasis on city planning. More and more municipal governments are turning to zoning. New factories and office buildings, for instance, may be restricted to certain sections. Many cities are tearing down slums and replacing them with parks, playgrounds and attractive civic centers. In some cases the Federal Government has made grants for such purposes. Chicago, Philadelphia, Providence and St. Louis are pacing this trend. It seems that at long last economic necessity is forcing American cities to pay some heed to such critics of "aimless" expansion as Lewis Mumford and Walter Gropius.

The definition of the term "city" has always been a puzzle. Certainly it is a place where many people live together in a comparatively small area. But how large such a place must be before it can be called a city is still a question.

There are about 43 cities in the world with populations of more than 1,000,000. Of these, 5 are in the United States. About 10,500,000 people live in Greater New York City alone! Almost one fifth of the people of the United States live in some 150 cities of over 100,000. In this chapter we discuss only the country's larger or more important communities.

The number and great size of cities throughout the world is a relatively recent thing. Although there have been great cities for a very long time—even as long ago as the days of ancient Egypt and Mesopotamia—it is only within the last two hundred years that the world has seen their amazing growth. Cities today are changing, like boys who finally stop growing up and start filling out.

The modern American city depends upon vast transportation facilities for its existence. Food for the millions of people in and around Chicago, for instance, is not grown by the people of Chicago themselves. Rather, it is transported from farms in Kansas, Ohio, Florida or California. Since city people do not grow their own food, they must make something of use or value which they can sell or exchange for food. This explains the reason why the large modern manufacturing city came into being.

There are many kinds of cities. Some of the best known cities of the United States serve a governmental purpose. Washington, D. C., is the best example of this type, although most state capitals have government as one of their primary operations. Most cities are commercial and manufacturing communities. If we trace back to the origins of such cities as Boston and New York, we discover that they developed as port cities because they had protected harbors. Manufacturing and larger commercial activities came later. Some cities, such as Detroit, developed as manufacturing cities almost from the beginning. Others, such as Atlanta, have their origins in strategic locations with respect to routes of transportation. Cities often are born at the mouths of mountain passes and where rivers can be easily crossed.

The primary purpose of some cities is

STATE CAPITOL AT RICHMOND, DESIGNED BY THOMAS JEFFERSON

The central part of the Capitol was completed in 1792, and the wings added in 1905. The figure in Capitol Square in the foreground is of Washington, surrounded by six Virginia statesmen.

MEETING PLACE OF CHAMPIONS—THE COTTON BOWL IN DALLAS

The mammoth stadium, accommodating 75,000 people, is the site of the annual southwestern football classic. Its name is a reminder of the importance of Dallas in world cotton markets.

THE HOUSE THAT GLASS BUILT—BOTH FUNCTIONAL AND BEAUTIFUL

Designed to admit a maximum of light, the glass-walled building is not only beautiful, but also ideally suited to research. It is part of the General Motors Technical Center near Detroit.

MECCA FOR MERCHANTS—THE MERCHANDISE MART IN CHICAGO

The famous twenty-four-story building, two blocks long and one block wide, employs 26,000 people. Here thousands of manufacturers and wholesalers can display their "lines" for buyers.

recreation. Miami, Florida, grew in this fashion, as did Palm Springs, California. Some of the important cities in each state are cultural centers and are the sites of universities. For this reason such communities as Cambridge, Massachusetts, exert an influence much out of proportion to their size. Finally, there are military or defense communities. In Europe, many cities originated in particular places because their locations were readily defensible. In the United States, San Diego, California, is such a city; it has grown big because a military and naval base is located there.

In certain ways all large American cities are alike in their interior arrangement. Imagine a Typical City from which all other cities differ only in their details. In Typical City there is a central business area, in the center of which is a large park. Facing the park is the city hall. Wide avenues extend out from the main business section, and spaced along the avenues are lesser business centers. A river runs through Typical City. Along its banks, not far from the business center, is the industrial section. A dam on the river supplies factories with the necessary electrical power. Railroad lines haul heavy freight to and from the factories. Great wholesale warehouses store all the things the city people buy in the retail stores of the business centers. This railroad-manufacturing-wholesale section is the noisy, bustling, throbbing heart that enables the city to live. It is usually ugly, and often visitors to Typical City avoid this section where heavy trucks jam the streets, factories clatter and sooty smoke thickens the air. Yet if all this were to end, city bankers, grocers, bakers and others would soon find that they were unable to work or sell their goods.

Between the broad avenues of Typical City there are many blocks of homes. Those next to the noise and dirt of industry are rented cheaply. In this section closely packed apartment buildings house many families each. Farther away from

CALIFORNIANS INC.

LONGEST IN THE WORLD—SAN FRANCISCO–OAKLAND BAY BRIDGE

Eight-and-a-half miles long—half of it over water—the bridge passes through a tunnel at Yerba Buena Island in mid-bay. The view here is of the west half, from the island to San Francisco.

industry and business there are smaller individual houses. Many of these are owned by the families living in them. Still farther out from the business centers are mansions and large estates. Beautiful apartment projects and very large homes occupy a portion of the river bank. Scattered through the residential section are churches, schools, playgrounds and parks. On a bluff overlooking the river stands the state university with its broad, green campus. Typical City is imaginary but its features and arrangement are very like those of most American cities.

Look at a map showing all of the cities of the United States having over 100,000 people. You will notice at once that they form a pattern. About one-third are located within or near a triangle having its corners at Chicago, Boston and Richmond, Virginia. This great urban area has available a combination of raw materials, power, markets and labor necessary for big industrial development. Except for the Pacific coast cities, the western

half of the country has few large cities. The dry, grassy plains, the deserts and the Rocky Mountains are not conducive to big-city development.

During the twentieth century, the growth of cities in the United States has been remarkable and swift. Some have grown 50 per cent in the last ten years or so. The most rapid growth is seen in the South and along the Pacific coast. Cities lying in the urban triangle have also for the most part grown, but at a relatively slow rate. Few cities in the nation have lost population in the past ten years, but their expansion is taking an unusual form. Because of the increased use of the automobile, the central area of large cities is gradually being abandoned to business and people are moving their residence to the suburbs. Throughout the nation small towns adjacent to cities are gaining population more rapidly than the cities themselves. It is these small but growing towns that will some day help to swell the ranks of the great cities.

LOS ANGELES CHAMBER OF COMMERCE

CALIFORNIA'S ROOSEVELT HIGHWAY SKIRTING THE BLUE PACIFIC

The beautiful coastal highway passes through the popular beach resorts in Los Angeles County, paralleling many stretches of fine, sandy beach such as the Santa Monica section shown here.

IN BYGONE DAYS AUGUSTA, MAINE, WAS A TINY INDIAN VILLAGE
Now an industrial city, the capital of the Pine Tree State, it reflects a modern skyline in the Kennebec River. The products of its mills include lumber, paper, textiles and shoes.

CITIES OF THE NORTHEASTERN STATES

Although there are many communities of importance and renown in Maine, New Hampshire and Vermont, these states of northern New England have no really large cities. Maine's capital is Augusta, but its largest city is Portland. A fine harbor makes Portland a thriving fishing center. Bangor, named for a hymn tune, is a transportation city in the northern part of the state. Bar Harbor is one of many famous vacation resorts along the coast.

Concord, of Revolutionary War fame and the capital of New Hampshire, is located on the Merrimac River. Nashua and Manchester, also on the Merrimac, use power from that river in the manufacture of textiles and leather goods. At the mouth of the Piscataqua River lies the important port and naval yard of Portsmouth.

Burlington is the chief city of Vermont and a popular resort center. The city overlooks beautiful Lake Champlain and is noted for its fine parks. At Barre, Rutland and Proctor there are important granite and marble quarries. Montpelier is the state capital.

In contrast to northern New England, Massachusetts, Connecticut and Rhode Island include many large cities of industrial and commercial importance. Boston, the largest of these and the capital of Massachusetts, is noted both for its present industry and for its past history. Its name, like those of many New England towns, was drawn from old England, the home of the original settlers on Massachusetts Bay. Each year the city's historic landmarks attract thousands of visitors. Boston has long been a cultural leader among American cities, and its churches, museums and literary shrines are famous. Here lived such outstanding figures as Paul Revere, Longfellow, Louisa Alcott and many others who played prominent parts in the nation's history and cultural life. The bustling commerce of the modern city's port draws ships from all over the world, and Boston's fishing industry is a major activity. Cambridge, across the Charles River from Boston, is the site of Harvard University, Radcliffe College and Massachusetts Institute of Technology.

The industry of Worcester, the second largest city in Massachusetts, is greatly diversified; here steel wire, grinding wheels and looms are manufactured. This city is the home of Holy Cross and Clark universities. In southern Massachusetts, Fall River and New Bedford have developed as textile manufacturing centers. Metal and electrical goods are made in Springfield, which stands on the banks of

A PROUD OLD PORTLAND MANSION

The Sweat Memorial in Portland, Maine, has a collection of paintings and fine art objects.

FACTORIES AND SMOKE STACKS BESIDE THE CONNECTICUT RIVER

Springfield, Massachusetts, which in colonial days had only a few gristmills and sawmills, today turns out a long list of manufactured necessities from fine paper to heavy machinery.

COMMERCIAL SECTION OF VERMONT'S LARGEST CITY: BURLINGTON

The city is a port on the eastern shore of Lake Champlain whose southern end is connected with the Hudson River by the Champlain Canal. The University of Vermont is on the outskirts.

NEW HAMPSHIRE'S STATEHOUSE, MADE OF LOCAL WHITE GRANITE

The imposing statehouse in Concord is guarded by statues of Franklin Pierce, Daniel Webster, General John Stark and John P. Hale—all history-making sons of New Hampshire.

the Connecticut River in the midst of a rich agricultural region.

Providence, named by Roger Williams, is Rhode Island's capital and only large city. Providence is a producer of jewelry and silverware. Newport, south of the capital, is a wealthy residential and resort community.

Connecticut has three large cities. Hartford, the capital and the largest city, is a major center for insurance businesses. New Haven and Bridgeport are ports and, together with Hartford, are manufacturers of metal products. Yale University, the third oldest institution of higher learning in the United States, is situated at New Haven. Waterbury, a somewhat smaller city, is a leader in watch production and has a thriving brass industry.

New York City is so much larger than the other cities of New York State, indeed of the whole nation, that it deserves special mention. To people of other lands, it is the model of all American cities, and it is truly an amazing development. Over 7,000,000 people live within the city limits. The population of the entire urban

MONKMEYER

TOWN HOUSES ON BEACON STREET, IN BOSTON'S BACK BAY

The Back Bay is the city's most exclusive residential district and one of its most charming thoroughfares is Beacon Street. It breathes an atmosphere of quiet, gracious dignity.

ROGER WILLIAMS LOOKS DOWN ON THE CITY THAT HE FOUNDED

The memorial is on a hill and the raised hand of the statue seems to be blessing the city of Providence. In the center is the steeple of the church that Williams established in 1638.

YACHTS AT ANCHOR IN THE HARBOR OF NEWPORT, RHODE ISLAND

Though Newport's days of glory as an ultrafashionable resort have declined somewhat, it is still a center of yachting. Many races—to Bermuda, Annapolis—start from here.

concentration numbers over 12,000,000. More than one-fourth of these people are foreign-born, and so cosmopolitan is New York City that one may eat French, Italian, Chinese, Spanish, German and Hungarian food—to mention but a few—in Manhattan's restaurants.

Manhattan Island

That part of the city called Manhattan is an island lying at the mouth of the Hudson River. The present great city grew out of the small colony founded there in 1626 by Dutch settlers, who called it New Amsterdam. On Manhattan are located many world-famous landmarks, among them Times Square and Broadway, with their lights, and Wall Street, the center of America's banking interests. Central Park extends for fifty-one blocks down the center of the island, itself an island of open country in a sea of great buildings. Adjacent to the park is the Metropolitan Museum of Art and the American Museum of Natural History. The Public Library, some blocks south of the park, is one of the finest in the world. At the southern tip of Manhattan and up the western shore are long lines of docks where ships from all parts of the world load and unload their cargoes and passengers. Ships approaching the docks must first pass the gray-green Statue of Liberty which stands in the city's harbor, a symbol of freedom known the world over. Rail lines converging on New York handle vast quantities of goods coming from and going to the rest of the nation. The city is so large that there is a great variety of manufactures and businesses, including clothing, publishing and advertising.

Transportation in a Metropolis

Many people who have business in Manhattan live in residential areas adjacent to the island and ride to work each day. A system of bridges, tunnels, busses and subways makes possible the transportation of people and goods from one part of the city to another. From New York's two great airports flights leave many times a day for Europe, South America and all parts of the United States.

MIDTOWN LANDMARK OF NEW YORK

The tallest structure is the RCA Building. At in summer. In addition to the broadcasting fa-

THOMAS AIRVIEWS

CITY—THE STEEL AND STONE SKYSCRAPERS OF ROCKEFELLER CENTER

its foot is a sunken plaza, used as a skating rink in winter and as an open-air restaurant
cilities and countless offices, there are a theater, gardens, shops and some other restaurants.

THE ALBRIGHT ART GALLERY IN NEW YORK STATE'S SECOND CITY

Buffalo's imposing gallery copies the severely beautiful lines of classic Greek architecture, even to the caryatids—the draped female figures supporting entablatures—on either side.

WATER-FRONT GRAIN ELEVATORS

Buffalo is one of the chief Great Lakes ports, through which quantities of grain pass.

THE CITY HALL ON NIAGARA SQUARE

Niagara Square is the heart of Buffalo, marked by the civic edifice of thirty-two stories.

ON YALE UNIVERSITY CAMPUS, THIRD OLDEST IN AMERICA

A view of the old library building from Phelps Hall. The college was founded in 1701, and later named for Elihu Yale, who had given money to the school. In 1887 Yale became a university.

A VIEW OF HARTFORD FROM THE CONNECTICUT RIVER

Connecticut's capital and largest city, Hartford, is also a vital center of trade and manufacturing, and it enjoys a great volume of the world's insurance business.

THE PULASKI SKYWAY SOARS OVER JERSEY RIVERS AND MARSHES

The 4-lane highway, of steel and concrete, is 3½ miles long, between Jersey City and Newark. It crosses the Hackensack and Passaic rivers on bridges that are 145 feet above the water.

PITTSBURGH'S GOLDEN TRIANGLE—BIRTHPLACE OF THE OHIO

At the tip of the Golden Triangle, the Allegheny and Monongahela rivers come together to form the mighty Ohio. The Golden Triangle, or Point, is the business section of the city.

Buffalo, the second city of New York State, is located just south of Niagara Falls and is noted for flour milling and iron and steel working. Iron ore and grain are brought here by barges through the Great Lakes. South of Lake Ontario and along the Mohawk and Hudson rivers are Rochester, Syracuse, Utica and Schenectady, cities that have a variety of industry. Cameras and optical equipment are produced at Rochester, metal articles of all sorts at Syracuse, knitted goods at Utica and electrical appliances at Schenectady. Albany, the state capital, is also a commercial and industrial center.

The Cities of New Jersey

New Jersey, for its small size, has a number of cities. With the exception of Trenton, the capital, in the west center of the state, all these cities form part of a large urbanized area of New York City or Philadelphia. Newark, Jersey City, Elizabeth and Paterson lie close together and just across the Hudson River from New York City. Of these, Newark, a commercial and industrial city, is the largest. Camden, an important producer of canned soups and phonographs, is across the Delaware River from Philadelphia. Although Paterson is famous for its silk mills and Trenton for its pottery works, the industry of New Jersey cities is highly diversified. Atlantic City on the coast— with five sandy beaches—is a favorite summer resort for the people of the New York, New Jersey and Pennsylvania area.

Home of the Liberty Bell

Philadelphia, Pennsylvania's "City of Brotherly Love," has long been a shrine of American liberty. Here, in time-mellowed Independence Hall, the Declaration of Independence was signed in 1776. In and about the city are many other buildings and sites of historic significance which are visited yearly by thousands. The city's checkerboard pattern of streets was laid out when Philadelphia was founded and it remains today as one of the earliest examples of city planning in America. Located along the important Delaware River waterway, Philadelphia

PHILIP GENDREAU

THE "CATHEDRAL OF LEARNING"
The University of Pittsburgh's main building is a towering skyscraper with Gothic lines.

MAIN ENTRANCE TO THE VAST PHILADELPHIA MUSEUM OF ART

The museum has an unusually fine location on a hill overlooking the Schuylkill River at one end of Fairmount Park. Leading up to this entrance is the broad, tree-lined Parkway.

SKYLINE AND WATER FRONT OF BALTIMORE FROM FEDERAL HILL

Baltimore, on the west shore of Chesapeake Bay, is an important eastern seaport. The Pata-pasco River gives it a water front forty-five miles in length, with excellent docking facilities.

THE UNITED STATES NAVAL ACADEMY AT ANNAPOLIS, MARYLAND

The aerial view above gives a glimpse of the picturesque setting, the spacious grounds and the impressive buildings, in French Renaissance style, of the splendidly equipped Naval Academy.

WILMINGTON, CAPITAL OF THE DU PONT INDUSTRIAL EMPIRE

In the heart of the industrial city is the du Pont Building (left center) housing a hotel, theater and business offices. It is connected by a bridge with the Nemours Building (right center).

is a city of diversified industry, where shipbuilding and oil refining are major activities. Like Boston, Philadelphia has been one of the nation's cultural leaders for many years.

West of Philadelphia is Reading, a textile city, and Harrisburg, the state capital and an important railroad center for lines to the west. Scranton, on the Susquehanna River in northeastern Pennsylvania, is a leading anthracite-coal-mining city. In western Pennsylvania, where the Allegheny and Monongahela join to form the Ohio River, lies Pittsburgh, named for the English statesman William Pitt. It is the iron and steel capital of America. Great barges bring iron ore from the mines of Minnesota, through the Great Lakes, to ports along Lake Erie. From these points ore travels by rail to Pittsburgh to be made into steel. Coal to fire the roaring blast furnaces of the steel in-

dustry comes by rail from West Virginia.

Baltimore, on broad Chesapeake Bay, has one of the deepest and best harbors on the Atlantic seaboard and is Maryland's only large city. Characteristic of Baltimore are the many rows of red brick residences with white stone steps which line the streets. At nearby Sparrows Point are great steel mills and oil refineries. To the south, Annapolis, the state capital, is the site of the United States Naval Academy. St. John's College, for men, is also at Annapolis.

The home offices of many of the country's largest manufacturing corporations are situated in Wilmington, Delaware's only really large city. Dover, the capital, in the center of the state, has a charming colonial air. The statehouse, which dates partly from 1722, has been the capitol since 1777. Dover serves as a shipping point for a rich farming area.

CITIES OF THE SOUTHERN STATES

Richmond, the capital and largest city of Virginia and former capital of the Confederacy, is a beautiful city, with broad avenues, spacious parks and graceful monuments. Cigarette manufacture is its most important industry. Norfolk, located almost at the mouth of Chesapeake Bay, is the second city in size. Its harbor at Hampton Roads and its rail connections with the interior of the country have made it a major coaling and naval port. Nearby Newport News and Portsmouth are shipbuilding centers.

West Virginia has no large cities. Huntington is the largest but Charleston, somewhat smaller, is the state capital. Nearby coal deposits make metal industries important in both cities.

Charlotte in south-central North Carolina is the only large city in that state. However, widespread tobacco cultivation and manufacture make such cities as Ra-leigh, the state capital, and Durham significant. Greensboro is a textile city and Wilmington is a port for cotton goods and lumber. Asheville, in the Blue Ridge Mountains, is a delightful summer resort.

Charleston, a port city of South Carolina, is one of the old cities of the South. Its homes and flowers are magnificent and each spring tourists throng to its beautiful parks and gardens. Columbia, the state capital, is a commercial and industrial city.

Atlanta, capital of Georgia, is a primary railroad hub for the southeast. Lines converge here after running south along either side of the Blue Ridge Mountains. Destroyed during the Civil War and then rebuilt, it is now the site of automobile-assembly plants, cotton-goods factories and ceramic plants. Rail lines from north, south and west meet in Savannah, the major port city of Georgia; lumber, naval stores and cotton move from this

STANDARD OIL CO. (N. J.)

THE GOVERNOR'S MANSION IN CHARLESTON, WEST VIRGINIA

The residence is a gracious one, in a simple classic style, surrounded by lawns and gardens. To the right is the dome of the state capitol, one of the most beautiful in the nation.

NOT A ROLLER COASTER, BUT THE COLISEUM AT RALEIGH

The futuristic structure is an indoor arena in North Carolina's capital. It holds ten thousand persons and consists of concrete parabolas apparently supported only by green glass walls.

BUSINESS DISTRICT OF CHARLOTTE

The chief city of North Carolina is also the principal industrial center of both Carolinas.

port and from Brunswick farther south. Savannah's winding streets, small parks and pre-Civil War buildings make it an extremely picturesque city.

City growth in Florida has been particularly rapid in the past quarter-century. Jacksonville, at the mouth of the St. John's River, is the Atlantic port and rail gateway to the state. The lower east coast, with Miami as the major city, consists of a long series of resort towns where the winter warmth is in sharp contrast to the cold of northern states. Tampa, on the Gulf of Mexico, is a port for trade with countries of the Caribbean. Its population, partly of Spanish descent, is engaged in cigar-making and shipbuilding. St. Augustine, the oldest continually inhabited city in the United States, was founded in Florida by the Spanish in the year 1565. Tallahassee is the state capital. Pensacola is an important naval air base.

In Birmingham, Alabama, the iron and steel center of the South, huge blast furnaces glow red against the night sky. They are made possible by nearby sources of coal and iron ore. Montgomery, an older city than Birmingham, was once the capital of the Confederacy and today is the state capital. Located near the agriculturally important Black Belt of Alabama, it has been a commercial city of some importance. Mobile was second only to New Orleans as a southern port in 1850. After relative inactivity at the turn of the century, Mobile is now resuming its growth. Harbor deepening, coal traffic by barge from the interior and natural gas and oil supplied by pipeline combine to make Mobile attractive for such industries as shipbuilding, paper mills and aluminum manufacture.

Growth of Cities in Mississippi

It is only within about the last forty years that Jackson, capital and largest city in Mississippi, has shown rapid growth. Light industries of various sorts are characteristic of the city. Meridian is a commercial city serving the agricultural region around it. Gulfport, Biloxi and Pascagoula are beach resorts and fishing centers on the Gulf coast.

Of Tennessee's four large cities, two are in the eastern part of the state along the banks of the Tennessee River. Chattanooga, the larger, derives hydroelectric power from nearby dams. This power, together with neighboring coal and iron deposits, enables the city to produce a variety of metal goods. Knoxville is a center for marble quarrying, wood products and, most important, cotton textiles. The state capital, Nashville, located in a lush agricultural area, is the site of several colleges and Vanderbilt University. Tennessee's western boundary is the Mississippi River, and on its high bluffs is Memphis, the largest city in the state. Memphis has shipped cotton and timber up and down "Ol' Man River" since the days of paddle-wheel steamers.

The Ohio River flows along the northern boundary of Kentucky and on its banks is Louisville. Like Memphis, Louisville has been an important river port since its founding by George Rogers Clark in 1779. Together with Lexington, near the center of the state, Louisville is

EWING GALLOWAY

A RAILWAY INTO THE CLOUDS

The cable railway that ascends Lookout Mountain in Chattanooga is the steepest in the world.

BLACK STAR

JACKSON'S STATUE IN NASHVILLE

The bronze statue of the famous President is near his beautiful old home, The Hermitage.

OLD CHARLESTON SLAVE MARKET
The building was the source of house and field labor for a large area in South Carolina.

CHARLESTON'S PINK HOUSE
Among the attractions for visitors in the historic city is this pre-Revolutionary tavern.

PALMETTOS AND LIVE OAKS ALONG THE BATTERY IN CHARLESTON
The popular walk overlooks Charleston Harbor and the historic fortifications at Fort Sumter. Near the promenade is a small park containing monuments and mementos of the city's history.

JALOUSIED WINDOWS AND BALCONIES ON A SAVANNAH STREET

The old houses in Savannah all are built somewhat alike. Most of them rise three or four stories above a basement. From the street one must climb steep stoops with iron railings.

NIGHT SHIFT IN BIRMINGHAM

When the blast furnaces are run at night, the dramatic glare may be seen for miles away.

NEW CITY OF THE OLD SOUTH

Atlanta, built on the ashes of the ante-bellum city, has become an energetic industrial center.

MEMORIAL TO SOLDIERS AND SAILORS IN MOBILE, ALABAMA

Mobile is a city of beautiful parks. There are thirteen public ones, including Memorial Park (above) and famous Bienville Square, as well as several private parks open to visitors.

THE STATELY CAPITOL BUILDING AT MONTGOMERY, ALABAMA

One of the most magnificent structures in Montgomery is the classic domed capitol building with its portico of fluted columns, set high on beautifully landscaped grounds.

THE TERRITORIAL CAPITOL IN LITTLE ROCK, ARKANSAS

The white clapboard building was the capitol before Arkansas became a state. Surrounding it are private homes that have authentic furnishings dating from the territorial period.

YACHT BASIN IN MIAMI CITY WITH ITS CHARTER FISHING FLEET

Catering to the vacationer is the major industry of most of Florida. Miami, the glamour city, adds to its list of attractions one of the finest fleets of charter fishing vessels in the world.

TUNEIVORN HOUSE IN ST. AUGUSTINE, FLORIDA'S OLDEST CITY

Today the building contains relics of St. Augustine's history since its settlement by the Spaniards in 1565. The surrey (right) for leisurely sightseeing is in keeping with the city's mellow charm.

FLORIDA STATE NEWS BUREAU

VIEW OF JACKSONVILLE, FLORIDA, FROM MAIN STREET BRIDGE

Jacksonville, one of Florida's largest cities, is an industrial and commercial center as its skyline would indicate. It is an important world port as well as being the principal gateway to Florida.

EWING GALLOWAY

MUNICIPAL PLAZA IN BEAUTIFUL CITY OF JACKSON, MISSISSIPPI

Across the Municipal Plaza, landscaped with colorful, formal flower beds, is the Hinds County Court House. At the left is the City Hall that was built in 1864 during the Civil War era.

noted for the fine horses that are bred in the surrounding Blue Grass region. Frankfort is the state capital.

Louisiana has one major city, New Orleans, whose population is concentrated along the banks of the Mississippi and adjacent Lake Pontchartrain. Great wharves and warehouses line the city's harbor, and from here grain, cotton, pe-troleum and machinery are shipped to ports throughout the world.

New Orleans was founded over two hundred years ago by the French and many of its people are of French descent. No visitor should leave New Orleans without seeing the buildings in the French Quarter, where balconies of intricate iron grillwork lend an Old World beauty to

CHARTRES STREET IN THE ROMANTIC VIEUX CARRE OF NEW ORLEANS

The Vieux Carré, the old French quarter of the city, recalls the days when it was the capital of the French colony. Along the narrow streets there are rows of lacy grillwork balconies.

STANDARD OIL CO. (N. J.)

THE WIDE DAM IN THE OHIO RIVER AT LOUISVILLE, KENTUCKY

River traffic moves around the dam and nearby falls by means of a canal and locks. Overhead
is a bridge carrying tracks of the Pennsylvania Railroad.

TOWBOAT AND BARGES ON THE MISSISSIPPI OFF BATON ROUGE

Soaring up from the center of the city is the skyscraper capitol building. Besides being the
home of the state government, Baton Rouge is a busy river port with modern docks.

A STATUE OF A COWBOY OVERLOOKS OIL FIELDS IN OKLAHOMA CITY

Since oil was discovered in 1928, Oklahoma City has become a forest of derricks. More and more wells have been sunk until today they are within a few feet of the capitol building itself.

mellowed houses and gracious hotels.

Up river from New Orleans is Baton Rouge, the state capital and an oil-refining center. The capitol building is a towering skyscraper. Like Baton Rouge, Shreveport, on the Red River, is important because of its oil refineries.

Near the geographical center of Arkansas and on the Arkansas River is Little Rock, the capital and largest city in the state, as well as its commercial crossroads. Here goods from east and west meet for exchange. Farther up the Arkansas River is Fort Smith, a secondary commercial city. Southwest of Little Rock is Hot Springs, a health and pleasure resort adjoining Hot Springs National Park.

Oklahoma City, Oklahoma, was formerly a small community in an Indian territory. Then oil was discovered there, and the town suddenly began to grow in size and wealth. Today oil pervades its atmosphere, and great derricks used in drilling have covered nearly all of the city's available space, even invading the grounds of the state capitol building. In Tulsa, once a sleepy Indian town, the oil refineries vie with modern skyscrapers.

Texas is so immense that there is room for many cities. Houston, the largest of these, is the biggest port on the Gulf coast. Once it was an inland town, but the ship canal dug to Galveston Bay has provided it with a harbor. The port city of Galveston is on an island paralleling the coast and is connected with the mainland by causeways. San Antonio is the site of the historic old mission, the Alamo, and several military bases. Manufacturing and trade across the Mexican border are its chief occupations. Dallas, a major banking and insurance center, is also a rail junction point and a great cotton market. In addition to its cotton mills, nearby Fort Worth has large stockyards and meat-packing enterprises. El Paso, in the western corner of Texas, is located in the fertile irrigated valley of the Rio Grande. The many ranches in the area supply its stockyards with beef and cattle. El Paso, across the border from Mexico, has a Spanish atmosphere. Corpus Christi is the port for southwest Texas. Austin, near the center of Texas, is the capital.

CRADLE OF TEXAN LIBERTY

The Alamo (right) in San Antonio, scene of a tragic siege in the Texas-Mexico struggle.

FOLEYS—KING-SIZE DEPARTMENT STORE IN HOUSTON, TEXAS

A major attraction for shoppers is the mammoth emporium occupying a square block in Houston. There are few windows above the street floor, which permits more display space inside.

MUSEUM OF SCIENCE AND INDUSTRY IN CHICAGO'S JACKSON PARK

A domed rotunda and the Ionic columns of portico and colonnade rise impressively above Columbia Basin. The museum contains models and exhibits of industry's greatest inventions.

CITIES OF THE NORTH CENTRAL STATES

Ohio's many large industrial cities are grouped along Lake Erie, in the central part of the state, and along the Ohio River. The largest is Cleveland, the state's principal lake port and the home of a thriving steel industry. Iron ore is brought here by Great Lakes barges to feed Cleveland's furnaces. Some of it is shipped on by rail to the nearby industrial cities of Youngstown and Canton. Toledo, Ohio's second great lake port, is also a principal rail center, with lines extending in all directions. Akron, one of the world's largest rubber-manufacturing cities, is a major producer of tires and tubes for trucks and automobiles. Columbus, in central Ohio, is the capital and is industrially important for its clay products. United States Government testing laboratories are located in Dayton, which is a city of diversified industry that includes the manufacture of office equipment and refrigerators.

Cincinnati, on a northward bend of the Ohio River, has a history dating from the Revolutionary War. Set in the prosperous Ohio Valley farming area, it has grown from a frontier fort into a great rail and commercial center. One of the largest soap-manufacturing plants in the world is located here.

Indianapolis, in Indiana's rich corn belt, is the capital and largest city in the state, with important flour mills and meat-packing plants. Fort Wayne and South Bend, in the northern part of the state, are

THE LOOP—A HIVE OF COMMERCE IN STEEL, CONCRETE AND STONE

A maze of surface transportation—broad auto expressways and streets, bridges that open for boats on the Chicago River, railroads everywhere—forms the apron of Chicago's Loop.

AUDITORIUM IN BATTLE CREEK

The auditorium in the breakfast-food city is the gift of the cereal-maker W. K. Kellogg.

LINCOLN, IN THE CITY HE LOVED

Andrew O'Connor's statue of Lincoln before the capitol building in Springfield, Illinois.

known for their flour production and the manufacture of farm machinery, sewing machines and clothing. Gary, on the south shore of Lake Michigan, is primarily a steel-producing city.

Illinois is dominated by one gigantic city, Chicago. Spreading out along the southwest shore of Lake Michigan, it is second only to New York in size, with over 3,500,000 people dwelling within its city limits. Over 5,500,000 more live in the metropolitan area of Greater Chicago. The meeting here of the industrial East and the agricultural West has made it possible for a lakeside village to develop into a leading metropolis of the world within a single century. Today Chicago is the major rail hub of the Midwest and from its heart a complex maze of lines reaches out in all directions like the spokes of a wheel. Cattle and hogs from the nearby corn belt fill its stockyards and make it the principal meat-packing city of the nation. Iron ore and grain brought in by lake barges supply its steel and flour-milling industries. For many years it has been a big manufacturer of farm machinery. Between the massed skyscrapers of

THE EDISON INSTITUTE

HENRY FORD'S LASTING TRIBUTE

A replica of Independence Hall is the entrance to Edison Institute in Dearborn, Michigan.

its business section and the lake shore is a long park containing museums and art galleries. Here the people come on hot summer days to be cooled by lake breezes. However, these same breezes blow cold and strong in winter and have given Chicago its nickname of the "Windy City."

Springfield, the state capital in central Illinois, was the home of Abraham Lincoln and is the site of his tomb. Each year it is visited by many who come to pay their respects to the great leader. Peoria, between Springfield and Chicago, is situated in a rich agricultural region and is the center of an enormous grain trade.

Although it is noted chiefly for its automobile manufacture, Detroit, Michigan, is also a port city. Founded by the French on the Detroit River, it has water connections with Lakes Erie and Huron and is the largest city in the state. Nearby Flint is also an automobile-factory city. Grand Rapids, on Lake Michigan, has been nicknamed the "Furniture Capital" of the nation. Kalamazoo, widely known because of its odd name, is the site of an important paper industry. Lansing is Michigan's state capital.

BLACK STAR

TO THE BRAVEST OF THE BRAVE

On the capitol grounds in Des Moines is a heroic column to Iowa's Civil War veterans.

TOWERS ON THE DETROIT RIVER—THE CITY THAT CARS BUILT

The buildings of downtown Detroit turn inward from the Detroit River, the busy strait between Lake St. Clair and Lake Erie. The names of Detroit's founder, Antoine de la Mothe Cadillac, and of the men who gave impetus to its growth at the start of the automotive age— Ford, Buick, Dodge, Olds, Chrysler—are known in every corner of the motoring world.

PLANE'S-EYE VIEW OF COLUMBUS, OHIO

Columbus, capital of Ohio, was named for Christopher Columbus. The town was laid out in 1812 and became a city in 1834. The state capitol building is of local limestone, built in Grecian style. Columbus is the site of Ohio State and Capital universities, and of Starling Ohio Medical School. Fourteen railroads converge in this city at the Union Station.

THE UNIVERSITY OF CINCINNATI

The Student Union Building represents a graceful combination of modern building methods and traditional styles of architecture. The campus is in picturesque Burnet Woods Park.

THE BUSY, BACKYARD CUYAHOGA

A tipple loads a lake ore boat with coal for Detroit in Cuyahoga River Flats—the cluster of blackened mills, factories and rail yards a stone's throw from downtown Cleveland.

CINCINNATI'S IMPOSING UNION TERMINAL

This handsome building is one of the most modern railroad stations in the world. The huge clock is a landmark. The city is in an area of heavy population, and this has helped to make it a leading railroad center. More than a dozen eastern and southern railroad lines enter Union Terminal. The city also owns and operates the Cincinnati Southern Railway, to Chattanooga, Tennessee.

HEART OF INDIANAPOLIS—THE SOLDIERS' AND SAILORS' MONUMENT

The great shaft, 284 feet high, is in the center of the city and commemorates Hoosiers who have given their lives in service to their country. At the top is a gigantic statue of Victory, 38 feet high. On the eastern and western sides of the base, water cascades down into pools. Looking up the broad avenue from Monument Place, you can see the handsome domed Capitol.

Milwaukee is by far the largest city in Wisconsin and, like Chicago, it is a port on Lake Michigan. It manufactures heavy machinery and has many large flour mills and breweries. Madison, the state capital and seat of the state university, is a pleasant city located amid lakes and rolling hills.

Minneapolis and its twin city St. Paul lie on either side of the Mississippi River in Minnesota. The former is noted for its great flour mills. St. Paul, the state capital, is a rail center and an important meat-packing city. There are many ponds and lakes about the "Twin Cities" that add a fresh and attractive air to the bustle of metropolitan life. In northern Minnesota, at the extreme western end of Lake Superior, stands Duluth, through which flows iron ore from the nearby Mesabi mines to feed the country's blast furnaces. Wheat from the Dakotas and lumber from Minnesota also come to Duluth for shipment by lake barges to the states farther east.

Near the center of Iowa is the state capital and largest city, Des Moines, a

FREDERIC LEWIS

A BIT OF VENICE IN INDIANA

The dome is the culminating point of the Fort Wayne Court House, which has a look of Venetian baroque. It is in the center of the city— a railroad hub and heart of a farming region.

NORTHERN PACIFIC RY.

THE WHITE CITY OF ST. PAUL ABOVE THE FATHER OF WATERS

A stern-wheeler excursion boat, riverside retaining walls, the piers of Robert Street Bridge and the massive buildings of St. Paul cast a glow on the Mississippi. St. Paul grew up as a banking and railroad center; its cross-river twin, Minneapolis, as a flour- and saw-milling town. Today they work together as the industrial capital of the northern states.

COFFMAN MEMORIAL UNION OF THE UNIVERSITY OF MINNESOTA

The forthright-looking building is a fitting tribute to a former president of the university. It is a social center for the students, a place for them to come in their hours of leisure.

FOUNTAINS SPLASH IN FRONT OF UNION STATION IN ST. LOUIS

More than twenty railroads pass through the huge station, as the city is a crossroads for the whole country. The four-story building, of stone, is in a modified Romanesque style.

FISHING CONTEST FOR SMALL FRY IN KANSAS CITY, KANSAS

There are a number of lakes in the city which are open to young Izaak Waltons for one morning a week during the summer. This is Big Eleven Lake, kept stocked by the state fish hatchery.

ACRES OF STOCKYARDS ALONG THE KAW RIVER AT KANSAS CITY

Stockyards and packing houses are on both sides of the river, some in Kansas City, Missouri, and some in Kansas City, Kansas. They can process thousands of livestock in a day.

MONUMENT IN TOPEKA   **WISCONSIN'S CAPITOL**

A pioneer mother guards her children, with a rifle across her knees, on the grounds of the Kansas state capitol. The handsome structure in Madison, Wisconsin, has a ribbed dome.

A DREDGE REMOVING SILT FROM THE MILWAUKEE RIVER CHANNEL

The river flows through Milwaukee and is a feeder for the city's sheltered harbor on Lake Michigan. In the background the Wisconsin Avenue Bridge, a movable one, is raised.

LAWNS BETWEEN COUNTY AND CITY BUILDINGS IN OMAHA

On the farther side of the street, at the corner, is the rather massive-looking City Hall. The smooth lawn, with star-shaped beds, is in front of the Douglas County Court House.

THE FRONTIERSMAN STATUE ON THE CAPITOL GROUNDS AT BISMARCK

In the distance is the capitol building of North Dakota. It is a structure in the modern style and seems all the taller for the open space and low buildings that surround it.

corn-belt community of meat-packing houses, creameries and farm-equipment factories. The Iowa State Fair, held in Des Moines each year, is one of the country's big agricultural events. Other important food-processing and commercial cities in Iowa are Sioux City, Council Bluffs, Cedar Rapids and Dubuque.

Two of the nation's great Midwestern cities lie in Missouri, St. Louis and Kansas City. St. Louis, near the junction of the Mississippi and Missouri rivers, is a great river port. It was founded by the French, and its industrial history goes far back to the days when trappers brought their furs down the Missouri to its market. Today it is a prominent flour-milling and meat-packing city. Kansas City, on the Missouri, has a twin, Kansas City, Kansas, just across the river. Both are food-processing cities. Jefferson City, in central Missouri, is the state capital.

The largest city in Kansas is Wichita, on the Arkansas River. Set in the winter-wheat belt, the city does a large milling business. The prosperous farms of the region provide a great and ready market for the farm supplies in which Wichita dealers specialize. The state capital, Topeka, is just up river from Kansas City.

Ever since the days of the covered wagons, Omaha, Nebraska, has been a key point in transcontinental traffic and today it is a railroad center for lines running west. It is also a great agricultural and livestock market, and its food-processing industry is large. The thriving commercial city of Lincoln is the capital of Nebraska. Its capitol building combines the skyscraper and classic forms in one of the country's more beautiful government buildings.

The Dakotas have none of the very large cities that generally develop from an industrial economy. Sioux Falls, South Dakota, is a grain city with many flour mills, and Pierre, almost in the exact middle of the state, is the capital. The tourist trade is drawn to Rapid City by the famous carvings of United States presidents on a mountainside in the nearby Black Hills. Fargo, on the Red River, is North Dakota's largest city and a commercial and wheat-handling center for the surrounding agricultural belt. The state capital is Bismarck.

CITIES OF THE WESTERN STATES

Transportation, mining or livestock have been largely responsible for the growth of cities in the less densely populated Rocky Mountain states. Although the region covered by these states is generally arid, local supplies of irrigation water have made intensive farming possible in some areas. In such sections, agricultural communities have developed.

Despite its vast area, Montana, the largest of the mountain states, has no very big cities. Butte, the largest, is a world-famous city of copper mines and smelters and was once nicknamed the "richest hill on earth." In order to ship its ores and metals, Butte has developed fine railroad facilities. Mining is also carried on at Great Falls and Missoula. Billings, on the Yellowstone River, is a trade center for southern Montana. Helena, the capital, is a distributing point for a large stock-raising region.

Wyoming is a state of spectacular scenery, where cattle and sheep herding are the most important activities. Cheyenne, the capital and largest city, is situated in the midst of good range land and is a shipping head for beef cattle and sheep to eastern markets. Casper, the next town in size, is a producer of petroleum. Cody, named for "Buffalo Bill" Cody, is the eastern gateway to Yellowstone National Park and is a stopping place for tourists.

Colorado is another state of scenic grandeur and variety and is somewhat more densely settled than Montana and Wyoming. Denver, "The Mile High City" and capital, lies just at the foot of the Rockies and commands a superb view of the mountains. Its cool summers attract many vacationers. The surrounding irrigated farmland and pastures make it a great market city and it also has some

BLACK STAR

CENTRAL AVENUE, ALBUQUERQUE, METROPOLIS OF NEW MEXICO

Mission and frontier Spanish architecture stand side by side with classical Greek and modern American on Central Avenue. Albuquerque is a health resort and business center of a rich area.

light industries. It is the home of the University of Denver and several other institutions of higher learning. The Denver Art Museum contains an outstanding collection of American Indian art. The city also has a fine civic symphony orchestra and other musical and art organizations. A United States mint is located in Denver. Colorado Springs, near the base of Pike's Peak, is a famous health resort. Deposits of iron and coal near Pueblo are responsible for that city's steel mills.

Santa Fe is the oldest city in New Mexico and the state capital. It was founded by the Spanish in 1605, and its picturesque pueblo-type architecture makes it an interesting place to visit. Before the coming of the railroads to the southwest, it was the terminus of the Santa Fe trail from Missouri. Today its elevation makes Santa Fe an important health resort. Al-

BUTTE, MONTANA—COPPER TOWN

Marcus Daly, copper-mining millionaire, looks over the city his enterprise helped to build.

buquerque, on the Rio Grande, is the commercial heart of the state and to it come the products of the nearby irrigated valley farms and ranges.

A bright green oasis in the desert is Phoenix, Arizona's capital and largest city, situated on the Gila River. Its rail connections make it a major distributing point for the southwest. Tucson, formerly capital of the state, is a commercial city near the copper-mining district of southeastern Arizona. In the northern part of the state, Flagstaff and Williams serve as gateways for tourist traffic to the Grand Canyon region.

Much of Utah's population is concentrated on the eastern shore of Great Salt Lake, where the Mormons founded Salt Lake City in 1847. Rich irrigated land that produces grain, sugar beets and other vegetables surrounds the city. Wide avenues and Mormon churches add to the attractiveness of the city. Ogden, to the north, is a rail center. Bingham is the site of one of the nation's biggest copper mines.

Idaho has no large cities. Boise, the state capital, is the major commercial city and lies at the heart of an irrigated farm area. Pocatello has great railroad shops,

ADOBE DWELLING IN SANTA FE

The "Oldest House in U. S. A."—built perhaps before 1600—recalls an Indian settlement.

364

DENVER'S CITY AND COUNTY BUILDING AND THE GREEK THEATER

Columns of the Greek Theater frame the graceful tower of the City and County Building. Denver, the "mile-high city," has several colleges and a lively interest in the arts.

AT BOISE—IDAHO'S MAJESTIC COPY OF THE NATIONAL CAPITOL

The dignified façade and the columns of the tower seem to hold high the central dome. Within
are legislative chambers, government offices and the state historical museum.

stockyards, cement plants and food-processing facilities. Coeur d'Alene is both a mining center and resort town.

Nevada has two well-known cities, Las Vegas and Reno, both mining towns that are also amusement and tourist centers. The capital, Carson City, was once a Pony Express station. A hundred miles northwest of Las Vegas is Frenchman's Flat, where the Atomic Energy Commission uses five thousand square miles of wasteland as an atomic testing ground.

In contrast to the mountain states of the interior, the more populous Pacific coast states of California, Oregon and Washington have many large cities. Southernmost of these is San Diego, California, which developed from an old Spanish mission and is the oldest city in the state. In many ways its atmosphere reflects the peaceful and colorful spirit of mission days. Landlocked San Diego Bay is an excellent natural harbor. It is a naval base and the dry, warm climate makes year-round naval and air operations possible.

Farther north along the coast is Los Angeles, commercial and tourist center of southern California and the largest city

west of Chicago. Almost 2,000,000 people live inside the city limits and the metropolitan area contains over 4,000,000. Founded in 1781 as a tiny Spanish settlement, it has spread out until today it embraces the greatest area of any city in the United States. It is the hub of the motion-picture industry and leads all other cities of the state in wealth, manufacturing, commerce, aviation and ocean shipping. The delightful, sunny climate has made it one of the nation's outstanding recreational spots. The University of Southern California and the southern branch of the University of California are also in Los Angeles.

The second great city of California is situated on San Francisco Bay, which is separated from the Pacific Ocean by the Golden Gate channel. San Francisco takes its name from a Spanish mission founded about 1776, but it did not begin to grow until the gold rush days of 1849. It had already become a prosperous community by 1906, when it was devastated by fires following an earthquake. Its citizens immediately began to rebuild their city, and today it is a major supply base and distribution center for Pacific coast

BRIGHAM YOUNG MONUMENT BASE

The figure is on a Salt Lake City statue to the
man who led the colonization of Utah.

TO "THE MIRACLE OF THE GULLS"

Tribute in Temple Square to gulls that saved
the pioneers from a grasshopper plague.

THE MORMON TABERNACLE AND TEMPLE IN SALT LAKE CITY

Six ornate spires of the Mormon Temple rise in stately watchfulness over the broad, fertile
valley of Great Salt Lake. The rounded, white roof shelters the famous Mormon Tabernacle.

367

agricultural, manufacturing and mining industries. Its landlocked harbor is one of the finest in the world. The famous Golden Gate Bridge suspended across the outer mouth of the harbor has the longest span of any bridge in the world. It is really a series of bridges, with a total length, including its approaches, of eight and a quarter miles. Ocean liners can easily pass beneath it. So steep are many of the hills on which San Francisco is built that street cars run on cables.

The capital of California is Sacramento, set in the Great Valley which extends north-south through the center of the state. The fruits and vegetables that grow around the city are canned in its large food-processing plants. Stockton and Fresno are located in good agricultural areas. The former, once a gold rush city, now manufactures farm machinery. Fresno is known as a "raisin capital."

In Oregon most of the population is in the beautiful Willamette and Columbia

SAN XAVIER DEL BAC MISSION
The Indian mission church near Tucson is an example of Spanish baroque in America.

FREIGHT YARD OF THE UNION PACIFIC IN CHEYENNE, WYOMING
Cheyenne, a city that grew up as a main division point of the railroad westward, thrives today as the shipping and trade center for a region rich in the production of minerals and food.

ARIZONA'S STATEHOUSE AND THE CAPITOL PARK IN PHOENIX

In the park grounds before the state capitol, a memorial to the sons of Arizona who served in World War I stands in quiet dignity among the swaying palms and clipped evergreens.

A GUEST RANCH OF PHOENIX WITH AN AIR OF MOORISH SPLENDOR

At a New World retreat in an Old World, Moroccan key, vacationists bask beneath a bright desert sun. Phoenix is lively all through the winter with the comings and goings of tourists.

STATE LIBRARY AND SUPREME COURT BUILDINGS, CARSON CITY

Nevada's State Library and Court House stand in dignity where once was the surge of frontier life. Carson City, the smallest state capital in the United States, has had history enough for a town several times its size. Named for Kit Carson, intrepid scout and soldier, it was a center of supply during Indian wars and the great gold and silver booms.

A DAYTIME VIEW OF VIRGINIA STREET, THE WHITE WAY OF RENO

Reno's slogan and the neon signs announcing night clubs and bingo parlors tell but a small part of the city's story; and its assembly-line divorce court, but a fraction of the remainder. The University of Nevada, the banks, the ski slopes nearby in the Sierra Nevada make it an educational, commercial and recreational center for the state and bordering counties.

A BEACON IN NIGHT-TIME LOS ANGELES

The Los Angeles City Hall, dramatically lighted at night, is part of the city's beautiful Civic Center. Proud of its rapid growth and the beauties of its scenery and climate, Los Angeles is the fourth largest city in the United States. Much of its growth can be traced to the motion-picture industry, which chose Hollywood, part of Los Angeles, as its center.

371

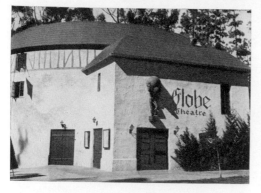

IN BALBOA PARK, SAN DIEGO

A long way from Elizabethan London is San Diego's replica of Shakespeare's famous playhouse, the little Globe Theater.

valleys. Portland, built on both sides of the Willamette River near its confluence with the Columbia, is the state's major city. Since the Columbia River is large enough for sea-going vessels, Portland is an important west coast port. Farm and forest products are among the principal industries, and the city's wool textile mills employ many people. Because of its beautiful location, Portland is sometimes called the "City of Roses." Salem, the capital, is an agricultural, textile and food processing city.

Seattle, on Puget Sound, is Washington's largest city and an important port for trade with Asia and Alaska. Tacoma's lumber industry is one of the largest in the country, and paper mills, copper smelters and electrochemical plants add to the city's industrial might. Spokane, in the fertile wheat area east of the Cascade Mountains, is a leading commercial and rail center.

We have looked at all the large and most important cities of the United States. However, the list of them will not remain

PHOTOS, BLACK STAR

WHERE VINE CROSSES SUNSET IN THE TOWN THEY CALL COLOSSAL

West coast studios of NBC stand at one of Hollywood's busiest intersections. In and around the city, actually a part of Los Angeles, are other stations and many motion-picture studios.

FISHERMEN'S WHARF	SAN FRANCISCO, FROM NOB HILL
Masts and a tangle of rigging lace San Francisco's water front where the fishing fleets put in.	Skyscrapers stand out against San Francisco Bay and hide the approach to Oakland Bridge.

HOLLYWOOD'S MODERN TELEVISION CITY, FOUR STUDIOS IN ONE

The Columbia Broadcasting System's home on the west coast, Television City, brings together all the various CBS departments of TV production under one big roof.

PORTLAND—SHIPPER OF WOOD AND WOOL, PAPER AND GRAIN

On the west bank of the Willamette River, near its union with the Columbia, stand the sky-scrapers of Portland—trading headquarters for the industries of the Northwest.

STATE CAPITOL IN SALEM—A MONUMENT TO THE PIONEER WEST

In white marble, of modern design, Oregon's capitol serves the needs of government and pays tribute in sculpture and murals to the hardy men and women who helped to build the state.

the same over a long period. Within a few years many towns and smaller cities not mentioned here will have grown large.

Now that you have seen the large communities in some detail, imagine yourself in an airplane flying high over the land. Just below is the Mississippi River and St. Louis. Off toward the setting sun, beyond the Rocky Mountains, is the Pacific. To the east, in dark shadow, sprawl the Appalachian Mountains, and past them roll the waters of the Atlantic. Here and there, like tiny ant hills scattered through the patchwork of forests, fields and desert land, lie the great cities. You can see how few miles out of the total they occupy. Yet their seeming tininess belies their importance, for in them stirs the nation's industrial power.

By JOHN R. DUNKLE

UNITED AIR LINES

FLOATING BRIDGE AT SEATTLE
The longest floating bridge in the world steps across Lake Washington on concrete pontoons.

NORTHERN PACIFIC RY.

SEATTLE'S MODERN PIERS AND THE WATER FRONT ON ELLIOTT BAY
Freighters, tankers and liners dock at Seattle, metropolis of the Northwest, beautifully situated on an isthmus between the Pacific inlet, Puget Sound, and fresh-water Lake Washington.

United States Parks ... *conservation of natural beauty*

FEW people realize that the United States national-park system is constantly growing and changing. Each year the Interior Department's National Park Service adds a park or monument here, discards one there. Much more land is being added than dropped. Between 1955 and 1960 the system grew by 500,000 acres to reach a grand total of nearly 24,500,000 acres. This immense stretch, larger than each of several whole nations in Europe, incorporates not only national parks (over

376

13,000,000 acres), monuments (9,000,-000 acres) and recreation areas (about 2,000,000 acres) but several other categories. These include historical parks, battlefield sites, military parks, historic sites, parkways and so on. The Department of Agriculture also maintains a number of national forests to protect and develop timber resources.

The park service's housekeeping job has become enormous. In 1947, some 25,-000,000 tourists visited the parks. By 1959 the figure had more than doubled. By 1966 the service's golden anniversary year, it is expected that 80,000,000 people will be using the system. In 1956 the service began, in a project called Mission 66, to increase facilities to meet the expected influx. The Congress responded by increasing the service's budget. A number of private donors also contributed, enabling the service to improve trails, roads, utility systems, campgrounds, trailer courts and parkways throughout the nation.

A major aim of Mission 66 is to promote understanding of the park system. Several visitor centers have been built near parks and sites. Such a center offers lectures, displays maps, distributes pamphlets and even shows motion pictures about the area. Jamestown and Yorktown, in Virginia, each has such a center, modeled on the one at Williamsburg, Virginia. Mission 66 has also built roads linking the three historic spots, the whole forming the new Colonial National Historical Park.

Among the many additions made to the park system late in the 1950's were the Cumberland Gap National Historical Park, comprising 20,100 acres in Kentucky, Tennessee and Virginia; the Virgin Islands National Park in the Virgin Islands; and two sites honoring national leaders—Theodore Roosevelt Memorial Island in the Potomac River, Washington, D. C.; and Booker T. Washington National Monument near Rocky Mount,

Virginia. The latter was a combined donation of the Booker T. Washington National Monument Foundation and the state of Virginia.

The park system has deep historical roots. Before the adoption of the Articles of Confederation several of the states claimed unoccupied lands west of the Alleghenies. These they ceded to the national Government; and as additions were made to the United States, the ownership of all land (except in Texas) not already in private hands was vested in the Government.

Most of these lands have now passed into private ownership. However, the Government still owns millions of acres scattered through many states of the West. Some of them are open to settlement (though all the best agricultural land is gone), but much of them have been set aside for the recreational use of all the people. The first of the national parks was Wyoming's Yellowstone, created in 1872. Such parks are created by Congress for the sake of developing and perpetuating them for the public enjoyment. National monuments, on the other hand, are proclaimed by the president to conserve some restricted area of unusual scientific or historic interest. Most of the national monuments are small, though some include large areas. Parks, monuments and forests welcome thousands of vacationists every summer.

A map of the national forests would show vast areas reaching from Canada to Mexico along the rocky backbone of the continent and from the desert to the mountain meadows. Most of the national parks and nearly all of the national monuments would show up as mere dots here and there, although Yellowstone Park has an area of 3,458 square miles, chiefly in Wyoming, though spreading into Montana and Idaho; and Glacier Park on the Canadian border is nearly half as large. Several others are of considerable size. Exact figures are given at chapter's end.

The Nation's Pleasure-grounds

The national parks may be roughly classified as of four kinds—(1) those remarkable chiefly for their extraordinary scenic beauties, as stupendous waterfalls, gigantic trees of prehistoric age, the highest mountain peak in North America and the marine vistas of historic Acadie; (2) those displaying such evidences of erosion as remarkable limestone caves and stupendous canyons wonderfully carved and colored; (3) those illustrating glacial action; and (4) those containing volcanic phenomena, geysers and hot springs. The names, location and area of these parks are given in the summary, together with the dates of their creation. Instead of describing them in their chronological order, it seems more interesting to group them according to characteristics. The nation has provided roads, trails, supervised camp grounds and hotels.

Yosemite Valley, the best known feature of Yosemite National Park, cut by the Merced River and by glacial action, is a canyon seven miles long with walls in places three thousand feet in height down which pour the world's highest waterfalls. The Yosemite Falls is shown on page 394. Vernal Falls are unsurpassed for sheer loveliness. The Merced River here descends for 320 feet in a sheet of jade-green water to foam white among the bowlders at its foot. The trail from the valley rim leads one down among the spray-wet cliffs through a veritable rainbow which, every afternoon the sun shines, seems to follow one from step to watery step. Bridal Veil Falls, aptly named, drops 620 feet and the slender Ribbon Falls makes a straight drop of 1,612 feet. Nevada Falls drops 594 feet behind the evergreens. Equally spectacular are the summits that rise from the valley floor. Cathedral Rocks, El Capitan and Sentinel Dome are exceeded by Half Dome, which towers a sheer 4,892 feet, and Clouds Rest, 5,964 feet.

A Land Beloved of John Muir

But Yosemite Valley occupies only eight square miles out of a total of over eleven hundred which constitute the park. Above the valley's rim lies a region less well known save to groups like the Sierra Club and to individuals like John Muir, its first president, because well marked trails, canvas lodges and a motor road have only recently made it easily accessible. Lying on the western slope of the Sierra Nevada Mountains, Yosemite Park reaches Mount Lyell, the crest of the range, and the waters which feed the falls take their rise in the eternal snows. Glacier Point, on the valley rim, gives one a panorama of domes and pinnacles unsurpassed for its loveliness as the fingers of sunrise touch each in turn with gold.

The little known Waterwheel Falls of the Tuolumne River leap "high in the air in wheel-like whirls." The explanation of these falls is that the river, rushing down its canyon, encounters shelves of rock projecting from its bottom and throws enormous arcs of solid water upward, in some cases in a fifty-foot arc. One can but mention the government ranger-naturalist talks, the half-tame deer and brown bears, the carpets of wild flowers, the snow plant that pushes up like giant red asparagus, and the nightly bonfires that shower sparks to the moon. Yosemite Valley was discovered in 1851 by the Mariposa Battalion while pursuing Indians but was for long unknown save to miners and surveyors, soldiers and sheepherders.

Great Sequoias Saved from the Ax

Although Yosemite National Park includes a large grove of "big trees" (the Mariposa Grove) and Kings County National Park to the southward preserves a mammoth one in its extensive General Grant Grove Section, it is Sequoia Park which is most noted for conserving these oldest and biggest living things. The Sequoia gigantea, big cousin of the coast redwood or Sequoia sempervirens, is for the most part set apart in the Giant Forest of Sequoia Park. Before 1916 these trees were the property of individuals, but were purchased by Congress, aided by the National Geographic Society, and so saved from the possibility of falling before the

STEADY, THERE! It is a sheer drop of 4,892 feet from the summit of Half Dome where hikers in Yosemite National Park have an inspiring view of the valley of the Merced River.

lumberman. The oldest of these forest giants is unquestionably between three and four thousand years old, several hundred of them rise to three hundred feet in height and large numbers measure from twenty-five to thirty-seven feet at their base.

Brown bears, shy by day, roam the Giant Forest and sometimes raid campers' larders in the wee sma' hours. One moonlight night a two-yearling cub was seen running away on his hind legs hugging to his chest an outsize fruit cake, pan and all, for which he had overturned the kitchen cabinet of someone's motor camp; and several of the rascally fellows got into the Sierra Club commissary department and were routed in a smother of flour and a trail of bacon rinds. At that same camp a three-prong buck used to beg the campers for melon rinds. The wild life which is protected in all of the national parks is a unique source of entertainment.

A Land for Pack-horse Trips

From Giant Forest eastward up the forested slopes of the Sierras, Sequoia Park has been extended to include Mount Whitney, 14,496 feet, which drops almost sheer on its eastern front into the desert just north of Death Valley. To reach it, pack-horse campers negotiate the canyons of the Kaweah, Kern or Kings rivers, a wild region of castellated peaks, where brief afternoon thunder-showers brighten the aromatic conifers, and sun-baked middays are succeeded by chill nights. The Kern, unlike most Sierran streams, flows southward and its glacial-hewn canyon embraces more than forty peaks over 13,000 feet in height. The neighboring Kearsarge and Junction Passes were used by the California Forty-niners. Mount McKinley National Park in Alaska contains the one peak in the United States that towers higher than Mount Whitney —20,300-foot Mount McKinley, climax of an ice-coated range more fully described in the chapter on territorial possessions. Three scenic parks are in the East. Acadia, in Maine, was first established, then the Great Smoky Mountains in North Carolina and Tennessee, and the Shenandoah in Virginia.

Discovered by Champlain

Acadia (formerly Lafayette) National Park, occupies old French territory on the coast of Maine, with the ancient Mount Desert Mountains as its nucleus. "L'Île des monts deserts" (meaning, not "barren," but "wild and solitary") was discovered by Champlain in 1604 while exploring to the southward of De Monts' colony at the mouth of the Bay of Fundy. The Island, Mount Desert, was in 1688 presented by Louis XIV to the Sieur de la Mothe Cadillac, who left it for his governorship of Louisiana; and in 1713 the French king was obliged to cede this part of Acadia to England. After the capture of Quebec the island fell to the lot of the Province of Massachusetts, but Massachusetts gave it to Sir Francis Bernard; and although the property was confiscated during the Revolution, Bernard's son later secured a half interest in it—and sold it to American settlers. The other half, Marie de Cadillac, granddaughter of the original owner, regained for her family, but sold it bit by bit.

Acadian Woods and Waters

On this island, long inaccessible, fishing hamlets sprung up and the felling of the giant pines vied with the lobster industry. No steamer came until 1868. In the meantime, a few people of means discovered its delights of boating, climbing and buckboarding, and it became a favorite summer haven. Now the lands composing the park have been given to the nation from various sources. Though not yet fully developed, the Great Smoky Mountains Park, and the Shenandoah offer some of the most beautiful and impressive mountain scenery in the country, though the mountains do not tower so high as those in the West. The largest remaining hardwood forest is in the Great Smokies.

Of the parks remarkable as works of erosion (Zion and Bryce canyons, which are shown in pictures, Wind Cave and

ALONG THE BRIGHT ANGEL TRAIL IN THE GRAND CANYON OF ARIZONA

Travelers may reach the floor of the brilliantly colored Grand Canyon by a nine-mile ride on mule-back down the steep Bright Angel Trail. It starts out from the south rim of the canyon.

MONTEZUMA CASTLE, national monument in Arizona. The five-story, ash-pink adobe structure, 40 feet high, is one of the best preserved of the prehistoric cliff dwellings. It was dug into a natural cave at the top of a sheer cliff 145 feet high. White visitors who first saw the place incorrectly associated it with the Aztec Emperor of Mexico, Montezuma.

the cavelike shelters of the Mesa Verde cliff-dweller ruins), the Grand Canyon of the Colorado in Arizona is by far the most extraordinary. On viewing a sunset from Pima Point, a noted traveler and writer once said, "Peaks will shift and glow, walls darken, crags take fire, and gray-green mesas, dimly seen, take on the gleam of opalescent lakes." We depend upon the illustration on page 395 to give an idea of its weird carving and gorgeous coloring. Throughout the ages the Colorado River and its tributaries have gouged out of the sandstone a network of mysterious chasms and at one point the water flows red-silted nearly six thousand feet beneath the canyon's rim. The great natural barrier is more than two hundred miles in length, but in places one may descend on mule-back by trails that loop in zigzags. The total area of the park is over a thousand square miles.

A Perilous Journey

A Hopi Indian legend says that the first human beings ascended from the underworld by way of the Grand Canyon. While a number of white men had already seen and reported on its grandeur, the canyon was not explored until 1869 when Major John W. Powell with nine men in four small rowboats set out on a journey down the Colorado River. Four men gave up the hazardous trip through turbulent water before the party reached the lower end of the canyon.

Mesa Verde, Colorado, is a green table-land on which Richard and Alfred Wethrell, searching for lost cattle in 1888, came upon a hidden canyon and discovered—in a shelf under the overhanging edge of the opposite brim—a prehistoric cliff-dweller ruin that they called Cliff Palace. In a neighboring canyon they discovered Spruce Tree House, another of the best-preserved prehistoric ruins in America. A quarter century later an exploration conducted by Dr. J. W. Fewkes of the Department of the Interior unearthed Sun Temple on a mesa opposite Cliff Palace. The latter is the largest of many cliff-dwellings, each of which had living and storerooms for numerous clans, as well as kivas or rooms for religious ceremonials. The park was created in 1906.

Streams of Boiling Water Erupt

The national parks distinguished first for their volcanic origin include Hawaii, with two active volcanoes, a lake of boiling lava and an extinct volcano (described in the chapter on these islands), Crater Lake and Yellowstone Park. This park contains more geysers than are found in the rest of the world put together. Our five pictures of Yellowstone Park include one of the canyon through which the Yellowstone River foams. Not far distant, along the Lamar River, and elsewhere, there are fossil forests. Yellowstone is also one of the largest wild life refuges in the world. Some of the black bears actually permit automobile tourists to feed them and grizzlies come nightly to the garbage dumps. There are herds of elk, deer and antelope, moose and bison, buffalo, eagles and mountain goats. The buffalo were at one time in danger of complete extermination, as the settlers' fences cut off their pasturage and as the coming of the railroads caused them to be increasingly slaughtered. Now tourists riding quietly a little off the beaten trail often see a line of sentinel bulls rising black against a hill crest. Ranger-naturalists take parties on lecture-walks or talk about the nightly bonfires. The first white man who recorded a visit to the Yellowstone was John Colter, a member of Lewis and Clark's Expedition in 1807. Joseph Meek, W. A. Ferris, Father De Smet and James Bridger also told of it, and a government expedition was sent to explore it in 1859; but it was not until a large expedition went out in 1870 under H. D. Washburn and N. P. Langford that public incredulity was overcome and steps taken to create a park of the area.

One of the World's Deepest Lakes

This largest park was preceded by forty years by the smallest, the radioactive Hot Springs of Arkansas, which in De Soto's time the Indians constituted a Land of Peace. Lassen Volcanic National Park

ANSEL ADAMS

A MERRY DOG-SLED RIDE past the vertical face of Half Dome, in Yosemite National Park. The park is open all year round and attracts numbers of winter-sport fans.

ELIZABETH HIBBS

YELLOWSTONE'S FAMOUS "OLD FAITHFUL" SPURTS UP ON TIME

With almost clocklike precision this geyser sends a column of steam and water into the air at regular intervals to the delight of tourists and camera fans. Yellowstone National Park, high in the Rocky Mountains where Wyoming, Montana and Idaho meet, has some three thousand springs, pools and performing geysers, as well as vast forest reserves for wild animal life.

RAY ATKESON

LOGAN PASS, in Glacier National Park, Montana, is on the Continental Divide, the spine of North America. Within the park there are more than sixty creeping rivers of ice.

THE ONYX CHAMBER in Mammoth Cave, Kentucky, is so called because impurities have tinted the limestone purple and brown.

W. RAY SCOTT FROM SHOSTAL

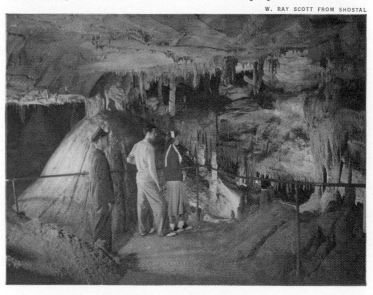

AMETHYST, rose and blue—stone-hard logs in the Petrified Forest, Arizona, that were living trees millions of years ago. Silica has replaced the wood.

JOSEF MUENCH

MAX HUNN FROM SHOSTAL

A WALKWAY through the Everglades, Florida. The area's swamps, sluggish streams, and sawgrass savannas teem with wildlife, particularly birds—ibises, pelicans, herons, egrets and the rare roseate spoonbills.

SAPPHIRE CIRCLE—Crater Lake, Oregon. It lies in a pit caused ages ago by a volcanic eruption and has no inlet or outlet. The water level is kept constant only by rain and snow.

RAY ATKESON

in northern California was created just before the eruption of Lassen Peak in 1916. Once a row of fire mountains blazed along the mountains of the Pacific Coast states. Of these, Mount Mazama, in southern Oregon, underwent some terrific cataclysm in which the volcano fell into itself, jamming its vent and leaving a thousand-foot rim of cliffs about the cavity. In the ages that followed, cold springs poured in their waters until a lake covered all but the peak of one small cone. The result is Crater Lake, which varies from turquoise to blue-black; and the one tiny cone emerges as tree-clad Wizard Island.

The parks characterized by glaciers are Glacier Park and Rainier, while Rocky Mountain Park, in northern Colorado, and Grand Teton, in Wyoming, show signs of glacial action. Rainier rears its solitary white crown in Washington, where it towers 14,408 feet above Puget Sound, bearing a great cap of ice with ragged border. Its glacier system exceeds all others in the United States in both size and grandeur. Twenty-eight imperceptibly moving rivers of ice which have been explored and named, in addition to unnamed smaller glaciers, flow down its sides until their terminal moraines lose themselves in alpine fields of wild flowers. Rich forests of fir and cedar clothe the lower slopes, but from every open space on road or trail the great white dome glistens until one understands why the Indian name for deity, Tahoma (Tacoma) has been applied to it. Some prehistoric explosion has left a crater a mile wide in the mountain top, and the winds from the Pacific, suddenly cooled against its snow crown, deposit their moisture in terrific storms.

On Hoary-crowned Rainier

The snowfalls, settling in the crater, press themselves into ice and slide, of their own weight, down the rocky slopes, here grinding down the softer rock strata, there rumbling over precipices until the air of lower altitudes melts them to rivers milky with sediment. As there is less

to impede the ice-flow in mid-stream, crevasses are formed which yawn, green and clear, for hundreds of feet, and climbing-parties are safe only with experienced guides.

Glacier Park has all of sixty glaciers, but is considered even more remarkable for the beauty of its rugged peaks and precipices and its several hundred glacial-fed lakes, the beds of which have been carved by glaciers of past ages. At Iceberg Lake, where there are miniature icebergs, even in midsummer, a glacier once hollowed a bowl beneath a rim of cliffs two thousand feet in height, and, curiously, another glacier hollowed a similar bowl so close on the other side of the mountain that, had they met, a mountain pass would have been created.

Amid Alpine Lakes

From the Continental Divide a dozen great valleys open gradually along the leisurely western slope, while seven drop abruptly on the east; and each of these valleys leads to some large lake. St. Mary Lake and Lake McDonald, Lake McDermott with its minarets and Two Medicine Lake are too lovely for words, and even pictures leave out their aroma of spruce woods and the feeling of incredible freshness and soothing silence. Among the crags mountain sheep and goats watch while trout dimple the placid waters.

Rocky Mountain Park, "at the top of the world" in Colorado, was fathered by Enos A. Mills, and a huge glacier at the foot of a precipice of Long's Peak has been named for him. Many are the glacial-watered gorges. Those north of Long's Peak are called the Wild Garden and those south of the peak, Wild Basin. The many thickets of white-stemmed aspens make the region a favorite with beavers, who live on the bark.

Stalactites Like Stone Icicles

Caves as well as canyons have been formed by erosion, and numbers of limestone caverns have been preserved in the national monuments of the West. All have been formed by the action of under-

DEVILS TOWER, in Wyoming, is a great fluted column of volcanic rock. From the base it is 865 feet high. It tapers from a diameter of 1,000 feet at the bottom to 275 feet at the top.

ROCK CANDY MOUNTAIN looms over the scenic Zion-Mt. Carmel Highway in Zion National Park, Utah. Part of the park is a canyon, cut by the Virgin River.

JEWEL COLORS—Emerald Pool in the Black Sand Geyser Basin of Yellowstone National Park. The water is tinted by the presence of various minerals.

CLIFF PALACE, Mesa Verde National Park, Colorado. The structure was built into and on top of the cliff by Pueblo Indians a thousand years ago.

PHOTOS, RAY ATKESON

RAY ATKESON

GLOWING like opals —limestone spires in Bryce Canyon National Park, Utah. The canyon is a huge natural amphitheater, broken up into a maze of cliffs, pinnacles, towers and domes. In slanting sunlight, hues are dazzling.

JOE CLARK FROM SHOSTAL

A DEEP BLUE HAZE often veils Great Smoky Mountains National Park (North Carolina–Tennessee) and gave the lovely mountain range its name.

ground waters, perhaps through ages of time; and all are more or less characterized by stalactites formed by the drip of water impregnated with carbonic acid and by stalagmites formed by the ground splash from the stalactites which has caused them to grow slowly upward beneath them.

Visitors enter the Carlsbad Caverns in the Guadalupe Mountains of New Mexico through a musty-smelling hole that takes them directly from a noonday heat of more than a hundred degrees to an even, cool fifty-six. A trail almost a mile long down the main hall leads to a chamber called the King's Palace. Smooth paths, gentle stairways and electric lights, cleverly concealed behind rocks, make the going easy. Beyond the King's Palace, the Queen's Chamber and the smaller Papoose Room is the Big Room, a tremendous vaulted chamber more than half

a mile long, six hundred feet wide and nearly three hundred feet high. There, in the Big Room, is Giant Dome, a leaning stalagmite thought to be more than fifty million years old.

Another wonder at Carlsbad is the swarm of millions of bats that billows from the entrance every summer evening at dusk. They consume tons and tons of insects before returning at dawn to their upside-down daytime life on the roof of a chamber hundreds of feet below the entrance.

Wind Cave of South Dakota and Mammoth Cave of Kentucky are two other national parks. The national monuments include several additional caves of great beauty—Jewel Cave in South Dakota, Lehman Caves in Nevada, the Oregon Caves, Shoshone Cavern in Wyoming and Timpanogos Cave of Utah.

The log cabin in which Abraham Lin-

THE GRANITE PEAKS of the Grand Tetons stand in scenic splendor beyond Jackson Lake in northwestern Wyoming. Sparkling glaciers lie in many of the ravines and gorges.

MOUNT RAINIER explorers take time out for a breather before hiking up Paradise Glacier, part of the ice sheet that envelopes the peak rising 11,000 feet above the forested base.

coln is believed to have been born, now enclosed in a protective memorial building, is typical of national monuments to great Americans. In Washington, D. C., are memorials to Washington, Jefferson and Lincoln. These three presidents, along with Theodore Roosevelt, are also memorialized in the form of huge figures carved on the face of Mount Rushmore in South Dakota.

Many famous battlegrounds—Yorktown, Gettysburg, Chickamauga, Richmond and Little Bighorn, to name only a few—are marked by parks, cemeteries and monuments. One of these monuments is Appomattox Court House in Virginia where General Robert E. Lee's surrender to Ulysses S. Grant in 1865 brought an end to the bloody Civil War. Some other historical sites that have been set aside as national monuments include that of the first permanent English settlement at Jamestown, Virginia; Fort McHenry in Maryland, where the national anthem was inspired; Fort Laramie, Wy-

oming, which guarded the Oregon Trail; and Kill Devil Hill in North Carolina, scene of the world's first successful airplane flight, by Wilbur and Orville Wright.

When the United States Government first awoke to the need of forest conservation, an act of 1891 gave President Harrison authority to set aside ungranted land as forest reserves. The Yellowstone Park Timberland Reserve became the first of a series of such reserves. In 1905 the Forest Service was organized under the United States Department of Agriculture. In 1907 the name Forest Reserves was changed to National Forests. President Theodore Roosevelt showed special zeal in adding forests to the conservation areas.

The national forests of the United States and its territories cover approximately 180,000,000 acres—more than one acre for each inhabitant, on the average. Each year they yield millions of dollars to the Federal Government, chiefly from their timber crop, partly

INDIGO SHADOWS emphasize the modeling of rocks and sand dunes in Death Valley National Monument. At Badwater, the California-Nevada valley is 280 feet below sea level—lowest point in the Western Hemisphere.

MOSS CARPETS the aisles of the great rain forest in Olympia National Park, northwest Washington. Some of the trees—fir, spruce, cedar, hemlock—grow out of the decaying trunks of other trees, long since fallen.

PHOTOS, RAY ATKESON

MOUNT RAINIER mirrored in one of Mount Rainier National Park's lovely lakes. The glaciers that rest on the peak have a total area of about forty square miles.

DELICATE BALANCE in Arches National Monument, Utah, where wind and weather have carved hundreds of odd shapes out of sandstone.

TEMPLE OF THE SUN, one of the magnificient limestone chambers in the Carlsbad Caverns of New Mexico. It is remarkable for its delicately colored stalactites and stalagmites.

A TREE GROWS IN MARIPOSA GROVE—AND GROWS AND GROWS!

Nowhere does man feel more insignificant than amid giant sequoia trees such as those above in Yosemite National Park, California. Fully grown trees average about 275 feet in height and 25 feet in diameter. Some have been known to grow between 350 and 400 feet tall and 96 feet in circumference. One stump, converted into a dance floor, can hold 40 or more people.

WHERE SEA and mountains meet —Acadia National Park, Maine, which is mostly on Mount Desert Island. Spray keeps the rocks moist and they swarm with almost invisible forms of plant and animal life.

WITH A MIGHTY ROAR, the Yellowstone River plunges into a canyon 800 to 1,000 feet deep, in Yellowstone National Park. The river makes three great drops in passing through the 15-mile canyon.

398

RECORD OF THE AGES. As the Colorado River has gouged out the Grand Canyon (Arizona), it has exposed layers of rock that tell a story aeons old of the earth's crust. The colors of the rocks seem to change constantly as they come into sunlight or shadow.

SENTINELS of the desert—giant (saguaro) cactus in Saguaro National Monument, Arizona. The saguaro is the largest cactus known and its creamy white blossom is Arizona's state flower.

bec and Ontario, embrace immense regions of sky-high mountains, shining glaciers, and unspoiled forest and lake country where wild animals roam freely, safe from human enemies. Two of the parks were originally established for no other reason than to protect certain species of big-game animals that were threatened with extinction. Others preserve places of importance in the early history of Canada. There are so many provincial and national historic parks, each with noteworthy attractions, that we can mention only the more outstanding ones here.

The national parks

Perhaps Canada's best-known park regions are the national parks of Canada, administered and maintained by the federal Government. Eighteen of these are scenic parks and nineteen are historic parks. They not only stretch across the width of the continent but range north to

Hudson Bay and south to a latitude matching northern California's.

Seven of the magnificent scenic parks cover extensive mountain regions of the Rockies and Selkirks in British Columbia and Alberta. Four have been established in the Atlantic Provinces. Two prairie parks—not truly "prairie" in character —are large areas of virgin forests and sparkling blue lakes in the central sections of Saskatchewan and Manitoba. Two wild-animal preserves—Elk Island National Park and Wood Buffalo National Park—are in Alberta. Three smaller recreational units, on the shores of the Great Lakes and in the Thousand Islands of the St. Lawrence River, complete the national-parks system.

Apart from their value as a means of conserving the natural beauty of the land and its wildlife, both plant and animal, Canada's national parks are also "dedicated to the people of Canada for their

BY WATERTON LAKE, in Waterton Lakes National Park, Alberta, a member of the Royal Canadian Mounted Police gives motorists reliable directions.

benefit, education and enjoyment." Many of them have been developed for outdoor recreation and are linked to the main centers of population by road, rail and air. There are some seven hundred miles of motor roads in the various parks; and thousands of miles of trails have been cut through the wilderness sections, which lead to observation points with breathtaking views. Wild mammals of almost every Canadian species seek safety in the national parks, and their plant and bird life is also protected.

Parks from west to east

Suppose we travel in imagination from west to east across Canada, visiting some of the more important parks in each of the ten provinces.

In British Columbia, Canada's most westerly province, there are 117 provincial and four national parks. The national parks are Yoho, Kootenay, Glacier and Mount Revelstoke in the Selkirk and Rocky mountains. The provincial parks include E. C. Manning, on the Hope-Princeton highway east of Vancouver; Garibaldi, north of Vancouver; Wells Gray, north of Kamloops; and Strathcona, in the central part of Vancouver Island.

There are three classes of provincial parks in British Columbia. The 79 Class A parks are equipped for recreation. The 7 Class B parks are reserved for future development. Most of the 31 Class C parks are picnic grounds, playgrounds or small beach areas.

Mount Revelstoke

The most western of Canada's national parks is Mount Revelstoke, on the western slopes of the Selkirks, in British Columbia. It is easy to reach by main highways from Vancouver. At 6,000 feet above sea level, the park is almost literally in the clouds. A road from the town of Revelstoke climbs in easy stages up to the summit, rising 4,000 feet in 18 miles. From the top there is a superb view of the Illecillewaet and upper Columbia rivers.

Wild flowers grow in profusion in the open meadows, and countless little lakes lie in the rocky hollows carved by ancient glaciers. The whole area stretches across the Clachnacudainn Range, and from the lookout point at its summit visitors have a breath-taking view of three mountain ranges ringed with smoky clouds and topped with glistening snow fields. Far below, in the shadow of the mountains and cradled in the fork made by the Columbia and Illecillewaet rivers, is the town of Revelstoke.

More than forty miles of improved trails fan out from the summit to such interesting places as Lakes Eva and Miller. They are crystal-clear pools, well-stocked with cutthroat trout. Another trail leads to the Ice Box, a great cleft in the rock that is filled with ice and snow even at the height of summer.

Glacier National Park

Northeast of Revelstoke and also in the Selkirks is Glacier National Park. It is a superb alpine region of towering peaks, glittering rivers of ice, and forests. The area receives extremely heavy snows in winter. Most awe-inspiring of the glaciers is Illecillewaet which creeps down from an ice field almost ten miles square. The park remains a wilderness. There are no roads or hotels. The only way of seeing it is by railway. For part of the way the tracks go through a major engineering feat. Connaught Tunnel. Bored under Mount Macdonald it is almost five miles long.

Both Yoho (the name is an Indian word meaning "it is wonderful") and Kootenay national parks, which share a boundary, are on the western slope of the Rockies. Yoho is noted for its dramatic scenery: lofty peaks, magnificent waterfalls and colorful lakes. Kootenay was established to preserve the natural landscape along the Vermilion-Sinclair section of the Banff-Windermere Highway, the first motor road built across the central Rockies.

Kicking Horse Pass

Yoho lies astride the Trans-Canada Highway, which goes through Kicking Horse Pass (on the British Columbia-Alberta border) and thus over the Continental Divide. The pass was discovered by Dr. James Hector, on a geological expedition in 1858, whose own horse kicked him there. The highway runs by Wapta Lake, a favorite fishing spot and a starting point for trail trips to Lake O'Hara, whose beauty rivals that of famed Lake Louise, at Banff. Fed by melting glaciers, the blue-green waters of the lake reflect mountains that climb steeply from its wooded shores to lofty crowns of snow. The peaks offer a challenge that lures many mountain climbers. Two deep valleys are gouged in the park by the Yoho and the Kicking Horse rivers. Park headquarters are at the town of Field.

There are many spectacular waterfalls in the mountain parks, but Yoho has two of exceptional beauty. Twin Falls, which is fed by the Yoho, Wapta and other glaciers, seems to pour right out of the blue sky and plunges 600 feet in two cascades to the floor of the Yoho Valley. Lower down the Yoho Valley, Takakkaw Falls leaps over a massive limestone cliff and tumbles in a curtain of green water and silvery spray down to the Yoho River, 1,500 feet below. Takakkaw is one of the highest cataracts on the North American continent and one of the most impressive sights in the Rockies.

Kootenay National Park

Kootenay National Park, just south of Yoho, extends five miles on each side of the Banff-Windermere Highway for sixty miles. This splendid road is one of the main arteries of travel from the Canada–United States boundary line to the parks in the Canadian Rockies. It links with the Trans-Canada Highway and the Banff-Jasper Highway. The road winds beside the brilliantly colored walls of Sinclair Canyon, a spectacular cut in the mountains, where the perpendicular cliffs tower to a height of more than one thousand feet above the rushing waters of Sinclair Creek. The road also takes the motorist along the base of the Iron Gates, towering red rocks on either side of the Kootenay River, and the winding course of the Vermilion River to Vermilion Pass. This marks the boundary between Koote-

nay and Banff (Alberta) national parks.

Radium Hot Springs, today a resort, is on the southwestern edge of Kootenay park. As the name implies, the waters are radioactive—but not dangerously so. Hot mineral springs are one of the main attractions in several of the western national parks.

Kootenay is a big-game sanctuary. Such mammals as big-horn sheep, Rocky Mountain goats, elk, moose, mule deer, and black, brown and grizzly bears live there, safe from hunters.

Kootenay has a number of other interesting features. In summer, Floe Lake is dotted with small icebergs that have broken off from the tongue of Floe Glacier. The Paint Pots are ocher springs, once a source of ceremonial paint for the Indians of the region. In Marble Canyon the rushing waters of Tokumm Creek have worn through layers of white and gray marble to a depth of two hundred feet, leaving the canyon walls striped with mottled color. At the head of the canyon there is a seventy-foot waterfall. The gorge also boasts a natural bridge of rock.

Canada's best-known parks and some of the most widely used outdoor recreational regions lie in Alberta. Besides scenery, they offer splendid hotels, exciting skiing, and fighting trout in the swift streams. Within Alberta the Canadian Rockies soar to their grandest heights. The most accessible national parks in Alberta are Banff, Jasper and Waterton Lakes.

Banff, a sea of mountains

Banff (first called Rocky Mountains National Park) was established in 1885, the first of Canada's national parks. It then consisted of just ten square miles of land, surrounding the sulfur springs. It has been extended since, from the eastern foothills of Canada's Rocky Mountains to the Continental Divide. It embraces a sea of mountains, with ranges rising one behind the other in parallel lines. Lofty peaks and wooded valleys, rivers, glaciers, meadows of wild flowers, lakes, waterfalls, canyons, hot mineral springs and mountain wildlife have made this region world famous. Beautiful Lake Louise,

»

CANOEING and swimming are among the pleasures of a summer vacation at Fresh-water Lake in Cape Breton Highlands National Park, Nova Scotia.

tucked beneath the towering cliffs and gleaming snow fields of Mount Victoria, and Lake Moraine, in the impressive Valley of the Ten Peaks, are among Banff's outstanding attractions.

The town of Banff is a typical western resort town with wide streets, holiday hotels, modern restaurants, a wild-animal corral, and liveries where boats as well as horses may be rented. The summer climate is superb, cool and dry, the air redolent of the scent of balsam fir. Nearby are hot sulfur springs. A gay winter carnival is held at Banff every year. In summer it has a widely known school of fine arts, an extension of the University of Alberta.

Jasper park's grandeur

Banff's sister park Jasper has many of the same features but on an even grander scale. The 4,200 square miles of Jasper make it the largest national playground in North America. Its story is a fascinating chapter in the early history of western Canada. Along the famous Athabaska Trail, which winds through the area's green valleys and along its rugged mountain passes, came the explorers, fur traders, botanists, prospectors, missionaries and a host of other pioneers of a bygone era. The trail followed in part the course of the Athabaska River, which rises in the southern section of the park. Even today much of the park is an unexplored mountain wilderness.

The town of Jasper is the park headquarters. Almost thirty-eight miles from Jasper, down the Jasper-Edmonton Highway, some of the hottest natural springs in North America bubble from the banks of Sulphur Creek, at Miette Hot Springs.

Joining the two great parks is the 186-mile Banff-Jasper Highway. It follows the broad valleys of the Athabaska and Sunwapta rivers and passes through some of the most awe-inspiring scenery in the Rockies. The road sweeps across the floors of the valleys in long, straight runs and climbs the sides of wooded mountains, to heights of nearly seven thousand feet, by easy switchbacks. At the summits there are views of exceptional beauty. The highway skirts such spectacles as Johnston Canyon, Mount Eisenhower, Lake Louise and Panther Falls. Still other heights loom up—the Snow Dome, the Dolomite Peaks, Mount Hector and Mount Edith Cavell.

The Columbia Icefield

The vast Columbia Icefield is partly within Jasper park, on the south. In existence for perhaps a million years, the awesome mantle of ice that lies on the shoulders of the Rocky Mountains covers some

«

SETTING UP CAMP at Quetico park, Ontario. The park takes in 1,750 square miles of the beautiful country that stretches to the north of Lake Superior.

A SMOOTH BEACH and rowboats keep small fry busy at Oastler Lake, Ontario.

406

«

AN ELABORATE TENT—it even has a window—nestles among the trees on the shore of Clear Lake, in Riding Mountain National Park, in west-central Manitoba.

Campers' joy—woods, sparkling water

DEVIL'S HALF ACRE, in Fundy park, New Brunswick, attracts hikers seeking a camp site.

NATIONAL FILM BOARD OF CANADA

150 square miles and in places reaches a depth of 2,000 feet. Glacial tongues licking down the warm valleys drain to form the headwaters of the Athabaska and North Saskatchewan rivers. The Athabaska Glacier, between Snow Dome and Mount Athabaska, is second largest of the frozen rivers that emerge from the ice field. A spur of the Banff-Jasper Highway leads motorists to the very edge of Athabaska Glacier. Aboard snowmobiles, visitors may cross a three-mile stretch of the ice field in the neighborhood of Sunwapta Pass.

The Athabaska River, which rises in the Columbia Icefield, gathers tremendous volume from its many tributaries. It then tumbles into a gorge, creating a fall eighty feet deep. The main body of the river strikes the wall of the canyon with tremendous force and is hurled back into midstream where it boils and churns and swirls in great whirlpools flinging curtains of spray. The scene is wildly beautiful in a setting of alpine grandeur.

Canadian-American wonderland

Since 1932 Waterton Lakes National Park, in southwestern Alberta, has been joined to Glacier National Park, Montana, to form Waterton-Glacier International Peace Park. The Canadian park lies on the eastern slopes of the Rockies and has soaring peaks, and fir-carpeted valleys dotted with sprawling lakes. Many of these lakes straddle the international boundary line so that it is possible to cruise deep into Glacier park from Waterton starting points.

The park takes its name from upper Waterton Lake, a seven-mile-long body of water cut by the international border. The sparkling blue body of water is cradled in a deep trench between two lofty mountain ranges. Little more than a hundred years ago the region was an Indian hunting ground. White men did not discover it until 1858. Deer, grizzly and black bear, Rocky Mountain sheep and goat, elk and moose all find sanctuary in the beautiful wilderness.

The mountains of Waterton park have been shaped by the grinding action of ancient glaciers and by wind and weather. Their coloring is unusually rich, shading through purple, green and gold, particularly at sunrise and sunset. Seen from the plains of Alberta at those hours, the peaks are an awesome sight.

We have already mentioned the other two national parks in Alberta, Elk Island and Wood Buffalo. Both are big-game refuges. Elk Island, thirty miles east of Edmonton, the largest fenced animal preserve in Canada, is a delightful region of meadows, forest, lakes and marshes. The park's main attraction is its magnificent herd of plains buffalo. They share lush pastures with large numbers of elk, mule deer and moose. The park is also an important bird sanctuary where more than two hundred species have been counted in recent years. Though originally intended only as a wildlife preserve, Elk Island park's many lakes and rolling, wooded terrain make it particularly appealing to lovers of outdoor life.

Far to the north in Alberta and extending into the Northwest Territories is Wood Buffalo park, the largest big-game preserve on the continent. The park takes in 17,300 square miles of forests and plains and was established in 1922 chiefly to protect a large herd of wood buffalo. Other big-game and fur-bearing animals live there as well. Wood Buffalo park is so remote that it is rather out of bounds for casual visitors. However, there is air service between Fort Smith (Northwest Territories), park headquarters, and Edmonton and Prince Albert (Saskatchewan).

Both Wood Buffalo and Elk Island parks are classic examples of wildlife conservation in Canada. Early in the century, when the plains buffalo had virtually died out on its native prairies, the Canadian Government purchased the greater part of the only remaining herd in North America in order to save the species from possible extinction. Two Montana rangers had built up the herd from a pair of calves captured by an Indian in 1873. In 1907 this herd was transferred to a fenced enclosure in the Elk Island area and the park was established in 1913.

Today there are more than a thousand buffalo in the park.

Small herds of wood buffalo, which are larger and a darker color than the plains buffalo, were seen along the wooded banks of the Slave River by the earliest explorers in the Mackenzie River district of Canada's Northwest. Measures to protect the animals were taken as early as 1893. Nevertheless many of the animals were still being slaughtered every year in that period. Not until the park was established in 1922 was their preservation ensured. In 1924 there were only some 1,500 head. Then several thousand selected surplus animals from the plains herds were shipped north in 1925 and 1928. Today the total number of buffalo in the park is about 10,000.

Alberta's provincial parks

Alberta has 35 provincial parks scattered through its mountains and plains. They take in 96,134 acres. An additional 10,000 acres are held in reserve by the provincial government for future parks. Typical of Alberta's provincial parks is one of the latest to be incorporated into the system: Big Hill Springs. It is northwest of Calgary in a picturesque region of steep wooded ridges. The sparkling cold waters of Big Hill Springs Creek tumble through the sixty-two acres of park in a delightful series of thirty-two waterfalls, dashing past many small islands.

Dinosaur Park, in the badlands of Alberta's Red Deer River, just eighty-eight miles north of Calgary, is surely one of Canada's most unusual parks. In the fantastic rock formations of the red-shale hills, ravines and flats are the fossils of great prehistoric reptiles and oyster beds. Once living forests stand petrified. Fifty million or so years ago, before the Rocky Mountains were formed, the area was a steaming swamp where giant reptiles— the monstrous dinosaurs, with tiny brains —and fierce saber-toothed tigers roved at will.

Eastward from the Rocky Mountains, backbone of the continent, stretch a thousand miles of great plains across Alberta, Saskatchewan and Manitoba. The plains are a grassy, generally level expanse, with here and there charming islands of wooded hills and lakes to break the monotony.

Cypress Hills provincial park in the southwest corner of Saskatchewan is such an island. The park is 4,300 feet above sea level—only a little less high than Banff—and is heavily wooded with lodgepole pine. Thousands of years ago when the great glaciers swept down over the continent, then much warmer, Cypress Hills remained above the flood of ice, and its plant life was hardly disturbed. Thus the region is particularly interesting to naturalists because it has semitropical trees and some other kinds of plants ordinarily found only much farther south.

Prince Albert National Park

The largest national park in Saskatchewan is Prince Albert. In the center of the province, the park is a large forested region dotted with lakes. In the early days of the fur trade its waterways were paddled by trappers, hunters and traders from the north country and Hudson Bay. Today the park draws those who take to canoes for pleasure alone. There are hundreds of lakes, from small ponds to bodies of water twenty miles long. As many of them are connected by channels and streams, some waterways continue for hundreds of miles. With only a few short portages it is possible to make a complete circuit of the park by water, passing through nearly a score of lakes on the way. Largest of the lakes in the park are Halkett, Waskesiu, Kingsmere, Crean and Lavalee.

The park is just thirty-six miles from the city of Prince Albert, Saskatchewan. The summer-resort town of Waskesiu, park headquarters, is thirty miles farther north over a paved highway. There are facilities for seaplane landings on Lake Waskesiu.

Four miles south of the city of North Battleford, Saskatchewan, is one of Canada's western national historic parks— Fort Battleford. This is where the North West Mounted Police (today the Royal Canadian Mounted Police) won its first round against the wild Canadian West.

DRIFTING CLOUDS wreathe the summits of the Monshee Range—a magnificent view from Mount Revelstoke National Park, B. C.

Nature's spirit-lifting grandeur

TONGUE of the Athabaska Glacier, part of the Columbia Icefield, in Jasper park, Alta.

A MOTORBOAT cruises among the Thousand Islands, St. Lawrence Islands park, Ontario.

WILD FLOWERS carpet a valley in Glacier park, British Columbia.

ROCKY HEADLANDS and restless sea along the Cabot Trail of Cape Breton Highlands National Park, in Nova Scotia.

SUNSET over the rippling waters of Greenwater Lake in the Saskatchewan park of the same name.

SASKATCHEWAN PHOTO SERVICES

411

The fort, NWMP headquarters for the Saskatchewan district, was squarely in the Indian country. Powerful tribes of plains Indians lived there, whose leaders included such influential chiefs as Poundmaker and Big Bear. There were also many métis (half-breeds). However, the presence of the fort encouraged a steady stream of settlers from the east into the plains territory.

There was constant friction. For one thing the métis feared they would lose their land. The situation finally erupted in 1885 when the métis, stimulated by their leader Louis Riel, openly rebelled. During the Northwest Rebellion, Fort Battleford provided a precarious refuge for many of the early settlers. It lay within striking distance of several thousand Indians, whom Riel had been trying to draw into the conflict on the side of the métis. Instead Riel's defeat induced the Indians to surrender, and the fort never had to meet an attack.

Today the historic fort contains many interesting relics of the North West Mounted Police, the early settlers and the fur trade. The buildings are surrounded by a log stockade.

Playlands in Manitoba

Manitoba has nine provincial parks and one national park. The provincial parks include Whiteshell Forest Reserve, in the southeast corner of the province; and Porcupine Forest Reserve and the Duck Mountain Forest Reserve, in the west-central section.

Riding Mountain National Park, in southwestern Manitoba, is about 125 miles north of the international boundary. The park was established in 1929. Its plateau location, the highest spot in the province, makes the park a delightful playground. This broad plateau is the summit of Riding Mountain, which rises more than a thousand feet above a smooth patchwork of green and brown farmlands. The park

NATIONAL PARKS

NAME	LOCATION	FEATURES	AREA IN SQ. MI.*	YEAR EST.
Scenic				
Banff	Rocky Mts., Alberta	Lake Louise; Valley of the Ten Peaks; sulfur springs; winter carnival	2,564	1885
Cape Breton Highlands	Nova Scotia	Rugged coast and highlands; Cabot Trail	390	1936
Fundy	Bay of Fundy, New Brunswick	Forests; wildlife sanctuary	80	1948
Georgian Bay Islands	Georgian Bay, Ontario	Grotesque rock formations on Flower Pot Island	5	1929
Glacier	Selkirk Mts., British Columbia	Peaks and glaciers; climbing and skiing	521	1886
Jasper	Rocky Mts., Alberta	Columbia Icefield; hot springs; wildlife	4,200	1907
Kootenay	Rocky Mts., British Columbia	Canyons; hot springs; Vermilion-Sinclair section of Banff-Windermere Highway	543	1920
Mount Revelstoke	Selkirk Mts., British Columbia	Mountain-top plateau; alpine meadows; skiing	100	1914
Point Pelee	Lake Erie, Ontario	Excellent beaches; plant life; on flyway of bird migration	6	1918
Prince Albert	Central Saskatchewan	Many lakes and streams; canoeing	1,496	1937
Prince Edward Island	Northern Prince Edward Island	Famous beaches, on Gulf of St. Lawrence	7	1937
Riding Mountain	West of Lake Winnipeg, Manitoba	Lakes, forests, wildlife sanctuary on mountain summit	1,148	1929

* 1 square mile equals 640 acres

is densely forested and has a number of woodland lakes with sandy beaches. Deer, elk, moose and bear all find sanctuary in the heavily timbered uplands; and a show herd of buffalo grazes peacefully near Audy Lake. On the park's eastern side, a great cliff, 2,200 feet above sea level, provides visitors with a striking panoramic view of the plains.

The mountaintop playground stretches for nearly 70 miles westward, taking in an area of 1,148 square miles. Among the thick stands of spruce, pine and Manitoba maple are meadows carpeted with wild roses, marigolds and Indian paintbrush. The mountain tarns were shaped by the great glaciers of the ice age. Clear Lake, largest and most beautiful of the tarns, teems with pike, lake trout, and perch. The lake is nine miles long and in places almost two miles wide. Along the forty miles of shore line are smooth sandy beaches, and winding trails and bridle paths to lure hikers and horsemen.

Whiteshell Forest Reserve, a two-hour drive east of Winnipeg, is on the fringe of Canada's Precambrian Shield. The park (officially, a forest reserve) covers miles of deep woods threaded with some two hundred lakes and streams. They form a network that makes the region wonderful canoeing country. Whiteshell also has good roads. They wind by the shimmering lakes where great volcanic cliffs rise straight up out of the water. The subtle coloring of the forest, ranging from the dark blue-green of spruce to the yellowish green of poplar and the silver of birch trunks, attracts many artists and photographers. The southern half of the park is a game preserve harboring moose, deer, beaver, muskrat and many species of birds who make their homes among the wild-rice beds. For human visitors there are many lodges, cabins, campsites and trailer parks.

Although it is outside the national and provincial parks system, another park,

NATIONAL PARKS—*continued*

NAME	LOCATION	FEATURES	AREA IN SQ. MI.*	YEAR EST.
St. Lawrence Islands	Thousand Islands area of St. Lawrence, in Ontario	Camping and recreation	0.30	1914
Terra Nova	Bonavista Bay, Newfoundland	Wilderness; rich wildlife	156	1957
Waterton Lakes	Southern Alberta	Peaks and lakes; part of Waterton-Glacier International Peace Park (Alberta-Montana)	204	1895
Yoho	Rocky Mts., British Columbia	Lofty peaks; Takakkaw Falls; mountain climbing	507	1886
Wild Animal				
Elk Island	Central Alberta	Largest fenced animal preserve in Canada	75	1913
Wood Buffalo	Alberta-Northwest Territories	Largest wild-animal park in North America	17,300	1922
Historic			AREA IN ACRES	
Batoche Rectory	Near Prince Albert, Saskatchewan	Headquarters of Louis Riel and site of main battle in Northwest Rebellion of 1885	1	1957
Bell, Alexander Graham	Baddeck, Nova Scotia	Bell's summer home and burial place	14	
Fort Anne	Annapolis Royal, Nova Scotia	Early Acadian settlement	31	1917
Fort Battleford	Near North Battleford, Saskatchewan	North West Mounted Police post, 1876	37	1951

* 1 square mile equals 640 acres

The biggest fish I ever caught . . .

»

RODS AND REELS are checked before the start of a fishing trip on Lake of Two Rivers in Algonquin Provincial Park, Ontario.

NATIONAL FILM BOARD OF CANADA

HYDROPLANE TRANSPORT to Quebec's La Vérendrye park.

PROVINCIAL PUBLICITY BUREAU, QUEBEC

MANITOBA BUREAU TRAVEL & PUBLICITY

»

WAITING for a nibble from the placid depths of Clearwater Lake in Cormorant Forest Reserve. It is near The Pas, Man.

414

LAKE TROUT, or namaycush. It and its relatives are valiant fighters.

PHOTOS OF FISH, ONTARIO DEPT. LANDS & FORESTS

RAINBOW TROUT, so named for the shimmering iridescence of its scales.

NATIONAL FILM BOARD OF CANADA

« NETTING a trout in Fundy park, New Brunswick. Only flies, usually artificial, are used as trout bait.

STILL FLAPPING, a good sized catch is hauled out of a lake in the Nipigon area, Ontario.

ONTARIO DEPT. TRAVEL & PUBLICITY

A MOOSE splashes its way ashore in Fundy park, N.B.

Creatures of the wild find haven in the parks

BEAVERS rest a moment.

EAGLE fluttering its wings.

GRIZZLY in Jasper park.

BUFFALO, Elk Island park, Alta.

SURE-FOOTED on heights
—Rocky Mountain goats.

WAPITI, or American elk,
bear majestic antlers.

A SHY RACCOON.

FOX—furry and bright-eyed.

GANNETS nest on Bona-
venture Island, Gaspé area.
«

ENDEARING FAWNS cuddle up to a small "nursemaid" in Fundy National Park, New Brunswick.

dymion and Gordon); and Georgina and Constance, which lie side by side a short distance east of Ivy Lea. Grenadier Island, one of the largest, is almost a mile east of Rockport. From the Thousand Islands International Bridge there is a thrilling view of the wooded isles rising from the blue-green waters of the St. Lawrence. With the opening of the St. Lawrence Seaway, ocean-going vessels are now weaving through the channels.

Many of the parks in Ontario are particularly suited for canoe trips. Countless lakes and rivers, winding through deep woods, invite the dip of paddle and the curling smoke of campfire. Quetico park, in the Rainy River District, and the streams and lakes of Algonquin park and the Timagami Forest Reserve all sound a call to canoeing adventure.

Upper Canada Village

With the building of the St. Lawrence Seaway, many historic landmarks in the upper valley were in danger of vanishing. To save them, Ontario is creating more provincial parks and moving the historic buildings there. The focus of the plan is Crysler Memorial Park, upriver from Cornwall. In it Upper Canada Village is being erected. The village consists of thirty buildings that have been moved from hamlets now flooded. Most of the buildings are associated with the migration of United Empire Loyalists to this area in 1783. The village is intended not only to preserve the buildings but also to reflect the early life and achievements of the pioneers. A shallow-draft canal with an early-type lock, along with a batteau, will be constructed, giving added charm to the village.

Quetico is a vast forested wilderness whose lakes and rivers were highroads for early French traders and explorers heading west. The region is almost 40 per cent water. It straddles the Ontario-Minnesota border. The Canadian section

---

PROVINCIAL PARKS—*continued*

NAME	LOCATION AND AREA
British Columbia	
Alice Lake	Squamish; 104 acres
Anthony Island	Southwest of Moresby Island; 345 acres
Antlers Beach	Peachland; 3 acres
Apodaca	Bowen Island; 20 acres
Beatton	Fort St. John; 770 acres
Beaver Point	Salt Spring Island; 40 acres
Bijoux Falls	John Hart Highway 135 miles from Dawson Creek; 100 acres
Boundary Creek	Greenwood; 7 acres
Brentwood Bay	Near Victoria; 1 acre
Bridge Lake	East of 91 Mile House; 15 acres
Bromley Rock	Princeton (two areas); 368 acres
Brothers Memorial	Gibsons Landing; 5 acres
Cameron Lake	Parksville-Alberni Highway; 733 acres
Canim Beach	100 Mile House, off Cariboo Highway; 13 acres
Champion Lakes	Trail; 3,520 acres
Chasm	Clinton; 315 acres
Cinnemousun Narrows	Shuswap Lake, north of Sicamous; 319 acres
Clearwater	Hedley; 260 acres

NAME	LOCATION AND AREA
Colleymount Community	Burns Lake; 26 acres
Cottonwood River	Near Quesnel (called Cinema Campsite); 164 acres
Cultus Lake	Chilliwack; 950 acres
Darke Lake	Summerland; 5,472 acres
Dead Man's Island	Burns Lake; 1 acre
Dry Gulch	Radium Junction; 57 acres
Echo Lake	Near Lumby; 380 acres
Elk Falls	Campbell River; 2,565 acres
Elk River	Fernie; 10 acres
Emory Creek	Hope (Hope-Yale Highway); 37 acres
Englishman River	Parksville; 240 acres
Exchamsiks River	Terrace; 38 acres
Fillongley	Denman Island; 57 acres
Garibaldi	Haney and Squamish; 966 sq. mi.
Golden Community	Golden; 368 acres
Goldpan	Spences Bridge; 12 acres
Hamber	Big Bend Highway; 3,799 sq. mi.
Inkaneep (formerly Oliver Campsite)	Oliver; 7 acres
Inonoaklin	Edgewood; 6 acres
Ivy Green	Ladysmith; 52 acres

forms the 1,750 square-mile Quetico Provincial Park. It is strictly controlled by the Ontario government in order to keep its wilderness character. No building is allowed in the park, planes can land only at special points outside the park boundary, and access roads into the region are limited. However, these restrictions make the park a thrilling retreat for naturalists and other lovers of untamed land. Algonquin provincial park is about two hundred miles north of Toronto. In this region of lakes, rivers and forested hills, wildlife is protected strictly. Along the paved highway that winds through the southern section, wild deer feel so safe that they amble down to the road to watch passing motorists. The park is another ideal region for canoeing and camping. Hundreds of lakes, connected by rivers and streams, are scattered throughout the park. The fishing is excellent; lake trout, speckled trout and bass test the angler's skill.

In Ontario there are a number of his-

toric forts that have been established as national historic parks. Fort Malden (about sixteen miles from Windsor, Ontario) and Fort Wellington (near the town of Prescott on the St. Lawrence River) are the most notable. Both forts played prominent roles in the War of 1812. Fort Malden was the rallying point for the British in their attack on and capture of Detroit in 1812. Fort Wellington was built during that war to defend the lines of communication between Montreal and Kingston. It, too, was used as a headquarters for attacks, these against the town of Ogdensburg across the St. Lawrence River. Both forts are kept in excellent repair; and Fort Malden has an interesting museum containing exhibits of the early history of the region.

Quebec's parks and reserves

In Quebec, the largest province in Canada, 52,254 square miles of scenic territory are set aside for parks and preserves.

PROVINCIAL PARKS—*continued*

NAME	LOCATION AND AREA	NAME	LOCATION AND AREA
Jimsmith Lake	Cranbrook-Creston Highway area; 124 acres	McDonald	Sidney; 26 acres
John Dean	Sidney; 104 acres	Mackenzie, Sir Alexander	Ocean Falls; 13 acres
Johnstone Creek	Bridesville; 58 acres	Maclure Lake	Telkwa-Smithers; 60 acres
Kelowna	Kelowna; 3 acres		
Keremeos Columns	Keremeos; 50 acres	MacMillan	Parksville-Alberni Highway; 337 acres
King George VI	Rossland; 400 acres	Manitou	Naramata; 3 acres
Kitsumgallum	Terrace; 109 acres	Manning, E. C.	Hope-Princeton Highway; 179,313 acres
Kitty Coleman Beach	Merville; 21 acres	Maquinna	Near Sidney Inlet, Vancouver Island; 31 acres
Kleanza Creek	Terrace; 143 acres	Marble Canyon	Clinton (Pavilion Lake); 827 acres
Kokanee Creek	Nelson; 27 acres		
Kokanee Glacier	Nelson; 64,000 acres	Matheson Lake	Rocky Point, near Victoria; 401 acres
Lac La Hache	Clinton–Williams Lake; 54 acres	Memory Island	Shawinigan Lake; 2 acres
Lac Le Jeune	Near Kamloops; 138 acres	Miracle Beach	Oyster River, Vancouver Island; 326 acres
Lakelse Lake	Terrace; 11 acres		
Liard River Hotsprings	Alaska Highway; 1,650 acres	Monck	Nicola Lake; 111 acres
Little Qualicum Falls	Qualicum Beach–Hilliers; 249 acres	Monte Lake	Kamloops-Vernon Highway; 19 acres
Little Shuswap	Chase; 3 acres	Mount Assiniboine	Invermere-Golden; 12,850 acres
Lockhart Beach	Near Kootenay Bay Ferry; 7 acres	Mount Maxwell	Salt Spring Island; 492 acres
Long Lake	Nanaimo-Wellington; ⅓ acre	Mount Robson	Robson; 803 sq. mi.
Loon Lake	Cache Creek–Clinton; 8 acres	Mount Seymour	North Vancouver; 8,669 acres
McBride Community	McBride; 71 acres	Muncho Lake	Alaska Highway; 341 sq. mi.

Where history has left a lasting impress

NOVA SCOTIA FILM BUREAU

INTERIOR of Alexander Graham Bell museum at Baddeck, N. S. It has five sides.

AT FORT ANNE, Annapolis Royal, French, English and Indians fought for possession of Nova Scotia in the seventeenth and eighteenth centuries. In a present-day pageant the fort's colorful story is re-enacted.

THE CITADEL, a grim fortress, surmounts a hill overlooking Halifax Harbour, N. S.

THE MUSEUM AT Fort Battleford park, in Saskatchewan.

»
GREEN GABLES, the enchanting house on Prince Edward Island that was the setting for Lucy Maud Montgomery's memorable *Anne of Green Gables.*

CRUMBLING WALLS are all that remain of the (French) Fortress of Louisbourg, Nova Scotia.

423

Among them are Kipawa Reserve, in western Quebec near the Quebec-Ontario boundary; La Vérendrye park, northeast of Ottawa; Mont Tremblant park, about 140 miles northwest of Montreal. North of Quebec City is Laurentides park, and northwest again, near Lac St. Jean, is the Chibougamau Reserve. The Mistassini Reserve lies in the great forest and lake country north of Chibougamau. Farthest east of Quebec's parks is Gaspesian, in the heart of the great thumb of land—the Gaspé Peninsula—that stretches into the Gulf of St. Lawrence.

These parks and preserves are wildlife sanctuaries and oases of unspoiled scenery. Some of the parks surround charming French-Canadian towns and hamlets, first settled more than three hundred years ago. Just along the St. Lawrence River from above Montreal to Tadoussac, at the mouth of the Saguenay, there are some eighty historic sites.

From Gaspesian park rise the Shick-shock Mountains, the highest range in eastern Canada. The park offers a sporting challenge to mountaineer, photographer and salmon fisherman alike. From Mount Jacques Cartier (4,300 feet), the loftiest summit, there is an eye-filling view of the mountains rolling away to the horizon.

Laurentide park has an average altitude of two thousand feet above sea level and is noted for its spectacular speckled-trout fishing. In an open mountainous district that includes the upper basin of the Ottawa River lies La Vérendrye park, another wonderful fishing region. Mount Oxford park, in the Eastern Townships, and Mont Tremblant park, in the Laurentians, are year-round resort areas where skiing, golfing and mountain climbing are the principal attractions.

Historic sites in Quebec

As some of the earliest settlements in North America were established in Que-

PROVINCIAL PARKS—*continued*

NAME	LOCATION AND AREA	NAME	LOCATION AND AREA
Nakusp Hot Springs	Nakusp; 127 acres	Stone Mountain	Alaska Highway; 64,000 acres
Nakusp Recreation	Nakusp; 39 acres	Strathcona	Campbell River; 828 sq. mi.
Newstead	View Royal, near Victoria; ¼ acre	Strombeck	Alice Arm; 1 acre
		Sutherland Hills	Kelowna; 57 acres
Nicolum River	Hope; 60 acres	Swan Lake	Pouce Coupe; 166 acres
Okanagan Falls	Skaha Lake; 4 acres	Tow Hill	Queen Charlotte Islands; 480 acres
Okanagan Lake	Okanagan Lake; 198 acres		
Oliver	Oliver; 21 acres	Tweedsmuir	Bella Coola–Burns Lake; 2,424,400 acres
Osoyoos	Osoyoos; 21 acres		
Peace Arch	White Rock and Blaine; 16 acres	Vaseaux Lake	Oliver-Penticton; 13 acres
		Wasa	Cranbrook; 133 acres
Petroglyph	Nanaimo; 3 acres	Wells Gray	Clearwater; 2,032 sq. mi.
Premier Lake	Cranbrook–Canal Flats; 165 acres	Wendle	Wells; 640 acres
		Westbank	Westbank; 9 acres
Princeton	Princeton; 341 acres	Westview	Powell River; 10 acres
Roberts Creek	Roberts Creek; 102 acres	Whiskers Point	Off John Hart Highway, east side of McLeod Lake; 128 acres
Rosewall Creek	Bowser–Fanny Bay, Vancouver Island; 156 acres		
Salt Lake	Prince Rupert; 87 acres	Wilson, Ethel F.	Pinkut Lake (Burns Lake); 71 acres
Savona	East of Cache Creek; 4 acres	Yahk	Cranbrook-Creston Highway; 17 acres
Seeley Lake	Hazelton; 20 acres		
Shuswap Lake	West arm Shuswap Lake; 276 acres	Yard Creek	Sicamous-Revelstoke; 40 acres
Silver Star	Vernon; 21,888 acres	*Manitoba*	
Skihist	Lytton; 9 acres	Belair Forest Reserve	Lake Winnipeg; 54 acres
Sooke Mountain	Near Victoria; 912 acres		
Stamp Falls	Alberni; 424 acres	Cormorant Forest Reserve	Near The Pas; 575 acres
Stemwinder	Hedley; 9 acres		

bec, the province has many historic sites and shrines of importance to all Canadians. Just twenty miles from Montreal, on the banks of the Richelieu River, stands Fort Chambly. First erected in 1665, as a stacked wood enclosure, it had a long history of siege and capture in the early days of French control. Forty years after its completion the fort was burned by Indians while the garrison was away. In 1710 the French rebuilt the fort in stone. They continued to hold it until the Seven Years' War when it fell to the English, in 1760. In 1775 an American army under Montgomery captured it, and demolished it the following year. It was rebuilt for the last time in 1777 and garrisoned until about 1850. Today the fort is a national historic park, and much of it has been restored. There is a museum in the grounds with many interesting relics of the fort's exciting story.

Fort Lennox National Historic Park is on Ile aux Noix, in the Richelieu River twelve miles north of Lake Champlain. Though Fort Lennox is not the original structure, its site was a focal point in the Seven Years' War, the American Revolution and the War of 1812.

Atlantic Provinces parks

Canada's four smallest provinces—New Brunswick, Prince Edward Island, Nova Scotia and Newfoundland, all on the Atlantic seaboard—each has a national park of its own. New Brunswick's is Fundy National Park, along the bay of the same name. Nova Scotia has Cape Breton Highlands National Park, which takes in the northern part of Cape Breton Island. Prince Edward Island park includes twenty-five miles of red-sand beaches along the shores of the Gulf of St. Lawrence. Newfoundland has one of Canada's newest national parks, Terra Nova, about 150 miles north of St. John's.

Fundy National Park stretches for eight miles along the Bay of Fundy among val-

---

PROVINCIAL PARKS—continued

NAME	LOCATION AND AREA
Duck Mountain Forest	West-central Manitoba; 1,426 acres
Northwest Angle Forest Reserve	Southeast Manitoba; 280 acres
Porcupine Forest Reserve	Near Swan River; 787 acres
Whiteshell Forest Reserve	Southeast Manitoba; 1,088 acres

New Brunswick

NAME	LOCATION AND AREA
The Enclosure	Near Newcastle; 120 acres

Newfoundland

NAME	LOCATION AND AREA
Sir Richard Squires Memorial	Upper Humber River; 3,840 acres

Nova Scotia

NAME	LOCATION AND AREA
Chignecto Game Sanctuary	6 miles south of River Hebert; 85 sq. mi.
Liscomb Game Sanctuary	Eastern shore area; 200 sq. mi.
Tobeatic Game Sanctuary	Western end of province; 180 sq. mi.
Waverley Game Sanctuary	Halifax County; 65 sq. mi.

Ontario

NAME	LOCATION AND AREA
Aaron	East of Dryden; 110 acres
Adolphustown	West of Kingston; 30 acres

NAME	LOCATION AND AREA
Algonquin	East of Huntsville; 2,750 sq. mi.
Bass Lake	West of Orillia; 85 acres
Batchawana Bay	North of Sault Ste. Marie; 90 acres
Black Lake	West of junction of Highways 7 and 38; 10 acres
Blue Lake	Vermilion Bay; 5 acres
Burnham, Mark S.	East of Peterborough; 100 acres
Carson Lake	West of Barry's Bay; 15 acres
Clay Creek	North of Sombra; 20 acres
Costello Creek	West of East Park Gate
Craigleith	West of Collingwood; 27 acres
Dawson Trail Camp Grounds	East of Atikokan; 150 acres
Devil's Glen	South of Collingwood; 12 acres
Eel's Creek	North of Burleigh Falls; 48 acres
Emily	East of Omemee; 50 acres
Esker Lakes	Near Kirkland Lake; 7,000 acres
Fairbank Lake	Northwest of Whitefish
Finlayson Point	South of Timagami; 80 acres
Frog Rapids	South of Sioux Lookout; 13 acres

» BIRDS need sanctuary on their great spring and fall migrations. They not only delight our eyes and ears but feed on many of the pests that attack crops.

Conservation—

CANADA GEESE thrive, unmolested by man, safe within the limits of the parks.

» PLANT LIFE is also protected. Here a naturalist explains the value of a wild plant to an interested young audience.

WITHOUT SANCTUARIES, the mallard duck, prized by hunters, might now be extinct.

chief purpose of the parks

leys and wooded hills rising a thousand feet above the bay. Coves and inlets, carved by Fundy's tremendous sixty-foot tides, dent the rugged coast line. Inland the sound of water, rushing or murmuring, is ever present as swift streams and rivers crisscross the whole park. Point Wolf River winds along the southwest; Forty-five River, Laverty Brook and the Upper and Lower Vault brooks traverse the eastern section. In fact, rivers form part of the park boundaries: Upper Salmon River and the Goose River mark the east and west edges.

Even along the main highway, running directly through the center of the park, there are startling glimpses of wildlife in wilderness surroundings. Beaver, white-tailed deer, moose, bobcat, lynx and other large mammals haunt the lakes and the dense forests. The highway leads to Hastings Hill where the great sweep of the Bay of Fundy, Owl Head and Cape Enragé is an inspiring sight.

Just inside the park entrance is Devil's Half Acre, a 1,200-foot-high ridge that clings to the Bay of Fundy coast. In the deep crevices that crease the top of the ridge, quantities of ice and snow, sheltered from the sun, remain all summer long.

Red-sand beaches

Prince Edward Island is the smallest of Canada's provinces and yet one of its most appealing as a vacation land. Cradled on its north shore, facing the broad Gulf of St. Lawrence, is one of Canada's loveliest parks, Prince Edward Island National Park. It was established in 1937. Though the park is small, only about seven square miles, its smooth, red-sand beaches, separated by headlands, extend for almost twenty-five miles. There the waters of the gulf, rolling in over the gently sloping strand, are warmed in summer by the long hours of sunshine to a pleasant 76-degree average. On the landward side

PROVINCIAL PARKS—*continued*

NAME	LOCATION AND AREA	NAME	LOCATION AND AREA
Golden Lake	East of Killaloe; 2 acres	Marten River	South of Timagami; 102 acres
Greenwater Lakes	West of Cochrane; 11,000 acres	Mazinaw	North of Kaladar; 6 acres
Inverhuron	Tiverton; 300 acres	Mew Lake	East of West Park Gate
Inwood	West of Fort William; 60 acres	Middle Falls	South of Fort William; 10 acres
Ipperwash	Between Ravenswood and Port Franks; 109 acres	Mississauga Lake	Buckton; 15 acres
Kakabeka Falls	West of Fort William; 350 acres	Oastler Lake	South of Parry Sound; 30 acres
Kap-Kig-Iwan	South of Englehart; 300 acres	One-sided Lake	South of Nestor Falls; 270 acres
Kearney Lake	East of West Park Gate	Oshawa	East of Oshawa; 252 acres
Kettle Lakes	Porquis Junction; 2,472 acres	Oxtongue River	East of West Park Gate
		Pancake Bay	North of Sault Ste. Marie; 100 acres
Klotz Lake	East of Longlac; 115 acres		
Kramer Lake	North of Kenora; 15 acres	Pearce, John E.	South of Wallacetown; 28 acres
Lake Helen	North of Nipigon; 2 acres	Perreault Falls	Vermilion Bay; 65 acres
Lake Marie-Louise	East of Port Arthur; 20 acres	Port Bruce	South of Aylmer; 10 acres
		Presqu'ile	Brighton; 900 acres
Lake on the Mountain	Glenora; 2 acres	Quetico	West of Fort William; 1,750 sq. mi.
Lake of Two Rivers	East of West Park Gate	Racine Lake	North of Chapleau; 1,000 acres
Lake St. Peter	Near Lake St. Peter Village; 30 acres	Remi Lake	East of Kapuskasing; 110 acres
Lake Superior	North of Sault Ste. Marie; 540 sq. mi.	Rock Lake	West of East Park Gate
		Rock Point	Southeast of Dunnville; 34 acres
Long Point	Courtland; 25 acres	Rondeau	South of Morpeth; 5,000 acres
McLeod	Near Geraldton; 1,100 acres	Rossport	East of Rossport; 20 acres

the beaches are sheltered by sand dunes and high red sandstone cliffs. Small islands and shoals, across the mouths of several bays, also give protection to the inner waters.

The park shore has three main sections. On the east is the Dalvay-Stanhope Section where the park headquarters is located; on the west is Cavendish, one of the most popular beaches, and Green Gables; in the center is Brackley Beach. All are easily reached by good roads.

Anne's Green Gables

Green Gables is the house immortalized by Lucy Maud Montgomery in *Anne of Green Gables* and the other *Anne* stories. It is part of the park and the original buildings have been faithfully preserved in all details. Many other points of interest associated with the stories, including the "Haunted Wood" and "Lover's Lane," are easily reached by trails leading from the main building.

Cape Breton Highlands

Cape Breton Highlands National Park includes almost four hundred square miles of rugged mountain and seaside scenery in Cape Breton Island, Nova Scotia. The island lies between the Atlantic Ocean and the Gulf of St. Lawrence and is linked to the mainland of Nova Scotia by the Canso Causeway. This span was constructed across the Strait of Canso in 1955. In its wild grandeur, Cape Breton Island resembles to a marked degree the Scottish Highlands. The similarity is pointed up even more sharply by the island inhabitants. Many of them are direct descendants of the original Scottish settlers on the island. Gaelic, the old Scottish tongue, is still spoken; and Highland games are popular annual events.

The park of 377 square miles spreads out across the northern part of the island. In places great cliffs and headlands rear straight up from the sea for more than

PROVINCIAL PARKS—*continued*

NAME	LOCATION AND AREA
Rushing River	Southeast of Kenora; 390 acres
St. Williams	North of St. Williams; 5 acres
Sauble Falls	South of Sauble Beach; 25 acres
Serpent Mounds	East of Peterborough; 70 acres
Shuniah	East of Port Arthur; 12 acres
Sibbald's Point	East of Sutton; 495 acres
Sibley	East of Port Arthur; 58 sq. mi.
Silver Lake	West of Perth; 35 acres
Sioux Narrows	South of Kenora; 180 acres
South Nation	East of Ottawa; 12 acres
South Tea Lake Dam	East of West Park Gate
Springwater	At Midhurst Forest Station; 100 acres
Sturgeon Bay	North of Point au Baril; 7 acres
Tea Lake Dam	East of West Park Gate
Two Rivers Picnic Site	East of West Park Gate
Whitesand Lake	East of Rossport; 257 acres
Windy Lake	Northwest of Sudbury; 322 acres
Wolf River	East of Port Arthur; 3 acres

NAME	LOCATION AND AREA
Quebec	
Chibougamau Reserve	Northwest of Lac St. Jean; 3,400 sq. mi.
Gaspesian (including Chic-Choos Reserve)	Gaspé Peninsula; 1,414 sq. mi.
Kipawa Reserve	Southwest Quebec; 1,000 sq. mi.
La Vérendrye	North of Hull; 4,746 sq. mi.
Laurentide	North of Quebec; 4,000 sq. mi.
Mingan Reserve	Saguenay, opposite Anticosti Island; 21,000 sq. mi.
Mistassini Reserve	North of Chibougamau; 11,000 sq. mi.
Mount Orford	Eastern Townships; 15 sq. mi.
Saskatchewan	
Cypress Hills	Southwest Saskatchewan; 18 sq. mi.
Duck Mountain	Eastern Saskatchewan; 82 sq. mi.
Good Spirit	West of Duck Mountain; 6 sq. mi.
Greenwater	Near Kelvington; 35 sq. mi.
Katepwe	Qu'Appelle Valley; 16 acres
Moose Mountain	Southeast Saskatchewan; 152 sq. mi.

» A BRISK HIKE relaxes the members of a drama class studying at the Banff School of Fine Arts, in Alberta.

« THE COURSE at Cavendish Beach, Prince Edward Island National Park, challenges the most ardent golfer.

FAMILY FUN in the gentle surf of Lake Erie, at one of the smaller national parks—Point Pelee, Ontario, not far from Windsor.

NATIONAL FILM BOARD OF CANADA

BICYCLING is exhilarating exercise down a road in Banff park, Alta.

Human benefit—
areas for healthy
rest and play

SKIERS in the Canadian Rockies. Above them looms Mount Assiniboine.

SOAKING UP THE SUN is part of a happy holiday at Katepwe Beach. It is in the historic, lake-filled Qu'Appelle Valley of Saskatchewan.

1,700 feet. The small bays and sandy coves of the rugged western shore have a backdrop of steep forested hills. Deep valleys cut inland from the broad bays of the eastern coast. It is these valleys, which the islanders call intervals, that give the park the look of the Scottish Highlands. Except for a barren plateau that is mostly muskeg, the park is well forested, and white-tailed deer, bear and moose all find sanctuary there. One of Canada's most spectacular highways, the Cabot Trail, goes almost all the way around the park, a winding route of 185 miles. Frequently the road passes through fragrant groves of perfectly symmetrical evergreens—red spruce, balsam fir—for which the park is noted.

Scenes of early strife

The provinces on the Atlantic played important roles in the early struggles between the British and French for possession of the North American continent. Many of the cities, towns and villages on the Atlantic seaboard were famous long before most of today's heavily populated sections of North America were even settled. Consequently there are hundreds of historic sites in the Atlantic Provinces. These are usually marked, and many of the old buildings have either been restored or reconstructed.

Four forts loom large in the story of Canada's early days: Beauséjour, in New Brunswick; Anne, Port Royal and Louisbourg, in Nova Scotia. All are national historic parks. The Fortress of Louisbourg, just a short distance from Sydney, Nova Scotia, was built by the French on the island of Cape Breton between 1720 and 1740. The French then believed that it could never be breached. From its walls, twelve feet thick and thirty feet high, arose seven large towers bristling with cannon. Nevertheless, only five years after it was completed, a band of sailors, tradesmen and farmers from Boston captured it with the aid of British naval units. The fortress was handed back to France in 1748. Ten years later, however, it was finally captured by the British. The next year, 1759, it served as

a base for General Wolfe's campaign against Quebec. In 1760 the once grand fortress was razed by the British, and only ruins remain today.

Fort Anne, at Annapolis Royal, is in Nova Scotia's beautiful Annapolis Valley. Around this fort eddied the struggle between the French and English for control of Acadia. The fort changed hands six times before it was finally captured by a force from New England, in 1710.

Nearby is Port Royal National Historic Park. On the grounds is a faithful restoration of the first permanent white settlement on the continent of North America north of the Gulf of Mexico. This was Samuel de Champlain's habitation, erected in 1605.

Fort Beauséjour, New Brunswick, is at the head of the Cumberland Basin. It was built by the French in 1751 to defend the Isthmus of Chignecto. British and American forces captured it four years later. Today the park is most interesting for the museum, where mementoes of those tumultuous years are on display.

Among the other historic parks in the Atlantic Provinces are the Alexander Graham Bell Museum; Grand Pré (the scene of Longfellow's *Evangeline*); the Halifax Citadel, in Nova Scotia; and Signal Hill, at the entrance to St. John's Harbor, Newfoundland.

Terra Nova National Park, in Newfoundland, is about 150 miles from St. John's and is largely a wilderness.

Park-program future

Although tremendous tracts have already been set aside as park lands, the rapid gains of Canada both in population and in industry have emphasized the need for a continuing policy of conservation. The national- and provincial-park programs will continue to grow with the country. More parks are being created each year, and other tracts are being held in reserve. Thus the physical beauty of the country and its hallowed historical sites will be preserved and restored, and its wildlife protected—for all the people of Canada to enjoy in perpetuity.

By R. B. deGrosbois